RISKS
AND
RETURNS

Creating Success in Business and Life

WILBUR ROSS

Since 1947
REGNERY
An Imprint of Skyhorse Publishing, Inc.

Published in the United States by Regnery Publishing, an imprint of Skyhorse Publishing, Inc.

Regnery™ and Regnery Publishing™ are a trademark of Skyhorse Publishing, Inc.,® a Delaware corporation.

10 9 8 7 6 5 4 3 2 1

Library of Congress Cataloging-in-Publication is available on file.

Print ISBN: 978-1-5107-8171-9
eBook ISBN: 978-1-5107-8187-0

Printed in the United States of America
Cover design by Brian Peterson
Cover photo by Getty Images
Insert photos courtesy of author

Regnery books may be purchased in bulk at special discounts for sales promotion, corporate gifts, fund-raising, or educational purposes. Special editions can also be created to specifications. For details, contact the Special Sales Department, Regnery, 307 West 36th Street, 11th Floor, New York, NY 10018 or info@skyhorsepublishing.com.

Visit our website at www.Regnery.com.

Please follow our publisher Tony Lyons on Instagram @tonylyonsisuncertain.

For Hilary

Contents

RISKS
AND
RETURNS

Introduction

As a boy, I was small for my age, and I often felt self-conscious about that. Sometimes I was bullied. One day, in my early adolescence, my dad helped to boost my confidence when he installed a punching bag and a hanging speed bag in our garage. As I began to work the bags, my body became a bit stronger. I never did grow into a he-man, but the positive transformation was evident. More than seventy years later, that lesson—effort produces results—has never left me.

My physique was one of my earliest challenges to overcome, but certainly not my last. In the decades since I worked the bag at my parents' house in North Bergen, New Jersey, I've faced plenty of adversity. My beloved father died prematurely while I was in college, forcing me to depend on student aid. As a young man who came of age in the 1960s, I experienced an unexpected extension of military service. My first employer after business school died suddenly before I even started, forcing a transition to my second employer. Later, the Securities and Exchange Commission (SEC)'s new rules on commissions caused me to give up what had been a very profitable partnership. In 2000, after working at the same investment bank for a quarter century, I left to start my own operation at age sixty-three, right when most people are thinking about hanging it up. Later, at age seventy-nine, I became the oldest individual to ever assume a U.S. Cabinet post. I then survived four years as a senior official in the tumultuous Trump Administration.

This book is my effort to share with the world the collective wisdom I have earned—often the hard way—in eight decades of business and life. No one will live a life free of difficulty. Nor, if you want to achieve anything great, will you be able to minimize all risks. Lifestyle issues, boring jobs, dumb bosses, work pressures, low pay, political issues—they are ultimately small hindrances in the overall scheme of things. Instead of concentrating on them, focus on what you can do to advance yourself in business and life. Drop the self-pity and get on with an affirmative direction, even if that means a temporary postponement of self-gratification. You are ultimately the only person who can hold yourself back, and you cannot build anything based on negativity. Do not be afraid of taking rational risks—I have found that accepting them is the essential ingredient to achieving high-level returns. Just make sure that you think them through.

The specific circumstances I faced in my life may or may not be relevant to you, but I think the anecdotes will illustrate some of the risk-tolerant, goal-oriented mentality that translates into success in business and life. This book is the story of how mentors at Yale and Harvard Business School helped transform a scrawny bookworm who parked cars during the summer into a successful businessman. It's the story of formative experiences in the Army, J.P. Morgan, Wood, Struthers & Winthrop, Faulkner, Dawkins & Sullivan, and the Rothschild banking empire. Acquaintanceship with larger-than-life entrepreneurs like Richard Branson, Carl Icahn, Mike Milken, Warren Buffet, and Donald Trump ultimately helped lead to my service as Secretary of Commerce. In looking back, I can see how unexpected, and often initially unwelcome, change has characterized my life. Seizing the opportunities wrapped within the challenges has made all the difference.

This book is also the story of my own political journey. Over the years, I transitioned from a liberal who was Treasurer of the New York State Democratic Committee to a moderate Republican supporting Donald Trump. The way that changes in American society occasioned my switch of political affiliation is covered in detail, as well as my perceptions of how Washington really works. The book also deals with world leaders such as Xi Jinping, Vladimir Putin, Recep Tayyip Erdoğan, and Angela Merkel, as well as various other officials. And I offer commentary on various political and social issues that will shape our American future.

Multiple people deserve credit for helping bring my thoughts to the page. I am deeply indebted to my wife, Hilary, and our joint families for their encouragement, as well as the many mentors, friends, and business associates who have nurtured me over the years. Madeleine Morel helpfully introduced me to my gifted writing partner, David Wilezol, who carefully transformed more than two hundred pages of assorted anecdotes into a manuscript. I am likewise grateful to Tony Lyons and Michael Campbell at Skyhorse Publishing for bringing this book to life and offering their thoughts on how to strengthen the final product. Ian Hyland and John Walsh at Quartet Books were also instrumental in the process of turning my ideas into reality.

Happy reading!

Wilbur Ross
Palm Beach, Florida
March 2024

CHAPTER 1

Foundations for Success

"Come in, Wilbur!"

Before my government service, Donald Trump had been an opponent at the negotiating table, and, later, a friend. Now he was my boss. On this day, his loud voice beckoned me into the Oval Office for my first detailed policy meeting with him as Secretary of Commerce.

The President was eager to discuss tariffs. In his view (and mine), it was time to impose them on foreign countries to correct long-running imbalances in America's trade relationships. We talked about different options, particularly the difference between a flat tariff on all foreign shipments and selective ones that would kick in only when a preset quota on a particular item was exceeded. I personally preferred the quota approach—it would cause less inflation for Americans but would be almost as effective as a blanket tariff. Trump said his preference was a flat tariff because it would be easier to explain to the public, easier to administer, and would produce more revenues for the government. He had a point.

Suddenly, President Trump took out two ceremonial pens that presidents use to sign legislation into law, and which are given as gifts to people who had played a role in crafting the bill. One of the pens was about twice the diameter of the other.

"Wilbur, which one do you think is better to use for signing things?"

Knowing his penchant for large signatures with Magic Marker–type pens, I replied, "The fatter one."

He exclaimed, "Yes! And they are less than $5 each! The Obama Administration paid $300 *each* for the skinny ones. I called the pen manufacturer myself and said, 'This is ridiculous! Fix it or we will buy our pens elsewhere!' We were getting ripped off!"

He then went on to say that he had just spoken to Boeing's CEO and had gotten a $100 million price reduction in the replacement for Air Force One that was on order. To the outside observer, the tariffs, the pens, and Air Force One might look like disconnected subjects. But Trump was making a point: "Look around your department for such wastage of money," he ordered. "We can save a fortune just by being streetwise."

He urged me to have a Diet Coke while we continued our discussion. The president never touched alcohol, but he did consume gallons of Diet Coke each day. I poked at the questionable health effects of this practice: "You know, when I was in the Army, we sometimes used Coke to clean our rifle barrels."

Ignoring this small swipe at his drinking habits, he instead turned the conversation to the North American Free Trade Agreement (NAFTA). This pact among the United States, Mexico, and Canada had come into effect in 1994, and the president viewed it as a raw deal for the United States. He remarked that some White House advisors were urging him to submit the contractually required six months' notice that he was terminating the agreement. They believed that pulling out would give us a stronger position in a renegotiation of the deal. I responded that the threat of termination would equally motivate Canada and Mexico to engage in a renegotiation. I also knew from prior conversations that the Mexicans knew concessions were necessary. I gave my opinion that there were domestic political risks to such a tactic, especially in the agricultural states, where certain farmers stood to lose—temporarily—from changing the terms of the agreement. But Trump kept coming back to the idea.

When the meeting ended, I called Sonny Perdue, the newly minted Secretary of Agriculture. "You should bring your famous map of agricultural states down to the Oval Office," I suggested. "It will help the President understand the impact of leaving NAFTA on the farmers." That advice carried the day. In the end, President Trump did not act rashly, and NAFTA was scrapped in favor of the superior U.S.-Mexico-Canada Agreement (USMCA).

The meeting was representative of hundreds more to come over the course of my four years. Donald Trump was so determined to fix everything that was wrong right away that every meeting presented a rapid-fire barrage of topics. His ability to focus on everything from truly major items like NAFTA to less significant ones like pens gave some observers the incorrect view that his approach was too scattered. I believe the opposite. He is a keen observer of everything and wants everything, large or small, to be done properly and immediately. That attention to detail, combined with his boundless energy, is why he was able to accomplish so much so quickly. Maybe all those Diet Cokes helped too.

———————————

My frequent visits to the Oval Office, of course, did not begin with my nomination as Secretary of Commerce. They did not begin with my friendship with Donald Trump. Nor did they even begin with any success I am grateful to have had in my business career. They began in the small town of North Bergen, New Jersey, where I was the first child of Wilbur and Agnes Ross.

From my earliest days, my mother and father's devotion and support were instrumental in all of my successes. To begin with, both my parents instilled by example the necessity of working hard. My mother was a teacher in North Bergen. Even though she left school around 3:00 or 3:30 p.m., her day was far from over. She'd do lesson plans after coming home, and then, after making dinner, would stay up correcting papers. As for my father, he ran a two-man law practice in Journal Square in Jersey City, so he was always busy. His work ethic was largely attributable to some hardscrabble times he had endured as a young man: Just as he was about to graduate from college in 1931, the Depression sank a chain of New Jersey butcher shops my grandfather had labored to build. My father suddenly had no money for law school, so he worked as a law clerk and tutored immigrants preparing for their citizenship exams during the day. At night, it was off to class at the local John Marshall School of Law. Today that campus is home to Seton Hall Law School.

My parents demonstrated that work was a normal part of one's life—there was no question of whether you would do it or not. The reflex to work is not automatic in today's America. Since the 1960s, some American politicians have been content to subsidize able-bodied people's lethargy. Too many working-age men in particular are unemployed or underemployed. The predictable result of rewarding such laziness are things like what I saw the other day: a Reddit thread with almost three million members devoted to "anti-work."[1] The notion that work is an undesirable or aberrant behavior is a terrible way of thinking. It pushes our country toward outright socialism. And those who refuse to work are depriving themselves of the satisfaction of a job well done. The mentality is even trickling into education. I read recently that legislators in Ohio have proposed a bill to pay kids to go to school. Why that is a terrible mentality to instill in a young person should be evident to all.

My first decade of life overlapped with World War II, and I saw my parents and my community rally to the war effort. At the time, my father was an executive at a manufacturing company called Tungsten Contact. Because his work was deemed essential to the production of war materials, he was exempt from uniformed service. But he still served his community in a semi-uniformed capacity as an air-raid warden. Occasionally, our town of North Bergen would stage air raid drills. My father would put on a World War I–looking metal helmet and venture outside, where he ordered homes and vehicles to turn their lights off. My school also held air-raid drills, where all the children would be ushered into a basement and told to sit quietly with their backs against the wall. The teacher, perhaps just trying to make conversation with a bunch of nervous kids, asked, "Do you know why we have everyone sitting against the wall?" I piped up, "Maybe to make it easy to count the bodies?" Everyone got very upset, but I wasn't trying to be funny. It was my intellectually honest conclusion.

The air-raid drills and other experiences drilled home the reality of a nation at war. I recall well the antiaircraft weapons in our local park that overlooked the Palisades, as well as school children pooling together "war stamps" they had collected in expectation of trading them for a single war bond. Lines to receive gasoline rations, Walter Winchell's war updates on the radio, and empty shell casings claimed as souvenirs from a local Army base were also memorable. Nor will I ever forget our neighborhood exploding in ardent jubilation on V-E Day and V-J Day. The further I get from that moment, the more I wonder if the United States will ever display that level of patriotism again. The regard that the American people have for their institutions in general—including the military—has continued to dwindle over time, especially in the coastal cities. What institutions do Americans still respect such that they would take up arms to defend them?

A National Record

After the war, as I began to approach adolescence, my parents encouraged me in my pursuits. I was a scrawny bookworm as a kid, with my nose always buried in the *Encyclopedia Britannica*. Recognizing that I would do well in a high-standard academic environment, in 1951 my parents sent me to a very good educational institution: Xavier High School on West 16th Street in Manhattan. Xavier is a school run by Jesuits, a Catholic order famous down the centuries for being excellent and rigorous teachers. Including the commute to and from school, my days routinely ran from 6:30 a.m. to 7:30 p.m.—quite a lot for a fourteen-year-old. The long day was emblematic of a broader culture of self-discipline that characterized Xavier. For one thing, it was a Junior Reserve Officer Training Corps (JROTC) campus, so we students had rudimentary military-style training that demanded fastidious attention to detail and precision. Student MPs manned the halls to monitor behavior, and infractions were punished with what we called "Jug": marching for hours in the courtyard with a loaded backpack while holding a rifle. It would not be long before your muscles quaked from exhaustion, but quitting was not an option. Some of my earliest lessons about discipline and focus were learned on the Jug grounds.

Recreationally, marksmanship—a sport that demands a surpassing amount of discipline—became my forte. My first exposure to the sport came in 1948, when I was ten years old. My paternal grandfather arranged for me to take rifle shooting lessons, infusing me with a love of shooting. The pace of practice and learning accelerated when I attended Xavier, which had a famous rifle team. We were undefeated all four years I was there, even against the West Point freshman team. At age fourteen, I won all eight matches in the New Jersey State Championship for marksmen under eighteen. Marksmanship, too, cultivated habits that served me well for decades: I became something of a perfectionist, to the point of weighing every cartridge to ensure an identical amount of gunpowder in each round. I used calipers to be sure that every bullet had the same dimensions. And most of all, being a top shooter demanded untold hours of tenacious, isolating practice—just you and the target. Intense concentration on hitting the target became a metaphor for my entire life.

Marksmanship also provided an early taste of how dedicated preparation and focus pays off. In 1954, the rifle manufacturer Winchester had become my sponsor, and was urging me to take time off from school to prepare for the next Olympics. At a trial event, Winchester provided me with a "counter," someone tasked with ensuring that I fired the correct number of rounds at the target in each position: prone, kneeling, and standing. It was helpful to have a counter because the match was outdoors and the winds fluctuated, so you had to adjust for them by shooting test shots at an adjacent practice target. The counter's job was to keep track of how many of my shots had been fired at the real target. I shot my rounds and felt confident I had done well.

At day's end, the event organizers posted the scores and announced something extraordinary: I had set a new national record for the Olympic 100-meter small-bore rifle course. That triumph, however, ultimately proved to be bittersweet. My score in prone position, the easiest one, seemed to be off by nine or ten points. It was very rare that I even shot as low as a nine, so Winchester paid a protest fee, and the counter and I examined the target alongside a field judge. Sure enough, it was one bullet hole short, and that counted as a zero. The counter had failed to count correctly how many rounds I had fired. The Winchester man was profusely apologetic, but there was nothing we could do about it. Fortunately, a record is still a record!

I learned a significant lesson that day: You can delegate authority, but not responsibility. My mistake was relying 100 percent on another person to keep count. That realization served me well in later life. Delegation is often necessary, because you cannot grow an organization without it. The problem is that those with delegated responsibility for a task often cannot do it as well as you can. Close personal supervision of any line of effort and a commitment to the success of the outcome is the solution.

Ultimately, I did not take time off from school to pursue the Olympics. During my senior year, my family's attention turned to where I would go to college. Xavier wanted their graduates to go to West Point, into the priesthood, or to a Catholic college, and preferably one run by Jesuits. To that end, they had me spend a weekend with some Xavier alumni in their Georgetown University dorm. The most memorable part of this experience was the "Sneakin' Deacon." School rules held that all students had to be in bed with the lights out by 11:00 p.m. The Sneakin' Deacon attempted to enforce the curfew in a creative way. As he ran down the hallway looking for offenders, he wore one regular shoe and one quieter tennis shoe, so it sounded like he was just walking. In one sense it was amusing, but I wondered if such deception was necessary or useful.

I decided instead to go to Yale, as my father had done. The case for my acceptance was strong: I was the best shot on the rifle team, I had been appointed a captain in my ROTC regiment, and I ranked high academically. Additionally, my SAT scores were excellent. In fact, the German language test score was so high that Yale later waived its two-year language requirement, a testimonial to the quality of Jesuit education. On paper, I seemed to be a shoo-in.

But there was one snag that could have compromised my admission, and it rooted in an instance of questionable behavior by Xavier's headmaster. When my father and I attended the entrance interview, I found the admissions director to be friendly (perhaps because my father had recruited lots of football players for the college). We had a nice, relaxed discussion for an hour, but then the director said, "I have to step outside for a few minutes. But while I'm away, take a look at this." He then handed us a transcript from Xavier. It read well until we got to the headmaster's recommendation: "We do not believe that the student would profit from the courses offered at your institution."

Both dad and I got very angry at this assessment. Clearly, Xavier was putting its thumb on the scale to try and direct me to a Catholic institution, which Yale was not. When the director returned to the room, he took the folder back and said, "We have seen other instances like this when a parochial school doesn't like the concept of one of their best students going to a nonsectarian college. Don't worry about it. Your grades and test scores are excellent, and you are a legacy here. I will see you in the fall."

No actual harm was done by the recommendation, or non-recommendation, but it seemed to me at the time to be both an abuse of power by Xavier and unnecessary. After all, I had been the Prefect of the Sodality, so they should have had more confidence that a strong Catholic upbringing could survive four years at Yale. I remained upset for quite a while, but when Yale's acceptance letter came in, the event became just another anecdote. Today I am thankful for all Xavier did for me, and have recommended it to many parents thinking about where their son should go to high school.

A Yale Man

My freshman year at Yale began in 1955. My two freshman roommates were both nice enough, though our classmates quickly nicknamed one Pogo, also the name of a zany comic strip character of the day. During Pogo's first night in the dorm, he put on his pajamas, just like everyone else. But, quite unusually, he put his street clothes on over them after he awoke. He repeated that process day after day until the pajamas got a bit ripe. He also spent part of each day in a local pool hall, where he regularly won money from local players. Sadly, Pogo suffered a bit of trauma in the spring, as the Yale Freshman Ball approached. He had been dating a girl from Smith College and was excited that she agreed to attend the Ball as his date. However, the day before the Ball he received a telegram from her that simply said, "I am sorry I will not be able to attend the Ball this weekend. I have to go to Pennsylvania with my parents, or something." He never heard from her again. Must have been a long trip.

The patterns of social engagement on Yale's campus were radically different from those that predominate today. Yale was a male-only college until 1969, so the freshmen at the time were bused to mixers, mixed-gender events with women's colleges. Everyone was given a numbered card and had to find the matching number. In those pre-internet days, that took a while. Sometimes the men did ridiculous, sophomoric things to impress the girls. At one country club mixer with Vassar, one Yalie—a flamboyant character known for practical jokes—rode a horse into the ballroom. Everyone had a great laugh until the horse dumped a large amount of manure on the middle of the dance floor.

I admit I participated in my fair share of tomfoolery as an undergraduate, as well. One day at the beginning of sophomore year, one of my friends was driving us down to New York City in his bright green Volkswagen Beetle. Volkswagen "bugs" were still novel machines in those days because of their diminutive size, and it was common for other drivers in much larger cars to give them a hard time.

This was exactly what was happening on this day as we cruised down Connecticut's Merritt Parkway toward New York. A big Cadillac was tailing us hard, so we decided to strike back. At the first toll booth, we handed the attendant the fare for two cars and told him, "Let the guy behind me through, and tell him it's a free day for Cadillacs." The toll taker did so, and we repeated the same process at the second booth. By now the Caddy was barely stopping whenever it approached a toll. At the third booth we just paid for ourselves, but the Cadillac blew straight through at fifty miles per hour, prompting a state trooper to quickly flag him down. We chortled at the thought of the driver saying, "But, Officer, they told me it was a free day for Cadillacs!" We could only imagine the officer replying, "Yeah, Mac, just give me your driver's license and registration."

I also got a little sneaky one weekend when a roommate from Pittsburgh and I went to a fraternity party at Penn State University. After gallons of beer, we and our hosts decided to play soccer on some local doctor's lawn at 3:00 a.m. The campus police stopped us and asked to see our IDs. The Penn State carousers handed over their college ID cards so they could be reported to the dean. However, we were from Yale and had no college ID, so the campus police fined us $100 each, which they would give to the aggrieved property owner. Naturally, as college students, we didn't have that much cash. The police said they would only take certified checks. My roommate correctly guessed that the cops did not really know what a certified check was, so he had me write on the bottom of his check "personally certified by Wilbur Ross." He did the same on mine. The checks cleared, and that was the end of that.

But the most memorable episode of my salad days came during my junior year. Three of us who had been selling ads for campus publications created our own project. We persuaded several attractive girls—one each from Smith, Vassar, Mount Holyoke, and Wellesley—to become prizes as dates for a Harvard-Yale game. The four Yalies who wrote the best 150-word pitches as to why one should be his date would have the honor of squiring these beauties to the game, with the girls themselves selecting the winners. We charged ten local stores $5,000 each for being locations where Yale men could pick up and return the completed applications. The stores loved the promotion.

To build interest in the contest, we ran one-column-inch ads in the *Yale Daily News*. Each one said something such as, "She Is Coming," "Wheneth Cometh She?" "Why Is She Coming?" and "What Will She Do When She Gets here?" for the five days preceding the Colgate football game. That

Saturday, a small chartered plane flew over the Yale Bowl at halftime with a streamer in tow declaring "She Is Coming." Late that Sunday evening, we hung on every dorm room doorknob a card describing the contest and giving the store locations. Attached to each one was a strand of blonde hair from a local doll factory. In our minds, we were poised for a sure success.

But it wasn't to be.

By Tuesday, a *Yale Daily News* editorial accused us of violating the Mann Act's prohibition against transporting women across state lines for purposes of prostitution. It was a ridiculous assertion, so we ignored it. Undeterred, we convinced some Yale alumni at *Life* magazine to cover our amusing scheme. But Dean Henry Chauncey was not amused. By 3:00 p.m. on Wednesday, he summoned us to his office and was very blunt: "Your contest is about to replace *Life's* planned coverage of Yale's Scholar of the House Program! I'm calling each of the girls' colleges to stop their participation in this stunt. You have twenty-four hours to call this off!"

"But Dean Chauncey!" we stammered. "The stores paid us money for the contest and will want it back, but we've spent most of it!"

"That's not my problem. It is your own fault. You cancel the contest, or I will expel you from Yale. You decide."

Not knowing what to do, I called my father for help. He sighed, "Wilbur, I have only one question: What the hell made you be part of this?!" He then hung up, so no help there.

The next morning, we went around to the sponsor stores. To our surprise, they were ecstatic because of all the traffic the contest had generated. When they heard of our problem, most were great sports and did not demand refunds. And fortunately for me, one of the girls ended up as my date for the Harvard-Yale weekend. We had a great time, so not all was lost. But the moral of the story is this: Whenever you believe you have a brilliant and innovative idea, think through its possible outcomes before you implement it. The law of unintended consequences is powerful, omnipresent, and sometimes vindictive. We were so infatuated with our own cleverness that it never occurred to us that Yale might object.

I might add another piece of commentary on hijinks like these: They were the most disruptive forms of on-campus behavior that Yale knew at that time. How the world has changed! Pranks pulled by people not yet twenty years old are not nearly as reprehensible as the violent pro-Hamas, anti-Israel protests which have taken place on American college campuses, including Yale's, after October 7, 2023. Hamas's brutalizing, raping, and killing of unarmed and nonpolitical civilians, many of whom were not even Israeli, is indefensible. Randomly victimizing a stranger may make the perpetrator feel empowered, but such senseless carnage is ultimately meaningless. I am not Jewish, and in fact have never been to Israel, and I am not pro-violence of any sort, but I can understand why Israel felt the need for a disproportionate response to the Hamas attack of 2023.

Despite the stories above, life at Yale was infinitely more than pranks and parties. World-class, highly dedicated professors complemented a rigorous curriculum. The Xavier faculty also had been highly skilled, but their approach mainly centered on teaching us the facts we needed to answer questions correctly. Yale demanded more and carried the learning experience further. The pedagogy encouraged students to ask questions about the material presented and, when warranted, to disagree with it. The emphasis on intellectual curiosity was brought home clearly in the first paper I submitted in philosophy class. The assignment was to write about a particular philosopher's tenets. My essay carefully summarized his key points, and I was proud of it. But it came back with a grade of 50. Scribbled on it was the instructor's critique: "It is nice that you know how to read, but in your next paper you must prove you can think about what you have read, and not just reiterate it." He was 100 percent correct. Yale did a **great job** honing my analytical skills. The work also imparted lots of facts, but developing an analytical ability was ultimately far more important to my professional life.

My dream during my first two years at Yale was to become a creative writer. I was admitted to the elite sophomore course Daily Themes, which required students to prepare a thousand words of fiction or poetry five days per week and **insert it** into a certain mail slot by 10:00 a.m. When the class met, the professor would read excerpts from each piece and provide constructive criticism. The first two weeks were exhilarating, but by the end of the third week I was completely out of material. Yale's strict requirements had surely saved me from a life of poverty. In a sense, this book is a wish fulfillment of my earlier failed writing aspiration, but at least now I am not dependent on it for my livelihood, so it is an affordable folly. And nearly seventy years have gone by since my sophomore year, so today I have a bit more material!

Yale also encouraged dissenting analysis. Students often would have lively debates on all sorts of subjects and the guest speakers at the university often disagreed with each other. This served me well in my business life by helping train me how to parse out good ideas from bad. The idea that dissenting voices should be heard—even if your own ideology was totally opposed—seems to be lost on campuses today, even at Yale. That is a very bad development. Each side of every highly

divisive issue most likely has some rationale for its views, however slender, and the cacophony of argumentation is valuable for
helping students reach their own conclusions. Thought police
are the mortal enemy of any real intellectual. The first rule of
propaganda is that if you tell the same lie over and over without
rebuttal, it becomes a "fact." It was shocking to read recently
that 80 percent of college students polled acknowledged that
they had engaged in self-censorship.[2] That self-imposed silence
is the ultimate goal of ideologues. Only by bullying can they
make sure that no dissident views will be aired.

Even more dangerous are the concerted efforts to rewrite
history. No matter how unhappy you are with historical
events, it is pointless to distort or ignore them. One professor in Wisconsin has for years quizzed his students on their
historical knowledge, and most believe slavery originated in
the United States.[3] Slavery obviously existed for thousands of
years before Christopher Columbus discovered America, so
such ignorance seems to be the product of an intentional or
unintentional disinformation campaign throughout the educational system.

This answer also points to academia's proclivity to demand
that race is the lens through which human beings should view
everything. Some progressive activists and educators in places
such as California have even insisted that the discipline of
mathematics itself is inherently racist, and have lobbied to
discard standards of objectivity. In their mind, white suprem-
acy is embedded in the proposition that 2+2=4. How will
America continue our technological leadership when many of
those responsible for teaching children regard math class as
a seminar on the views of David Duke? Our K–12 education
system ranks thirtieth in the world or lower in many subjects. Thirtieth place is not good enough for us to remain the
world's most prosperous and inventive country.

Moreover, I cast doubt on the wisdom of introducing ultrasensitive sociopolitical issues to schoolchildren. This too points to the politicization of the educational system. I remember when Blake, the then ten-year-old daughter of CNBC's Joe Kernen, came home from school one day and asked him, "Daddy, why are corporations always bad and unions always good?" That exchange led to them jointly publishing a book called *Your Teacher Said What?!* Blake later went on to become the Press Secretary for the Republican-led House of Representatives Budget Committee, so I surmise she escaped the worst effects of indoctrination. Similarly, when I asked the ten-year-old daughter of a friend what the most interesting thing she had learned at school was, she responded, "I don't have to remain with the sex the doctor assigned me at birth. But I am going to remain a girl because I like the pretty clothes." I don't believe it is necessary or useful to pose such questions to ten- or eleven-year-olds. It is much more important that they learn reading, writing, and arithmetic. There is plenty of time later for them to confront these kinds of issues.

The taint of identity politics in today's education system were unimaginable to us at Yale—the greatest social protests we had on campus were our pleas to reinstate the Good Humor Man the administration ejected from his traditional spot beside the university post office. But we did have other experiences common to almost every generation of college students. Having decided I did not want to be a creative writer in the middle of my sophomore year, I wasn't sure what exactly I would do for a career.

Then, on April 1, 1957, the phone in my dorm room rang. It was Horace Isleib, the advisor to the fraternity of which I was president, and a manager of Yale's exceptionally successful pension fund.

"Wilbur, what are you going to do this summer?"

"Well, Mr. Isleib, I was planning to park cars at the Monmouth Park Jockey Club in Oceanport, New Jersey, like I've always done."

"No, you're not! I'm leaving Yale to join an investment firm in New York City. You are going to come along as my clerk and learn about Wall Street. Don't waste your time with a job that leads nowhere!"

Since it was April Fools' Day, I wasn't completely sure that he was serious. I told him that I needed to consider it, and then called him back to confirm that he was serious about the offer. He was.

Little did I know then the effect this conversation was going to have on the rest of my life.

CHAPTER 2

My First Mentors

Summer 1959. I was now a summer employee at J.P. Morgan, and the bank had tasked me to be its sole representative at a deal closing—my first-ever solo assignment.

As fate would have it, this was no ordinary transaction.

The party on the other side of the table that day was the famous real estate developer William ("Bill") Zeckendorf Senior. In his day, as the head of Webb & Knapp, Zeckendorf was the king of the New York City real estate scene. Among other achievements, Zeckendorf had redeveloped the decrepit mid-eastside of Manhattan into the United Nations buildings and high-end office towers. His obituary in the *New York Times* years later stated that Webb & Knapp "traded in major hotels and office buildings with the ease of a housewife buying a loaf of bread."[4] He was a legend.

It was at one of these office buildings that I arrived a half hour before the appointed meeting time—I was determined not to be late. I went up to the penthouse—Zeckendorf's office—and, a bit nervously, waited in my best Brooks Brothers suit and freshly shined shoes.

Eventually, the receptionist ushered me into Zeckendorf's office, the walls of which were totally circular, with glass from floor to ceiling providing 360-degree views of New York City. Directly opposite his huge ebony desk was a table stacked several feet high with the closing papers. This was a gigantic real estate deal, one in which one of J.P. Morgan's clients was to receive a thirteenth mortgage. Remarkably, our client's mortgage was not the most junior one. There were also a fourteenth and fifteenth! Decades before Wall Street invented multiple-tier mortgage securitizations, it was a common Zeckendorf technique to pile multiple mortgages on top of one another. At the time, I could not understand how this many mortgages could be an asset. I was just excited to be the bank's representative at closing.

As I stood goggle-eyed at the breathtaking panoramic views, this great bear of a man holding a small Chihuahua came up and put his arm around me. He uttered in a hoarse whisper, "What's the matter, young man? You look upset."

"No sir, it's just that I've never seen an office with this shape."

He flashed a big smile. "Let me tell you, son. If you had been backed into a f—ing corner as often as I have, you would want a goddamn round office too."

The closing went fine. But it was simultaneously one of my most unforgettable early moments on Wall Street.

———————————

As I recounted in the last chapter, two years before my encounter with Bill Zeckendorf, Horace Isleib, a mentor of mine at Yale, had forcefully petitioned me to join him on Wall

Street. In the summer of 1957, after my sophomore year, we both went to work at Buckner & Co., a boutique investment advisory firm in New York City. Buckner occupied a floor in the Chanin Building on East 42nd Street, near Grand Central Station. The managing partner, Walker G. ("Pete") Buckner, was the son-in-law of an IBM founder, as well as the president of the Salvation Army Foundation and a board member of many charities. Pete's charity derived in great part from his religious beliefs. I would leave my parents' home every morning at 6:15 (the only bad part of the gig), to be on time for an 8:00 a.m. gathering every morning in Pete's office. Here, the team would listen to him read a passage from the Bible aloud. We would silently reflect on it for a few minutes and then discuss the most recent investment ideas.

Pete was also a very shrewd investor, whose successes illustrated to me the kind of future I could have in finance. Buckner often bought out-of-favor securities, the most memorable of which were defaulted, tax-exempt West Virginia Turnpike bonds. At first, it was unclear to me why buying a failed bond was a good idea. But Buckner's research had concluded that while unexpectedly low traffic and tolls caused the defaults, both metrics were growing, and the increases would soon support at least half the original principal amount of the bonds. We bought these bonds each day at 15 to 20 cents on the dollar, and the firm's analysis ultimately proved to be correct. By the time I understood the rationale, the bonds were restructured, and Buckner had made a fortune on them. The firm even helped negotiate a 50 percent reduction in the principal amount, thus more than doubling their money and receiving a 5 percent tax-free return on the enhanced value—a real home run.

By August, I knew that my future was on Wall Street. As a very junior clerk at the firm, my work was not exciting. But

I learned a great deal. My formal task was maintaining the records of Horace's accounts. Other clerks gave me a crash course on the intricacies of double entry accounting, and I had the privilege of sitting in on the investment committee meetings, where I gained invaluable knowledge. It was only many years later that I realized what a generous act it was for Horace to take me with him to Buckner. He had just made a major career change himself, and had the temerity to impose on his new partnership a totally inexperienced young man who would be just a summer employee. He undoubtedly intuited that I would turn into a real player on Wall Street. Horace was just one of the first mentors who helped shape and guide me during this stretch of my life—and to whom I abound in gratitude to this day.

I am also grateful to Yale for the way the school helped me in a time of need. During my freshman year, my father, who was then in his early fifties, suddenly died. As a partner at a two-man law firm, he did not have any kind of retirement plan and had never built up much of an investment portfolio, so with his passing the Ross family lived to a large extent off my mother's earnings as a schoolteacher. The loss of my father's income during his peak earning years meant it would be a struggle to pay tuition bills. Therefore, as the eldest child, I decided to put myself through the rest of my time at Yale and later Harvard Business School (HBS) to leave money for my siblings' education. Yale and later HBS were both very supportive of these efforts through financial aid, and in the case of Yale I also had an ROTC stipend to fall back on. I also took jobs during the summer and part-time during the school year. Later, at HBS, I wrote articles for *Financial World* magazine and research reports for a small brokerage firm called Gruntal & Co. These jobs worked well with my schedule because they could be fitted into what otherwise would be small segments of down time. It wasn't always easy, but I made it work.

J.P. Morgan

The summer after my junior year at Yale was dominated by six weeks of ROTC training at Fort Devens, Massachusetts, so there was no time for working on Wall Street. I was in ROTC at Yale because the United States at the time had mandatory Universal Military Training, and it seemed better to be an officer than a private. Even more importantly, the Army's monthly stipend was my main source of pocket money. And I began trading small amounts of money, so I had very little debt by the time I started on Wall Street a few years later.

The next fall, following graduation from Yale, and with Horace's generous support once again behind me, I applied to become a J.P. Morgan Trainee. It was at Morgan that I learned what a strong corporate culture really was—and why it is so valuable. Every Morgan trainee started out in the mailroom, exposing future executives to the nitty-gritty of banking and creating team spirit among the permanent clerks. My mail room assignment was to manage outbound monthly statements. One, for a wealthy widow on Long Island, had to be sealed with wax impressed with her family crest. She wanted that done to prevent her household staff from opening it and seeing how much she was worth.

In 1959, J.P. Morgan completed a "merger of equals"—in the words of our bosses—with Guaranty Trust. The essence of the transaction was that J.P. Morgan had the stronger relationships with major companies, but lacked a balance sheet sizeable enough to maintain the lead position with its largest clients. Guaranty was a solid institution with little flair, but had a big and clean balance sheet, so the deal combined brains and brawn. There were also economies of scale from merging duplicative departments.

The headquarters for the new entity remained J.P. Morgan's office at 23 Wall Street, the southeast corner of Wall and Broad Streets facing the New York Stock Exchange (NYSE), and the New York Federal Reserve Board. This location symbolized J.P. Morgan's place at the epicenter of global finance. During the Great Depression, an anarchist had thrown a homemade bomb at the building, slightly damaging the wall. But the company never repaired it. That was their way of saying, "We are impervious. We are J.P. Morgan." The door to the main banking floor was precisely at the corner and led to row after row of rolltop desks with polished brass spittoons beside them. At the rear of the floor was a huge safe whose door was generally left wide open as though to say, "no one would dare to try to rob us." This confident attitude characterized the Morgan enterprise, and its bankers—then and now—regard themselves as the best.

After the merger, some Morgan employees were relocated by necessity to the old Guaranty Trust headquarters at 140 Broadway. I was the first of the trainees to be sent over. Ahead of the merger, management at Morgan reminded each of us to retain our corporate culture, even though Guaranty had more officers than we had employees. It wasn't hard to do once I took one look at Guaranty's trust department. It had the same drab olive-green steel furniture that would belong in an old midwestern factory shop. That dismal visual was repeated floor after floor, ending any illusion one might have about a merger of equals. In the seat of power, the right rear of each floor, there was a single mahogany rolltop desk with a brightly polished brass spittoon to the left of it. Seated there was, of course, the J.P. Morgan man now running the group.

In those days, the Morgan secretaries were mainly alumnae of the Seven Sisters schools—female equivalents of the
Ivy League. They wore cashmere sweaters with little strings
of pearls, and carried copies of the *Wall Street Journal*. For
some, the main objective seemed to be to marry a successful
Wall Streeter, and many of them succeeded. In the meantime,
they took pride in being part of the firm just like the rest of us.
On the first morning I was moved to the Guaranty building,
a newly relocated Morgan secretary was in the same elevator
with me. A friendly Guaranty secretary asked her, "Tell me
dearie, how do you think you will like it here at 140?" The
Morgan girl instantly responded, "How would you feel if you
were working at Tiffany but were transferred to Woolworth?"
No one said another word until we got off.

J.P. Morgan bankers were especially choosy about their
customers. Their mantra was, "You can do good business only
with good people." Collateral was nice to have, but a trustworthy borrower was the best collateral. That is probably
why they had so few bad loans. In today's world of computer-
ized financial analysis, that attitude may seem anachronistic.
But I believe a corporate culture that emphasized prudence
contributed substantially to Morgan's reputation as the best
investment bank in the business. Indeed, I have seen many
otherwise successful investors hurt by being overzealous. Just
a year and a half after my encounter with Bill Zeckendorf Sr.,
he went bankrupt, a case of one mortgage layer too many.
Years later, I met his son, Bill Zeckendorf Jr., who became a
highly successful New York developer without loading fifteen
layers of mortgage debt on a property.

Later, when the subprime securitization phenomenon
arose in the early 2000s, I was very skeptical because it
imitated Zeckendorf's tiers of mortgages. Firms marketed
the lower tiers based on computer models showing their

creditworthiness. Miraculously, the sum of the parts totaled more than the original whole mortgage. The reason for this, to my mind, was systematic misallocation to the lower tiers of more risk than the interest rate implied. The underwriters touted their sophisticated algorithms. But the quality of algorithmic models is very dependent on the quality of underlying data put through them. The models generally had one characteristic in common: They assumed long-term appreciation in home values. The vivid memory of the Zeckendorf closing helped me avoid the pitfalls of the subprime mortgage crisis, so attending that closing in person proved to be an invaluable lesson for the future. In fact, in later years I made money restructuring these securitizations after they failed.

In the time since I manned the mailroom as a trainee, Morgan has continued to march to its own drumbeat. In recent years, it has successfully grown into retail banking through its acquisition of Chase Manhattan. While many big banks, especially Citibank, are shrinking, Morgan has opened large numbers of new branches, twenty-six in the Washington, D.C., area alone. At the same time, it has also expanded its investment banking and wealth management unit by acquiring large failing firms such as Bear Stearns and First Republic. I have been a regular customer of theirs for many years and therefore can confirm that their "Morganesse" has not been diluted by their immense scale.

Moreover, J.P. Morgan's expansion has not come at the expense of institutional excellence. Part of their success is the ability to absorb and channel the hyperproductivity of serious executives at acquired firms with extremely different cultures. For example, my friend of fifty years and business compatriot John Rosenwald, who had been President of Bear Stearns, became a highly productive Vice Chairman of J.P. Morgan Securities and continued to be effective well after his ninetieth birthday. Bear Stearns had a rough-and-tumble culture similar to that of Salomon Brothers, but his move to Morgan did not adversely affect his productivity. In fact, Morgan recently named a room in their new Midtown conference center after John.

Perhaps unsurprisingly, Morgan now consistently earns the largest profits of any U.S. bank. This sterling track record is very much the handiwork of the ultra-talented Jamie Dimon and the leadership around him. Throughout the several recent periods of banking turmoil, Morgan has consistently dodged the speeding bullets. I am proud to have worked there, albeit just for a short while. Once a Morgan man, always a Morgan man!

Harvard Business School

After this busy summer at J.P. Morgan, it was time to enroll in Harvard Business School. I had decided that business school was the best next step for my business career (though business school is certainly not a prerequisite for business success). I applied to both HBS and the Wharton School of Business at the University of Pennsylvania. I was admitted to both, and spent a day at each, but concluded that HBS was the superior choice. For one thing, it seemed to have a broader curriculum, and, based on published data, seemed to be more competitive in terms of the test scores of the students admitted. Finally, its most recent graduates were earning superior pay. That helped persuade me to go there.

September 5, 1959, was my registration day. As I waited in line to choose my classes, I noticed that the man in front of me was several years older, wearing a three-piece suit, carrying an Hermès briefcase with his initials in gold leaf, and wearing lizard-skin Gucci loafers. I was in my typical undergrad outfit: a Shetland sweater, chinos, and loafers. Obviously, I could learn a lot more from people like him than they could learn from me (as long as I could keep up with their pace). To that end, HBS did well to create contacts between students of all different backgrounds and interests through an arrangement that we referred to as the "Head Group." The first-year dorms were arranged with three rooms radiating from a central bathroom, or "head," to borrow a term from the Navy. The people in a given Head Group were each in different sections, so they felt free to trade ideas. In stark contrast, Harvard Law School was so fiercely competitive that students hid reference books from each other.

Much as business schools do today, the HBS curriculum emphasized real-life cases that we would study overnight. The next day we would debate our conclusions with our classmates. Every section—there were eight in total—did the same case on a given day. An instructor monitored the debate and at the end informed us of the outcome. We were also responsible for submitting a written analysis of a case (WAC), which we put into a slot in the administration building prior to each weekend. The WACs were graded by young female faculty members based on instructions from the professor. Some students reached deep into their bag of tricks to curry favor with the graders. One classmate enclosed an apple with his submission. Another arranged his text so that the capitalized first letter on each line spelled out, "I love you, Miss Adams." Others invited their readers out on a date. Every entreaty was rebuffed. The readers were too professional to be bribed or sweet-talked.

My section—E—was the most confrontational one. We earned our reputation because of what I will call the tinfoil ball escapade. People often brought candy or chewing gum to class to keep their energy levels high. On the first day, one student took the tinfoil off his and made it into a small ball. He suggested that everyone should add to the ball each day and pass it to whomever made a dumb remark in class, and continue to transfer it to whomever made the next malapropism. By the second week, the ball was the size of a grapefruit. Whenever someone would commit a flub, we would cry out, "the ball!" and it would promptly land on that student's desk until it was "awarded" to the next person to misspeak. The instructors never commented on the ball, but probably liked it because it put pressure on everyone to sharpen up. Eventually the ball game stopped.

Most students at HBS had conventional backgrounds, but one student was exceptional. Michael Coles had neither gone to college nor high school. He was an Englishman who had enlisted in the Royal Navy as a young teenager and educated himself by reading books while on active duty. At the time he applied to HBS he was a pilot flying fighter jets off an aircraft carrier in the Mediterranean. He had decided some years earlier to leave the Navy, but that took years to accomplish. Despite his lack of formal education, Michael graduated near the very top of our class. He later became the CEO of Goldman Sachs International and the author of the book *A Boyhood in Wartime Britain*. He later earned an MA in history from Columbia. Less exotic, but also unusual, was my second-year roommate Tom Winter, who was learned enough to do the *New York Times* Sunday crossword puzzle in ink. His main decision each time was whether to do the vertical or the horizontal boxes first. He later became the publisher of the right-wing magazine *Human Events*. Overall, my time at HBS yielded a solid network of peers on whom I could often rely in the business world—as the reader will soon see.

By far, the biggest influence on me during my HBS years was Georges F. Doriot, a French Army private in World War I who became a professor at HBS in 1926. During World War II, Doirot served as an American general with responsibility for planning and research. After the war, Doriot founded INSEAD, the most prestigious business school in Europe, and organized the first publicly listed venture capital company in history, American Research and Development Corporation (ARDC). This achievement earned him the monicker "the father of venture capitalism."

Doriot's course—"Manufacturing"— was unique because it eschewed case analyses. Instead, it consisted of working through an actual textbook on manufacturing and other business topics supplemented by lectures and informal discussions with the general. He loved using anecdotes to make his points, and he shared them liberally with his students. One story went like this: Shortly after ARDC went public, a five-foot-square painting of a human eye was delivered to him from a new shareholder with a note that read, "General Doriot, I will be watching you carefully!" Over the years, the thought of that painting reminded me that every investor should and must exercise painstaking oversight over his or her investments. I adored Doriot's idiosyncratic lectures and, even more, his occasional small dinners with a business leader. His first such invitation to me was to attend a dinner with the Governor of the Bank of England. Would I be free to join them? You bet! Additionally, as a way of gaining practical experience, each student spent several hours each week performing unpaid consulting for one of many local companies Doriot had lined up. At the end of the term, Doriot and the company's management would both critique the student's findings.

Doriot was a font of wisdom that I applied scrupulously throughout the rest of my life. One of his more interesting

pieces of advice was, "You must dress and act like the important person you want to become. The people who rule the
world wear long socks and Hermès ties and refer to others as
'gentlemen,' not 'guys.'" He insisted that your shoes be well-
shined and your clothes well-pressed. He hated speeches clut-
tered with ancillary phrases such as "What I mean to say,"
"You know," "That is to say," and verbal tics such as "ums"
and "ers." But above all, the worst speech defect was speaking too long. He viewed thank-you notes as very important,
because people so rarely send them. Above all, he demanded
that you be on time. If you were late for a meeting, you could
find yourself locked out of the room. His attitude was that a
latecomer was really saying that his time was more valuable
than that of the meeting organizer, a doubtful premise.

Doriot's focus on the concise transmission of information
also applied to charts and graphs. He loved those with simple and bold messages, understanding that the impact of a
chart varied inversely and exponentially to the amount of
data it included. He especially disliked speechmakers reading
from large-type slides. He drilled into us: "It is bad enough
if you *say* something dumb. But if you *show* them something
dumb and read it aloud, that shows you are *really* dumb."
He preferred speeches made with only brief reminder notes,
saying that if you really know your material you don't need
a script. This conviction was echoed in Walter Isaacson's
book *Steve Jobs*, wherein he quotes Jobs saying, "People who
know what they're talking about don't need PowerPoint."[5]
He urged us always to be polite, saying, "A gentleman is
someone who never insults another person unintentionally."
He also advised that at a cocktail party you should pick out
the one or two most interesting people and spend time with
each, rather than flitting about and shoving business cards
at everyone.

Another Doriot motto that was essential to my professional life was that the only stupid question in performing due diligence was the one you failed to ask. His emphasis on due diligence complemented a similarly strong view: "Never assume anything. Verify everything!" This mantra reinforced the need to be scrupulous in evaluating the premises for your decisions. As a sign outside the door of a famous Chicago newspaperman once read, "If your mother tells you she loves you, check it out!"[6]

Finally, Doriot encouraged students to pursue their intellectual interests. In my second year, the general permitted me to substitute two research electives under him for two normal courses. One of the reports was published by an affiliate of the Carnegie Endowment as a paperback book, and my Master of Business Administration (MBA) degree was awarded with distinction—another success for the general. All of Doriot's advice may sound rather elementary, or even simple-minded, but I have noticed over the years that people who follow his rules make more progress than those who don't. I cannot recall how many times during my early years on the Street that I referred to the notes I made regarding General Doriot, or called him for advice. When I was the honoree at the Harvard Business School Club of New York's annual fundraiser, my speech was essentially about Doriot. After it, many alums who had studied under him came up to me and confirmed how important he was to them, too. Unfortunately, he died in June 1987, and many of his protégés contributed to naming the French Library in Boston after him. That philanthropy was a sign of how his generous mentorship shaped not only my life, but hundreds more.

During the summer off from HBS, in 1960, I worked in the research department of McDonnell & Co., a brokerage house and major player in the analysis of growth stocks. Its research director, Sam Steadman, had developed algorithms for deciding whether an extremely rapid-growing company at fifty times earnings was more or less attractive than a slower-growing company at twenty times. His approach was basically one of using the discounted present value of his predicted future results. Usually, his conclusion was that the more rapid grower was the better buy, and this made his research a favored investor tool during the high-tech bull markets of the early 1960s.

McDonnell had much more of a go-go culture than J.P. Morgan and Buckner, my prior summer jobs. I wrote research reports, but the customers had no idea that the analyst was just a graduate student. In fact, one became irate when he called the firm for an update on one of my recommendations, and learned the author was back at graduate school. The salesman calmed him down by reminding him the stock was way up from his purchase price. This proves the old Wall Street adage: "Money Talks."

Unfortunately, McDonnell's own capital and financial management systems did not keep up with its rapid growth, so it failed during the next market crash. The failure of McDonnell and other broker-dealers was also due largely to the way Wall Street firms historically had moved people into high management positions. Promotions were based on how much profit an employee contributed from his specialized activity: analysis, trading, etc. Advancement did not have anything to do with management capability. As a result, many top executives lacked basic management skills. With the consolidation of the industry, that situation has improved somewhat. Individual productivity remains an important criterion for climbing the first few rungs of the executive ladder—and should. But a skill in steering a firm should be an essential competency for anyone aspiring to senior management, in addition to an ability to generate returns.

It was during this time that Doriot's philosophy of meetings, combined with some early experiences of enduring unproductive gatherings, helped me develop my own approach to meetings. Every meeting should have a limited set of objectives. Meetings that are unfocused consume vast amounts of time with little or no result. If everyone arrives at a meeting well-prepared, and with the intention of coming to a decision, the odds that they will achieve the goal are good.

The decision-maker in any meeting must avoid improperly influencing the direction of the discussion. Whenever I chair a meeting, my objective is to keep the discussion moving and focused. I try hard not to make my own views known until everyone else has expressed theirs. If the chair is too assertive, the group will lapse into being yes-men, thereby defeating the reason everyone got together. But if the chair does not guide the flow of the discussion, the meeting will take too long and go off in irrelevant directions. A wise man once told me that the best way to turn a dozen CEOs into blithering idiots is to place them as outside directors of a poorly managed board. The classic story is about a meeting that had only two agenda items: approval of a major acquisition and the design of recreational facilities for a new headquarters building. The first topic was approved in a minute, and the second took an hour; that was a poorly run meeting indeed.

When meeting with external actors, anticipating your counterpart's questions and preparing your answers in advance will also pay a healthy dividend. Proper preparation tends to result in responses that are thorough but succinct.

That concision is especially important when you are trying to convince the other party to buy something or make some other kind of decision. It's hard to take someone seriously if he or she meanders through a sales pitch.

But sometimes impromptu responses can be useful. This was illustrated to me during my second year at HBS. My younger brother Jim decided that he would like to go to Phillips Academy, a highly competitive prep school in Andover, Massachusetts. A classmate and close friend, Olin Barrett, who was very involved in the school's alumni fund-raising, generously arranged for an admissions interview, and accompanied us to it. The director exchanged a few pleasantries with Olin, asked about my own background, and had a dialogue with Jim. Jim, a wrestler, explained that he had read lots about the school and was especially interested in its highly ranked wrestling team. So far so good.

"And what do you like to read, Jim?" came the director's next question.

"I read the *New York Times* every day, starting with the sports section. But the most interesting part to me is the obituaries."

The director paused for a few seconds to think about this response. Olin and I rolled our eyeballs. We feared that the director would perceive this to be a weird answer, one that would crush Jim's chances for admission. After what seemed like forever, the director then asked, "What interests you about obituaries?"

"You cannot imagine what interesting lives so many people have led. Their obituaries make me think about what I could become when I grow up."

The director said with a smile, "That is such a sophisticated answer for an eighth grader. I am sure you will fit in well here."

Olin and I breathed sighs of relief. Had we rehearsed the session, Jim probably would have just given some canned responses and might not have been selected. While this is one of the few times in my experience that an impromptu response really worked, it is generally much better to try to anticipate questions and think through the responses before the meeting. As for Jim, he loved his four years at Phillips Academy and even won a few wrestling matches for them.

Wearing the Uniform

Years of ROTC training at Yale had helped instill in me a sense of discipline (and instill in my pocket some spending money). After graduation from HBS, it was time for me to fulfill my duty as an Army officer, which I was permitted to defer while I was still in graduate school. The locale for my service was Fort Dix, New Jersey, a large installation in the middle of the New Jersey Pine Barrens. Military organizations are very hierarchical in nature and punish insolence and disregard for rank. They probably couldn't function well otherwise. But this insistence on reflexive obedience to authority can create some problems, as I saw in a couple of episodes.

Most troops who trained at Ft. Dix were preparing to deploy overseas. Their point of departure was usually nearby McGuire Air Force Base, to which they were bused with their gear. One day, a sergeant overseeing the operation sold a previously discarded leather suitcase to a private about to embark. Strangely, McGuire had both a maximum and a minimum weight limit on luggage. But the private's belongings did not fill the suitcase, and the check-in clerk said it did not weigh enough to take it on board. He went to get his money back from the sergeant who had sold him the bag. Instead, the sergeant said, "Soldier, go find some big rocks and stuff them into the suitcase. Then it will weigh enough."

The private did so, but all the way to Germany kept thinking that it was not right for the military to pay for shipping useless rocks thousands of miles. After landing, he went to an MP lieutenant who took his statement, attached photos of the soldier with the rock-laden bag, and sent the complaint through his commandant up to the European High Command. It then made its way to the Pentagon and down through the First Army Area chain of command to Fort Dix. Everyone in the chain of command was upset by the incident, especially because noncommissioned officers were not supposed to be selling anything to privates, let alone a rock-filled suitcase. The Fort Dix commanding general ordered the Judge Advocate General to investigate his matter thoroughly and report back to him. The sergeant naturally denied the whole story, and they apparently believed him. This outcome likely happened because the military is very protective of career people. I never heard what happened to the private, but the minimum weight requirement was soon quietly canceled.

An episode in which I was involved also illustrated how the military's insistence on adherence to superiors can cause things to go awry. All military bases have officers' clubs that have recreational facilities and serve food and drinks (mostly the latter). Many junior officers, including myself, complained that more senior officers obligated us to go each Wednesday evening in full dress blue uniform to play bingo for the benefit of the officers' wives club. As mostly single young men, we didn't want to spend our precious free time playing bingo with each other. Consequently, a few lieutenants organized a proxy fight to oust the club's board, which had set this obnoxious rule. Since there were many more lieutenants than senior officers, they won, and their first act was to cancel bingo nights.

But this reprieve didn't last long. The senior officers had their own means of fighting back. The ringleaders of the ouster were soon transferred away from Fort Dix, making them ineligible for the board. And their assignments were not plum ones. One was shipped to frigid Thule, Greenland. Another was given casket duty, accompanying the bodies of deceased servicemen back home. The replacement board immediately reinstated bingo. There was nothing anyone could do.

One of the more humorous episodes of my life occurred during my time at the Fort. I was dating a girl from Jersey City at the time. One night we were out late and had a bit too much to drink. After dropping her off at her parents' home, I got back into my little white Plymouth Valiant, started back for my parents' house in nearby North Bergen, and lit up a cigarette. I guess I dropped it, because soon a smoldering fire broke out on the passenger's seat. Not thinking very clearly, I thought that by shutting all the windows in the car I would quickly deny the flames the oxygen they needed to be sustained. This brilliant idea naturally caused my car to fill with smoke and made it nearly impossible for me to see. Nevertheless, I proceeded like this for a few miles before I could go no farther. I soon got to the Journal Square Transportation Center in Jersey City and asked for help. The supervisor immediately activated the fire alarm, and within ten minutes a huge hook-and-ladder fire engine arrived. The firemen had thought the whole terminal was ablaze and were disappointed to find it was just a car seat.

Nonetheless, they did what firemen do. They pumped gallons of water into the car and tore the seats apart to ensure that no embers were hiding inside. While this action extinguished the fire, it also reduced the car seats to bare curved springs on which it would be impossible to sit. But I still had to make it home, so I broke down some old packing crates and put them on the seats. This solved one problem, but I had absolutely no idea how to address another: The car was filled with water from the firefighting effort. I had no choice but to take off my shoes and socks, roll up my pant legs, and set off with my bare foot on the gas and brake. The water sloshed back gently as I maneuvered the vehicle, but whenever I hit the brake at each red traffic light it splashed forward over me. The only good thing was that the ice-cold water was quickly sobering me up.

When I arrived at home, I couldn't find my house key, so I rang the doorbell at 4:30 a.m. Mom let me in but was astonished to see her bleary-eyed son barefoot with soaking wet pants. When I finally awoke the next afternoon, I explained what had happened. She delivered a tight-lipped tirade against drinking too much and ended the conversation by saying, "I never liked that girl, but I can't blame her for this incident. You are lucky you didn't kill yourself in an accident." The lesson from this escapade is obvious.

Notwithstanding these few odd events, military service taught me how necessary strict rules and highly repetitive training were to convert teenaged draftees into units sufficiently disciplined to survive in real combat situations. Historically, the United States has had the finest fighting people of any major military. But today, I am concerned about our readiness and ability to fight and win another conflict on a global scale, for a few main reasons.

First, one recent Pentagon study has shown that approximately 77 percent of young Americans are ineligible for service.[7] This mass ineligibility is largely due to mostly preventable health issues such as obesity, type 2 diabetes, and drug and alcohol abuse. Second, reinstating a draft to supply manpower in a time of national crisis would be extremely controversial. We have not had universal military training—the draft—for decades, so we don't know if youths today will resist military service as aggressively as they did during the Vietnam War. Our current level of men and women in unform is concerning. At present, we have only about 1.4 million active people in our volunteer military compared to China's more than 2 million, North Korea's 1.2 million, Iran's 1 million, and Russia's 800,000. (At least, Russia *had* 800,000 before heavy casualties in the Ukraine War.) Ukraine's largely volunteer prewar fighting force of 250,000 has greatly outperformed Russia's largely conscripted forces, suggesting that smaller, all-volunteer armies can hold their own against numerically superior conscript armies. But it is not a guarantee.

Finally, and perhaps most troublingly, American youths no longer trust our traditional institutions the way they formerly did. In the America of my youth, people respected institutional authority and respected the boundaries set for them. For example, it was routine at Xavier to have a school assembly in which everyone recited the Pledge of Allegiance. Although that kind of patriotic display still exists in many schools today, many also now cast doubt on whether we should feel good about being Americans. They overemphasize where the country has fallen short of its founding ideals in the maltreatment of various groups.

Hopefully, the United States will not have to test how well the present generation can fight. True, the next major conflict, if heaven forbid there is one, will be fought with drones, missiles, satellites, and cyberattacks. But, as the war in Ukraine has showed, boots on the ground will remain important, and so will be the quality of training and discipline of the people operating the sophisticated devices.

In total, the mentorships I was fortunate to have received from Horace Isleib, the partners at Buckner, Georges Doriot, and my U.S. Army comrades was instrumental to all I would later achieve. Any successful person who boasts that he or she is self-made is probably overestimating his or her own abilities or underappreciating those who have provided help along the way. As for me, by 1963, with my mind now shaped by wise counsel, my formal education complete, and my U.S. Army service fulfilled, it was time to apply all I had absorbed from my fine mentors. My formal, full-time career on Wall Street would now begin in earnest.

CHAPTER 3

Accepting Risks, Seizing Opportunities

Though it was a sharp contrast to my Wall Street and military experiences, I had learned a ton in my first-ever job, which I had held years before. In 1954, I was hired by the Monmouth Park Jockey Club in Oceanport, New Jersey, as a "parker," a car park attendant. Monmouth Park was near my family's summer rental home, and the ten of us youths who showed up early the first morning were greeted by Louie the Lot Boss. His look and personality was exactly what you'd expect from a man with a nickname like that. This large man with a gruff voice and an entrepreneurial bent began his "training" of that summer's team with a warning:

"OK, listen up. After the races end, everyone wants their car back fast. This is when crashes and damages happen. If a customer notices the damage and reports it before they leave, the track will have to pay. And you'll be suspended for a week."

That didn't sound good. Louie the Lot Boss continued:

"But you can avoid all this. Do something to distract the customer when you bring the car back. If it's a convertible, put the top up or down as you bring it back. They'll complain about it, but it'll stop 'em from noticing a busted headlight. If it's not a convertible, put the music on as loud as possible, or turn the windshield wipers on. Whatever does the trick."

Louie's hustler mentality went even further:

"You have two choices for getting paid. You can either just take the minimum wage of 50 cents per hour, plus piddly tips. Or you can buy concessions from me."

One of Louie's "concessions" was the right to park a patron's car in the first few rows to avoid the mob scene of gridlocked vehicles after the final race. Another would be to park it under a tree providing shade, so that children and dogs locked in a car would be less uncomfortable. (Believe it or not, leaving pets or children in the car was not unusual in those days.) A third concession was the right to wash the car while the owner was inside the track. The fees for performing these services—all charged to the car owners—ranged from $2 to $4. Half of every fee would go to Louie, and half to us. All of us parkers but one chose to get paid by concessions.

The exception was a lad we called "the Shark."

The Shark was a runty little guy from Brooklyn. Instead of signing up for Louie's concessions, he ran his own scheme. He would tell every patron that he knew which horse would win the first race. He told the first driver he met to bet on the "One" horse, the next driver the "Two" horse, and so on. He kept going until he had tipped all the entries repeatedly, leaving him with ten to fifteen patrons who would win the first race. The winners generally came back for more advice, but this time he charged $15 and again gave the numbers sequentially. The small number of customers who won two races now were flush with excitement and money, so he charged them $30 to reveal the "winner" of the third race. On most days his hustle never got past the third race, but by then he had generated a big payday regardless.

Somewhat amazingly, those drivers who were tipped but lost never returned to complain. Perhaps their wives had berated them for being so stupid to think that a teenage kid working in a parking lot could know which horse would win a race. The Shark also benefited from Louie the Lot Boss's willingness to turn a blind eye to the scheme—Louie was perhaps quietly respectful of its audacity. Years later, the Shark got into lots of trouble with the SEC. But that's another story.

Working the lot at the Monmouth Park Club was my first and most memorable job of all time. Besides the characters I worked with, it was formative for my business career. First, it provided an early exposure to an ethic of doing business which I sought to avoid (and, happily, I later realized, was not representative of the whole private sector). Second, the Shark's scheme reinforced the old adage: If something seems too good to be true, it probably is. Like many ruses, the Shark's had succeeded because it preyed on each victim's desire to believe he was in on something that he did not deserve but was too good to pass up.

Finally, those days at Monmouth Park taught me about risk. They discouraged me from ever patronizing racetracks or casinos, where the house always wins in the long run. Instead, I confined my risk-taking activities to investments. Far from being wildly speculative in nature, those investments were made after performing keen due diligence and leveraging the help of experienced professionals. And ultimately, they were made after summoning the risk tolerance to capitalize on opportunities. Every business decision entails a certain amount of risk. Decades of experience taught me that you can mitigate them, but virtually nothing is risk-free. Too many people think they can drive the risk factor in any decision down to zero by declining the opportunity. But then they remain trapped in a safe zone that doesn't get them very far. My early years on the Street helped forge my willingness to adapt to circumstances, evaluate and tolerate risk, and summon fact-informed courage to seize opportunities.

Early Twists and Turns on Wall Street

Every spring, recruiters swarmed the HBS campus. Although I was scheduled to go on active duty for six months in 1961 following my graduation, that did not deter firms from making job offers. I entered discussions with firms in both Boston and New York. Boston was intriguing from the perspective of lifestyle, but General Doriot counseled me, "If you go to New York first you can always go to Boston later. But if you stay in Boston, New York may never notice you." Given what I have learned subsequently, I think that analysis was flawed—one of the few times General Doriot was not on the money. But New York it was, and the decision worked out well.

The second decision was whether to join a large firm or a smaller, go-go firm. After considering a few opportunities, I signed on with a go-go money manager named Imrie de Vegh. De Vegh had an extraordinary record and promised me that I would report directly to him. That sealed the deal. Even though the Cuban Missile Crisis extended my tour of duty from six months to eighteen, Imrie was even kind enough to wait the eighteen months for me to start.

Then something unexpected happened. A few weeks before my arrival at the firm in early 1963, Imrie died. On his death bed, he sold the firm to Robert Winthrop, a major client. Thankfully, the new firm, Winthrop de Vegh, still wanted me to join. It was a bit weird for my new employer to change its name so quickly, but I shrugged it off. Then more unusual things started happening.

A few weeks after I arrived, Winthrop hosted a lunch for Jack Dorrance, the CEO and major owner of Campbell's Soup, as well as the company's pension fund staff. Both the company and the fund were multibillion-dollar clients. The lunch began well, since the fund's recent performance had been excellent. Nonetheless, our visitors were sizing up the new owner.

Dorrance asked Winthrop, "Bob, why do I and the pension fund both have large positions in Lucky Friday Silver Mines?"

Winthrop turned to me and asked if his personal portfolio had the same stock. I replied, "Yes sir, all of our portfolios do." I then explained why.

After a few minutes of me explaining the rationale, Dorrance said he understood, thanked us for lunch, and left. The following Monday, Dorrance pulled both Campbell's Soup's pension fund and his personal account from Winthrop. Imrie had been a very hands-on manager whose knowledge of each holding equaled that of the firm's analyst directly responsible for it. Winthrop was not of the same ilk, and Dorrance knew it. Lesson learned: Managers must have intimate knowledge of the products for which they are responsible!

The following week, Winthrop attended a Citibank board meeting. After the meeting, he sighed to the bank's CEO, Dick Perkins: "I made a huge mistake buying de Vegh."

Perkins immediately had a solution: "Sam Milbank is the major capital partner of Wood, Struthers & Company. It's an old-line investment firm. Sam wants to retire and withdraw his capital. If you buy out his $20 million and fold in de Vegh, they will rename the firm Wood, Struthers & Winthrop. And no one will ever again put you on the spot."

Two weeks later, the deal was done, and I changed employers inadvertently for a second time. Wall Street was looking to me like a wacky place filled with turmoil, but I decided to play the hand out rather than panicking and quitting. I had to endure some volatility to get where I wanted to go.

As it turned out, working at Wood, Struthers & Winthrop was a great personal opportunity. Imrie had a venture capital company called de Vegh International Corporation, from which Wood, Struthers & Winthrop promptly decided to exit. The firm fired its CEO and his whole staff. A partner at Wood, Struthers & Winthrop became the new president, and I was named vice president (as well as the only other professional employee). They gave me the task of selling off all the portfolio companies in three years, with a major bonus to follow if I hit the goal. My work had three conditions: no new capital from Wood, Struthers & Winthrop; no litigation against them; and no bad press coverage. It was exciting to become a corporate officer so quickly and to have so much delegated authority. In retrospect they probably did it because I was the newest and most dispensable person available. Yet another change—but I resolved not to be afraid of it!

This assignment provided wonderful on-the-job training. Some of the companies were very valuable, and sold for large prices. Others were essentially worthless, including one predicated on the idea that semiconductors could be made from cellulose. This could not happen, so that company ended up liquidated. Another company made miniature reproductions of objects in the Metropolitan Museum of Art's collection and sold them in the gift shop there. It was profitable, but had limited growth prospects, so a wealthy young dilettante bought it. Several other companies needed financial restructuring, so

I learned how to conduct workouts—renegotiations of failing loans—with banks. In the end, my task took only took two years instead of the prescribed three, so Wood, Struthers & Winthrop happily paid up and hired me in their research department as a metals analyst.

While Wood, Struthers & Winthrop was a professional environment, I realized it was not exciting enough for me. While selling off the portfolio companies, I had met a lot of people and learned a lot about investment banking. I decided that I wanted in. I had a growing hunger for seizing new opportunities that interested me, and I didn't want to get stuck in a solid but relatively static operation at such a young age.

I described my situation to Dave Williams, an HBS classmate and friend who had gone to Wall Street two years before me. Dave was now the Research Director of Waddell & Reed, a major mutual fund manager based in Kansas City. He introduced me to Dwight Faulkner, who had cofounded a very hot institutional brokerage firm with Dick Dawkins and John Sullivan named Faulkner, Dawkins & Sullivan (FDS). They hired me at a 50 percent jump in pay to create what Dwight said had to become the best airline stock research operation on Wall Street. In those days, airline stocks were very volatile, with millions of shares traded by institutions between the highs and lows. But little quality research on the sector existed on the Street, so FDS saw an opportunity to introduce a potentially highly profitable specialty to the market. If I could build a world-class research unit in two years, I'd be rewarded with a partnership at the firm. If not, I would be replaced. A high-risk, high-reward proposition.

I told them, "I'll do it!" Although my only prior experience in airline research was writing a few articles for *Financial World* magazine to help pay the HBS tuition, it never occurred to me that I might fail. That level of self-confidence and willingness to take risks while you are young is what propelled my career and the careers of many other successful people.

I began to build the airline research product by doing what has always served me well: tenaciously digging deep into the data. In the early 1960s, the Civil Aeronautics Board (CAB) required airlines to report monthly earnings. Those results caused big fluctuations in stock prices. But no Wall Street analyst was trying to forecast monthly earnings, lamenting that it was hard to do. In truth, I simply don't think the other analysts were working hard enough to obtain data they could use to make accurate forecasts. I began generating reports by obtaining weekly takeoff and landing data for each carrier at major airports and carefully tracking fares, fuel costs, and equipment changes. We utilized these disparate pieces of data to create holistic projections of future earnings. Airline CFOs were impressed with my bold efforts and gave me little veiled hints before each earnings report. The results were sufficiently accurate that the commissions from the sales of our reports rolled in from institutions buying and selling airline shares. Best of all, FDS soon made me a partner. My dogged pursuit of due diligence—as General Doriot had urged—had begun to pay off.

Meanwhile, Dick Dawkins had begun using our research to find venture deals in which we and our clients could invest. Working these deals gave me some of the first business travel experiences of my life—and I had plenty of exciting moments. One of the deals I found for Dick was with Wien Air Alaska, a local service carrier that had monopoly routes to and from Prudhoe Bay, a rapidly developing major hydrocarbon production area. We raised them the money to buy their first Boeing 737s. Consequently, I would fly up to Alaska for monthly Saturday board meetings, usually arriving just before midnight on Friday. Once, as I began to sleep, there was a loud rumbling noise and the Anchorage Inn floors trembled—it was a major earthquake. I got up and stood in the doorframe. Everyone else did so as well, in various states of disarray. Most upset were the prostitutes a few rooms down whose working hours were interrupted.

Alaska is a gorgeous landscape, but it was eerie to be in either twenty-four hours of darkness or sunlight, depending on the month. During the summer, daisies bloomed with stalks as thick as your wrist. Winters were so cold that parking lots had heaters so that car radiators wouldn't crack open as the coolant inside froze. Sometimes, Inuit people would go to the airport's bright lights to play softball with a red ball which made a loud clunk as the bat hit it. Watching people slide into first base in deep powder snow was exciting. So were the blanket tosses. The locals would put a young girl on a large walrus skin, flip her over the tail of a 737, and scramble to the other side to catch her in the blanket. They usually succeeded.

Eventually, we sold Wien, and I haven't been back to Alaska since then. The physical drain of so many long trips convinced me that a geographically remote investment opportunity needs to have the potential for unusually high rates of return to make up for the wear and tear of travel and for the greater difficulty of effectively controlling a business several time zones away.

———————

Over the next several years, FDS did lots of small initial public offerings (IPOs). When Dick Dawkins retired, I became president of Faulkner, Dawkins & Sullivan Securities Corporation at age twenty-nine. Once again, I trace that accomplishment to the assistance provided by my friend and fellow member of the "HBS Mafia," Dave Williams. He made that one introduction for me at a time when I really needed one, and it turned out well for both FDS and myself. For his part, Dave went on to become the CEO of Alliance Bernstein, a major publicly traded investment management firm. It was a well-earned achievement for a talented and generous man.

As the 1960s stretched on, business at Faulkner, Dawkins & Sullivan continued to boom. Late in the decade, we moved from 60 Broad Street to One New York Plaza, the southernmost building in Manhattan. We needed more space, but wanted to keep everyone on one floor. One New York had extremely large floors, so we had our solution.

The floors immediately above us were occupied by Salomon Brothers, the largest trading firm on Wall Street, and with good reason. Salomon partners were the classic high-testosterone swashbucklers for whom Wall Street is famous. One day, going up on an elevator after lunch, there were three Salomon partners in the car with me, one of whom was smoking a Montecristo cigar. A little old woman aboard asked him politely to put it out. Instead, he took another big puff. As the elevator climbed, the woman quietly reached into her purse, took out a mace gun and covered his face and his cigar with mace. As he cried out in pain, his partners ridiculed him all the way up. The woman got off at her floor and wished everyone a good afternoon. So much for being a Master of the Universe!

On this occasion, Salomon's aggressive mindset backfired. But adhering to it on untold other occasions is what gave them the courage to bid on blocks of stock that were tens or even hundreds of millions of dollars in size, being sold by the best-known institutional investors in the world. Their appetite to handle huge order flows benefited FDS. As institutions awarded us more and more brokerage commissions to pay for our research, they also asked us to handle larger blocks of trades. Ultimately, they wound up wanting large-volume sales executed as a single block trade, rather than many trades over several days. We lacked the capital to do so, but Salomon had it (as well as a hearty appetite to capture a higher percentage of order flows), so we joint ventured. Salomon put up most of the capital, but we shared equally in the gain or loss on the trade. We therefore got to know them well and had a mutually profitable relationship.

One of Salomon's partners was a relatively young Mike Bloomberg. Later, while still in his thirties, Mike was fired from Salomon and founded his namesake company using his $10 million golden handshake. Bloomberg's business was providing trading desks with extremely timely information about security prices and both financial and nonfinancial news, all delivered by a desktop device at the push of a button. There already had been full-time firms with the same objectives, and we at FDS had taken public one of them, Telerate. Mike beat out Telerate and other such companies in part by convincing Merrill Lynch to put up most of the original capital for the company and agree to place the terminals throughout their office network—the world's largest in the financial sector at the time. That gave his fledgling company the initial scale necessary for launching a superior information-gathering service globally. As an institution, Bloomberg also emphasized speed as the differentiator between the company and its competitors: A friend of mine who worked there as a reporter told me her boss measured how much quicker she was at getting news out on the desktops than the competition at Reuters and Dow Jones. Bloomberg won a high percentage of the time, and that made its service essential to any trading or investment operation.

Mike later went on to disseminate the same data through television, radio, and magazine channels. The combined scale led to an incredible fortress of information, and overwhelmed competition. It really wouldn't be feasible for a competitor to spring out of nowhere and somehow offer a faster or more comprehensive source of data on everything like Mike's company did. Moreover, most trading desks don't have the room for yet another device, so Bloomberg benefited from a "first mover" advantage. Later, Bloomberg added a message service among Wall Streeters. Mike kept his ownership of Bloomberg when he became the wealthiest mayor New York has ever had—as well as one of the greatest. We have remained friendly to this day. I might also add that he was not the cigar smoker in the elevator incident.

Business and Pleasure

As I worked my way up at FDS, I seized more opportunities to grow my networks of clients, friends, and colleagues. We had a lot of fun enjoying the fruits of our labor together.

The FDS crowd used to hang out at the Delmonico Restaurant, right on the corner opposite Lehman Brothers, to put down a couple of martinis before going on to the evening's activity. I spent so much time there that Oscar Tucci, the proprietor, became a good customer, buying bonds from us. One day I was having lunch with the Exxon Mobil pension fund managers. A few days earlier, FDS had underwritten a convertible bond offering for the technology company Recognition Equipment, and Oscar bought some of them. When he saw us at lunch, he approached our table, and in his broken English asked, "Mr. Ross, zee gold bond, how they doing today?" I said, "They're doing fine. They're up from where you bought them." He thanked me. The Exxon man asked, curiously, "What is this about you selling gold bonds?" I replied, "He asked me if the bonds were good. I told him they were as good as gold!" We laughed and went back to lunch.

Another happy story was the Listerine royalty deal. Listerine was first formulated in 1879 by Dr. Joseph Lawrence, a chemist in St. Louis, Missouri. He later licensed the formula to Mr. Jordan Wheat Lambert, whose company became Warner-Lambert. The product was grandiosely named after Sir Joseph Lister, a Scottish surgeon who pioneered antiseptic medicine. At various times Listerine was marketed as a foot remedy, a dandruff cure, and as a "beneficial remedy" for diphtheria, smallpox, and other diseases. Its efficacy for any of those uses was at best highly dubious.

Listerine's real success began in the 1920s when Warner-Lambert's advertising reinvented halitosis as a social disorder and Listerine as the cure. In just five years, the company's profits grew sixtyfold, and growth has continued to this very day. Dr. Lawrence wasn't just a talented chemist. He had also very cleverly made a one-page agreement with Warner-Lambert calling for him to receive a perpetual royalty on the product. Dr. Lawrence managed to pass the royalties on to his descendants and also devoted a large portion to the Catholic Archdiocese of New York. The Archdiocese was a good client of John Sullivan, who had me conduct due diligence on the product and prepare a private placement for their royalties. We concluded that dirty mouths were still a growth business and that Listerine in its various iterations still worked as well as any alternative. Every time there was a merger involving Warner-Lambert, lawyers for the acquirer attacked the contract. But as one complained to me, "There weren't enough words in the agreement to let us find a way to break it. The medicine man's draftsmanship was at least as good as his medicine making, maybe better." I have failed miserably over the years to convince various lawyers to simplify contractual language, but the Lawrence-Lambert contract shows the value of brevity.

FDS sometimes found itself at loggerheads with labor unions trying to cut themselves in on our deals. One story involved Aspen Skiing Company, known locally as SkiCo. SkiCo was founded just after World War II by Walter Paepcke and Paul Nitze. Paepcke ran Container Corporation of America, and Nitze became famous as one of the architects of America's Cold War strategy and a negotiator in the Strategic Arms Limitation Talks (SALT). Both men had been ski patrollers in the Army, and that experience led them to create SkiCo. While other ski resort towns were developed to provide destinations for railroad passengers (for example, the Union Pacific Railroad's creation of Sun Valley, Idaho), SkiCo only created, operated, and charged for ski lifts. By the early 1970s, the company was earning millions of dollars annually. Returns on equity were very high because they did not own the slopes. They rented them from the U.S. Forest Service, so the only capital expenditures were limited to more lifts, snowplows, and the rarely used snowmaking equipment. Additionally, people who had paid millions of dollars for a ski lodge didn't complain if the lift tickets increased in price each year. And every year there were more skiers.

One of Paul Nitze's sons, William, was a friend of mine and the Chairman of SkiCo. My firm managed its initial public offering. Right after we went into registration with SEC, the Teamsters suddenly sent several organizers to recruit the company's ski patrol into the union. As soon as this happened, I called Bill Coors, a SkiCo board member whose family brewery was the largest nonunion one in the country. He became furious that a big-time union was invading this peaceful little community. He said, "Give me a couple of hours to take care of it."

Within a few hours, six of Bill's burly security men arrived and, wielding shotguns, tied up the organizers, trucked them outside of town, and released them. A stern message accompanied this ejection: "Never set foot in this town again. You know the ski patrol has no interest in your union and you don't belong here." Not a word was ever heard from the Teamsters again, and both SkiCo and Coors remained non-union. Despite the dark humor of this story, I am not anti-union, and my investment firm later enjoyed good relations with several unions, as I will recount later in this book.

Because of our success with SkiCo, an unusual client decided to take its business public through FDS: the Harlem Globetrotters. A Chicago man named Abe Saperstein founded the Globetrotters in 1926 and made them a major attraction at arenas around the country. The Globetrotters were no ordinary team of hoopers: They had perfected dribbling and passing to the level of an Olympic sport, and put on a circus-like display of their craft. (They also almost never missed a shot because the baskets were just nine feet high instead of the regulation ten feet.) Initially, there were no Black stars in basketball, but the Globetrotters were all Black men. Saperstein's attraction was very progressive at the time, even more so because the Globetrotters won every game. But they never had any trouble from the Ku Klux Klan.

Abe loved to have sex with ballerinas, and one night in 1966 he died in flagrante delicto with a couple of them in a hotel room. Shortly after Saperstein's death, the players' contracts came up for renewal. The team selected Meadowlark Lemon, the all-time most fabulous basketball dribbler, to represent them to Continental Illinois Bank, the trustee for Abe's estate. Meadowlark showed up to visit the trust

officers handling the estate dressed in his Globetrotter outfit and dribbled two basketballs while they negotiated. The
bank immediately decided to sell the team. The financial
records were a mess, so they sold the team to an adventurous
and wealthy Chicagoan, Potter Palmer. Potter joined forces
with Warren Hellman, the president of Lehman Brothers,
and George Gillett Jr., who had helped manage the Miami
Dolphins football team. This trio also invited me in to take
a small piece.

George managed our new asset brilliantly. He divided the
team into two units so that they could play at twice as many
arenas, with the only extra expense being travel. That decision multiplied earnings. Gillett also had Hanna-Barbera, the
animation company, create a Saturday-morning Globetrotter
TV cartoon show for children. That built our audience and
was itself profitable. With our cash flow strong, we decided
to take the team public.

Then trouble hit.

One week after Faulkner, Dawkins & Sullivan filed the
Globetrotters' IPO with the SEC, a labor organizer convinced the team to have a real union, not the informal one
they had. This put us in a bind: We didn't want a union, but
we couldn't afford a strike in the middle of a public offering. George solved the problem by meeting privately with
the team and telling them they could have a real union but,
if they did, all mail sent to them at the company address
from the young ladies with whom they had dallied on the
road would be forwarded to their home addresses—where
their wives were. The players voted unanimously not to
have a real union. Meanwhile, our lawyers were hysterical. Such a threat was probably a gross violation of the
labor laws, but Gillett knew his men and the deal went well.
Nonetheless, it was remarkable that small-time operations

such as SkiCo and Harlem Globetrotters became the targets of union organizers.

My early years on the street also brought plenty of tough situations where I learned a lot about what *not* to do. I found myself in an uncomfortable situation one day when an FDS salesman and I flew out to meet with Investors Diversified Services (IDS), a huge mutual fund in Minneapolis. On the plane, the salesman mentioned to me that he didn't think that the fund manager we were meeting was particularly adept. The next morning, there was an IDS person in the elevator with us as we rode up to our appointment. He said, "I am the fund manager you were talking about on the plane, so there is no need for a meeting. My fund will never deal with people who are that disrespectful of their clients and so stupid as to mock one in a public place!"

The salesman tried to apologize, but it didn't work. We soon had to get rid of him because he made similarly indiscreet comments about other customers. The valuable lesson was that you don't get to grade your customers—they grade you. There is no upside to knocking them, especially in a public or semipublic setting.

Another cringeworthy episode occurred in connection with the Fur Vault. In the 1970s, the Fur Vault had the fur coat concession at Bloomingdale's stores, as well as its own chain of retail stores. Thus, the company was quite profitable. Since this stock would interest individual investors, and we had few retail salesmen, we brought in Prudential Bache, a major wire house, as comanager of the IPO. They were thrilled to be in on the deal, and invited me and a CEO who called himself Fred the Furrier to have lunch with their senior management.

As a goodwill gesture, Fred had created a funny little brown teddy bear holding a Prudential Bache sign. The most senior person from Prudential Bache was late for the lunch, so Fred placed the bear on the table in front of the man's plate. When the executive came in and saw the teddy bear, he stood up, picked up the bear, and said, "Fred, we are so happy to be in this deal that we have prepared for you this Pru Bache bear as a token of our appreciation." He then presented it to Fred, having no idea it was a gift to him *from* Fred.

We all quietly cringed. To avoid embarrassing this executive, Fred took the bear and thanked him. The Prudential Bache executive's staff got very red-faced, but they too did not want to embarrass their boss, so his error has been kept secure until now, well after his death. I learned from that how important it is to be on time and well-prepared. Nor did I ever partner with Prudential Bache again. One embarrassment like that was enough to convince me that I couldn't trust them with bigger matters.

Despite this faux pas (or perhaps I should say "fur pas"), The Fur Vault soon listed on the American Stock Exchange (AMEX). The antifur movement was in its infancy in those days, and we didn't take it seriously. However, in what should have been a warning to us, activists picketed the exchange on the first day the stock traded. As time passed, the antifur movement became increasingly aggressive, even to the point of spray-painting women wearing furs. The fur business was never the same. This was the first time I had seen a mob destroy not just one company, but a whole industry. It presaged the scene today of activists boycotting consumer companies because of their political views. These activists say such disruptive actions are merited because their policy objectives are so laudable. This concept that the end justifies the means remains as invalid in my mind as it always has been, but now the left wing widely accepts it. There must be a better way to achieve social objectives.

Even well-established Wall Street firms encounter their share of headaches from unscrupulous people who have no interest in creating value for others, only enriching themselves. One traditional firm I worked with was White Weld & Co. (long since gone). One day I bemoaned to its CEO, my friend Paul Hallingby, that FDS had underwritten a computer software company that lacked the capital to invest in large systems. He promptly said that he was on the board of the Philadelphia-based Sunasco, a real estate company with lots of assets, but not much of a business plan, and so its stock was pretty dead. After a few weeks of back-and-forth, we convinced the two companies to merge under the new name Scientific Resources Corp.

On the day of the Sunasco shareholders' meeting in Philadelphia to approve the merger, Paul and I sat together in the second row. Everything was going smoothly until a well-dressed older man approached us and asked in a very friendly way, "Are you Paul Hallingby? And are you Wilbur Ross?" We smiled, confirmed our identities, and reached out to shake hands with him.

Instead, he shoved a subpoena at each of us. A law firm had filed a class action suit against the deal. I was stunned, but Paul simply put the subpoena into his briefcase and turned his attention back to the meeting. The deal was approved, and we got into the White Weld limousine to go back to New York. The subpoena had me frightened, but Paul shrugged it off: "Don't worry about it, these suits happen all the time. The insurance companies providing the officers and directors coverage will ultimately settle the case by paying some money and our lives will go on without interruption." He then loosened his tie, laid back, and slept for the rest of the trip.

I was too nervous to do the same, but the next time a similar situation arose, I didn't respond in fear. Paul was right. It became almost ritualistic that every merger announcement brought a shareholder derivative suit. A few minor changes might be made to the proxy statement and the lawyers would get a fee, but they almost never succeed in blocking a deal. In fact, it wasn't clear that they really wanted to upset the transactions as opposed to just getting fees from them. What a racket. Some of the firms had legitimate concerns but their suits were invalidated, followed by "me too" complaints almost always word-for-word identical to the original ones.

A few months after the Sunasco shareholder meeting, another client, Peabody Galion, encountered a hostile takeover bid from Victor Posner. Victor was an infamous corporate raider best known for hostile takeovers of medium-sized companies (and a hostile personality). He loved to strip their assets while paying himself huge compensation. During a period of stock market weakness, Victor became Peabody Galion's largest shareholder and sought to take control. We didn't want that, so I was delegated to try to dissuade him.

I flew down to Miami early one afternoon to meet Victor, and his stretch Cadillac limo met me at the airport. It was parked just outside the gate on the sidewalk, and the driver's window was covered with tickets. As I got into the back seat, a policeman added another ticket. The driver screamed out, "My boss is Victor Posner, who doesn't give a f— how many tickets you give me!" He then honked his horn to clear the pedestrians away and drove recklessly to Victor's headquarters: the top floors of a seedy hotel he owned on Collins Avenue in Miami Beach. Upon arrival at the hotel, two security people frisked me and accompanied me into the elevator, pushing out of the way two elderly women who had gotten on first.

At the top floor, two more burly, shirt-sleeved men ostentatiously wearing .45s in shoulder holsters ushered me into a dimly lit bedroom to wait until "Da Boss" was ready to see me. After about fifteen minutes, they escorted me to the rooftop, which had an Olympic-sized pool and several cabanas. Victor was sitting in one of them, accompanied by a very young teenaged girl. About a dozen similarly dressed (or undressed) girls lounged around sunning themselves. Victor greeted me and announced, "I'm paying the college tuition for these lovely girls!" At this, the girl sitting by him giggled and said, "Yes, Mr. P. is very nice to all of us."

Victor told her to take a swim while he and I talked. For two hours he monologued about how he had never lost a proxy fight. I asked him why he was attracted to our company. He said he liked the business and our debt-free balance sheet. One could only imagine what he would do with it. When asked if he saw any synergies with his other companies, he responded, "I will be the synergy!"

After more arguing, he suddenly became conciliatory and asked questions about our plans for the company. By now it was early evening and he said, "I know you're booked on a late-night flight back to New York. I'll change and we can have a friendly dinner at my country club."

A few minutes later we piled into Victor's hulking Cadillac. Two of the swimming pool cookies had already gotten into it and were more or less dressed, although their more obvious features were quite visible. Victor explained, "These ladies wanted to make sure we had a nice evening together."

We drove to the club, which looked more like a disco than a country club. We had a nice meal during which both Victor and the girls were very friendly. As we got back into his Caddy, Victor said, "Lilly really enjoyed sitting with you, so why don't you stay over? You can get the morning plane back to New York."

I responded, "Thanks, but I have an early meeting there, so I really should go tonight."

This was an obvious setup to compromise me. For sure, if I had stayed over, everything would have been well-photographed.

Early the next morning, I told our CEO the story, and we decided to go on the offensive. We sued Victor and sub-poenaed him and the girls. The girls were very tough, and answered every question by pleading ignorance, which might well have been true. We were getting nowhere. But a bright young lawyer then piped up, "Let's subpoena the girls' mothers. They are probably not as hardened and may put pressure on the girls to make Victor stop." Nor did these mothers probably know that their young daughters were cavorting with a man decades older than them. We reasoned that they probably had never been subpoenaed before, so they would be terrified and blame their daughters.

It worked. Victor called me a few days later to say, "You bastard! You know their mothers don't have any f—ing idea what I'm doing, but I don't want to make this into a big war. Get me a bid 20 percent above my cost and I'll go away."

"Victor, give me thirty days."

He did and we bought him out. Our paths never again crossed, and I certainly never heard from Lilly again. Nor did I particularly want to.

By no means did all buyout artists have the lifestyle and modus operandi of a Victor Posner. Others I have encountered over the years, while just as aggressive and tough, are people you would be happy to have as dinner companions and friends. One example is my friend Paul Singer, the founder of Elliott Management. Paul famously had a ten-year battle with the Government of Argentina. Argentina had once again—for the tenth time—defaulted on their bonds. They negotiated a consensual restructuring in which virtually all the bondholders participated. But Paul felt it was not generous enough, so he held out and litigated fiercely, on one occasion foreclosing on an Argentine naval vessel when it docked in a jurisdiction that honored Paul's claim.

Eventually, the case was resolved, and Paul made an enormous profit. There are many similar tales of his dogged and successful persistence. But if you met him and his wife in a social setting you would be impressed by how polite and low key they are. The Victor Posners of this world and the villainous hedge funders of the type depicted in the TV series *Billionaire* are caricatures of most serious players in that game.

Looking back on it, Louie the Lot Boss's initial advice about concealing damage to patrons' cars, the concessions he created, and the Shark's fraudulent schemes represented the worst examples of bad behavior in the capitalist system—a degeneracy that would be embodied at the highest levels by the Victor Posners of the world. Yet, most of my experiences proved that these outliers are not at all representative of American business morality. In fact, the integrity of our ecosystem—and the people involved in it—is superior to that of any of the thirty-odd countries in which I have done business over the years. For example, Americans are far more likely to pay their income taxes than the residents of most other countries, and very few of our citizens regard bribery as a normal way of relating to government. Those ethics contrast with how business is often done in Asia, Latin America, and parts of Europe. The American commitment to the rule of law is one of the greatest advantages our nation has for creating opportunities and taking certain risks off the table. Let us continue to uphold it.

CHAPTER 4

Personal Assets

In 1963, as my first summer on Wall Street approached, two friends and I rented a house in Southampton from Memorial Day through Labor Day. We had great fun there, so we did so again in 1964. At the end of that second year's term the broker, Isabell Crocket, approached me.

"You've been very good as the signer for your group rental. You paid on time, and the houses were in good repair when you left, so I have a proposition for you."

I listened with great interest.

"The Sag Harbor Savings Bank is about to foreclose on a house at the corner of Ox Pasture Road and Halsey Neck Lane. The thing is, the present owner is politically connected, so they want to do it quickly and quietly."

"I see."

She continued: "If you pay the four months of overdue mortgage payments and give the owner $5,000 to walk away with, you will own the house and you can continue his old mortgage, which is already one-third paid down."

It sounded like a good deal. And then she made it even sweeter.

"To make it easy, I will find you a Southampton College professor whose rent from September through June will cover the mortgage payments, the property taxes, and the insurance for the whole year. You will own a lovely property with no carrying costs and lots of upside."

I bought the house. When I sold it many years later, the brokerage commission on the resale alone was many times my gross purchase price.

This unplanned foray into real estate should have made me more aggressive buying houses and renting them when I was young. But at the time, I merely thought of Southampton as a place for the summer, not as a business venture. In retrospect, I should have figured out that supply of oceanfront resorts is quite limited, but as more and more people become affluent, the demand side of the equation keeps growing. The long-term trend of prices can only be upward (with some temporary cyclical plateauing or downturns).

I missed out on more big returns from Southampton real estate, but my positive experience with that property and others reinforced the realization that some assets are smarter buys than others. Other purchases—as the reader will see—held less value.

Everything had worked out great with the Southampton house. But in 1964, I learned one of my first key lessons about acquiring new assets: Know what you're getting into before you buy them! In that year, now flush with some disposable income earned from early successes, I purchased a sailboat from a Wall Street friend who had just bought a larger one.

To receive my new prized possession, I drove to his home north of Hudson, New York, one Friday afternoon. I hitched the nineteen-footer and its trailer to my car and set off for Southampton. Then the trouble started. As I hit the road with the boat behind me, I instantly felt the vessel's length looming over my MGB—a tiny British roadster. Suffice it to say that hauling the boat through the mountainous terrain of New York State was a struggle. The MGB quaked with tension as it crept slowly up every hill, and trembled on every downward curve against the centrifugal force that threatened to whipsaw the car off the road.

As it grew dark, I decided to lay over at the Thayer Hotel on the grounds of the U.S. Military Academy at West Point. Here I ran into another problem: the Thayer doesn't let just any interloper obtain a room for the night. I explained to the MP at the gate that I had been an Army officer and hoped that the academy could accommodate this need. He was so amused at the sight of my little car towing a boat that he harangued the desk clerk into providing me a room. The next morning, I was fairly stunned to see an armed MP protecting the boat. As I approached, he barked out, "Halt, who goes there!" I said, "Lieutenant Ross! I have come to take my boat away!"

The next big obstacle was crossing the Hudson on the George Washington Bridge, the height and span of which renders traffic prone to the effects of high wind gusts. We started on the windward side, but gusts kept pushing us toward the leeward side. I had to navigate the MGB slowly across the fourteen-lane bridge. So far, so good.

On arrival at Southampton the boat was docked, and, after lunch, launched. As I had never sailed before, it took practice to tack successfully with the fluctuating wind. Eventually, I sailed to a drawbridge for Route 27, a major thoroughfare across Long Island. Knowing that the mast was too tall to go under the bridge, I used a claxon to ask the bridge operator to draw it up. He obliged.

But I immediately realized that I had made an enormous mistake.

When a boat travels between two enormous concrete pilings supporting a bridge, the pilings block the wind necessary to propel the boat through. I did not realize this at the time. What I should have done was to get a good "running start" by letting the momentum from a full sail carry me through. Instead, I had to paddle the craft through the opening against a hostile tide. As a result, the boat went a few feet forward on each stroke, but as the paddle came out of the water to begin the next stroke, we slipped partway back.

It was a minor inconvenience. But my inability to navigate my boat through the bridge had caused a lengthy delay for the hundreds of motorists who were waiting for the drawbridge to go back down. Drivers above could see the tip of the mast wobbling back and forth with little progress, and soon started honking and screaming. I finally made it through to the other side soaking wet from furious paddling, and went to a marina to dry off. After cruising around on that side of the bay for a while, it was time to go back home. On my second approach to the bridge, I again asked the operator to open up, but he refused. Soon I resorted to begging. He shouted, "No! I am never going to open up for you again. You screwed up traffic on a Saturday afternoon! You are too incompetent to sail!" I went back to the marina and called a friend, an experienced sailor, who eventually piloted the craft through.

After a few years, I got bored with sailing, so I docked it at a local marina and asked them to sell it for me. I even ran an ad in the Southampton press, but there were no takers.

People there had little interest in sailing, especially not an old Lightning, so I finally donated it to Southampton College. I was never tempted in later years to buy a motor yacht. It seemed to me that yacht owners spend one-third of their time, and lots of money, in dry dock. Another third of their time is devoted to dealing with captains who are drunk, hitting on a crew member, or taking another job. The final one-third of their time is spent trying to recruit guests to accompany them on voyages. Besides all this, how much free time do you actually have to be on the yacht? A few of my friends use their vessel as a second home, and that makes more sense. But with a house in Palm Beach and a house in Southampton, I was content to charter one occasionally for a week for so. A few friends who are immensely wealthy and retired are happy with their yachts, and for them it makes sense. For me, I was happy just to accept invitations to join friends.

The great lesson here is that anyone considering purchasing a boat should understand how to captain it. And while I could afford my boat and got good use out of it, there's an old joke that "boat" is in fact an acronym for "Break out Another Thousand." The costs of maintaining and storing one can be significant. A boat owner should carefully weigh how often he will take it out before buying it.

Helicopters are in a similar category as boats. FDS bought one when I was a young partner there. Dick Dawkins had gotten a contract to haul inbound checks from airports to the clearing banks via helicopter instead of trucking them, thereby accelerating the delivery and reducing the float on billions of dollars of uncashed checks. Dick's idea was that in between the contract runs, his friends who managed major Wall Street firms but lived out on Long Island would pay to commute by helicopter, and John Sullivan and I would buy weekend trips to Southampton. The chopper would be cash positive, and the depreciation would offset some of our partnership income.

In general, the concept worked well. Sometimes there would be a hiccup—the most notable of which happened on a Friday afternoon in the 1970s. When John and I got to the Wall Street helipad where our chopper was parked, we learned that President Richard Nixon, who was in New York at a fundraiser, would also be taking off from it that evening. Secret Service men were all over the place, and even had frogmen aboard boats in New York Harbor. Our chopper was on the tarmac along with the President's Marine One helicopter, and the Secret Service insisted that no one could use the helipad until Nixon took off a few hours later. We protested, but to no avail. Then the desk clerk piped up, "These two are regular customers and my boss told me to go ahead and board them. I am going to do so." Amazingly, the Secret Service just took our IDs, ran a quick background check, and then let us board with a warning: "We are only making an exception this one time. Now get out of here!"

A much more frightening event—which epitomizes more than any other factor the risk of owning a helicopter— occurred a few weeks later. The chopper was to take me to Southampton and then ferry three major FDS clients to Newport, Rhode Island, where they were weekending. One of these clients sat up front with the pilot, with the rest of us in the back. About ten minutes into the thirty-minute trip, he asked the pilot, "Why did that red light go on?"

"Oh shit, we're on fire!"

Panic swelled in everyone's chest. Fortunately, the pilot kept his cool. Even more luckily, we were near an airport close to Brookhaven National Laboratory, so we quickly landed and got out. What was meant to be a fun, brief ride turned into a nightmare. Not long after, there was another near mishap, so we donated the chopper to a private school, which sold it for a good price, giving us a tax deduction. Ultimately, a chopper can be an incredible force multiplier for saving time and money. But there are serious risks attached to climbing aboard.

Once FDS sold its helicopter, the summertime commute from Southampton became roughly three hours each way, far too long to endure each day. My family and I therefore decided to try the Jersey seashore. We bought a house in Deal, New Jersey, an eighty-minute commute to and from Wall Street. It worked out well—each evening my wife and daughters would pick me up at the train station. Even better, the house was close to the Deal Casino, a beach club right on the ocean. And our immediate next-door neighbor had two girls the same ages as ours, so they had ready-made playmates. Everything was off to a good start.

Life soon became complicated, however. Not long after we purchased the Deal home, Brooklyn Sephardic Jews built a synagogue in town and started buying local houses. At least once a week, one would ring our doorbell and ask to buy our house. Toward the end of the second year, they owned almost the entirety of our immediate area. Ultimately, sensing the high demand for property in the neighborhood, it seemed like selling was a good idea for me financially, so I called our broker. Within one day, an offer came in from a dealer in jade gemstones. He wanted to pay in jade objects, claiming that their value on the resale market would be far greater than the price of the house. I told him a neighbor of mine in New York dealt in jade, and that I would give him credit for whatever price he would pay me. The bidder got very upset, saying my friend would be unethical and just bid a lowball price. That ended that.

The next bidder asked if I would take all cash. By this he meant not just no mortgage, but literally a full payment in cash money. We disclosed this to my bank when I deposited the proceeds to avoid money laundering issues. He gave me an enormous number of hundred dollar bills whose authenticity the bank verified and arranged for a Brinks truck to pick up at the closing. It was a strange chapter, but had a good ending, and soon I decided to relocate back to the Hamptons for the summer.

Dakota Days

For all the good times my family and I enjoyed at the beach, my primary residence beginning in 1973 was The Dakota apartment building, at the northwest corner of 72nd Street and Central Park West. The Dakota was the first luxury rental apartment building in Manhattan, and is still one of the most stately and coveted residences in the city. The original developer was Edward Cabot Clark, a patent lawyer who helped bring the Singer Sewing Machine Company to life, and took stock in the company in lieu of fees, a wise decision indeed. At the time that Clark developed the building, only empty fields surrounded it. Its name supposedly came from a friend of Clark's who said it was so far away from the rest of the city that it could be in the Dakotas.

At the time, the Dakota helped establish a new standard of luxury: It had its own adjacent tennis court, and its own kitchen (in addition to those in each of the apartments). The kitchen published a daily menu and white-gloved ladies delivered meals to the apartments while other ladies staffed the hydraulic elevators. The apartments were two to a floor in each of the building's four quadrants, and featured ceilings more than twenty feet high and huge ebony doors. The Dakota's enormous iron front gates opened into a large courtyard, with two large turrets around which the horse-drawn carriages would turn. Clark's eleven-room personal bachelor apartment's ballroom could accommodate one hundred people in a sit-down dinner and still leave room for them to dance—leading one to deduce that he was quite active socially.

By 1960, the building was rent-controlled, and its cash flow was negative, despite present and future tenants such as Leonard Bernstein, Lauren Bacall (whom we knew as Betty), Paul Simon, Rudolph Nureyev, Roberta Flack, and Gilda Radner. The Clark Foundation, which then owned the building, announced the week before Christmas that William Zeckendorf wanted to tear it down and erect an eponymous high-rise. But in what may have been a prearranged gambit, another New York developer contacted the tenants and said he would organize a co-op purchase of the building for $4.5 million. In an act of seeming generosity, instead of reaping a cash fee for his services, he took ownership of the tennis court next door, which few residents used. He promptly sold the land for $2 million to a developer who built the Mayfair Apartments on it. Through this wily machination his fee was ultimately almost 45 percent of the sale price, an outlandish arrangement. But the purchase was successful, the new ownership board closed the restaurant to save money, and the Dakota was saved from extinction.

I soon realized after becoming a resident that a real camaraderie permeated the building, something very unusual in New York luxury dwellings. Every December, the Brooklyn Children's Choir would carol at the foot of each stairwell. Then we all would go to Leonard Bernstein's apartment for cocktails and hear the children carol while he played the piano. This great treat really embodied the spirit of Christmas. Another tradition occurred on the first Wednesday of October, when every resident would set up in our courtyard a table with each one's favorite food, a collective feast. Even the building's most famous residents, John Lennon and Yoko Ono, participated, in their case serving macrobiotic food. The whole atmosphere was remarkably like a country fair, but populated by very sophisticated people, including Princess Muna of Saudi Arabia, the pathbreaking dancer Mikhail Baryshnikov, and the Portuguese Ambassador to the United States.

Finally, the Dakota residents relished putting up elaborate Halloween decorations. When it was time for trick-or-treaters (limited to residents' children) to come around on Halloween Night, we left the door to our apartment ajar. Whenever it was opened a skeleton sprung out from a purple-lighted crypt with an eerie howling sound. Paul Simon's eight-year-old son came to our door in a Superman outfit the first year we did it. The apparition frightened him so much that he wet his pants and reeled backward, almost falling down the stairs. The Ross family subsequently switched to a slightly less scary display.

Besides the Halloween decor, the Dakota had, in fact, become infamous as a scary place because the 1968 horror film *Rosemary's Baby* was filmed there. The producer rented the use of the exterior and built studio sets to simulate interiors, so no actual filming took place inside. Nevertheless, I think the connection to the film played tricks on people's minds. When my daughter was young, she would sometimes have a playmate who, being afraid of ghosts, would suddenly insist on going home. Obviously, the ghosts weren't real, but one day, when I was the Board President, the superintendent called me to say that ghosts were causing a commotion in the basement. This claim was so outlandish that I went down myself to observe. Sure enough, every few minutes a garbage can would suddenly fly up and crash down or a mop would skitter across the floor. It was spooky, but most likely was somehow staged by teenagers living in the building.

Sadly, the Dakota community did experience real-world tragic horror. I was the board president the night John Lennon was murdered on December 8, 1980. Early in the evening, the killer had politely asked John to sign a record cover. John did so, and he and Yoko went off to dinner. But the killer lingered outside in the meantime and shot John dead without provocation after he got out of his limo. I was working at home when I heard the shots. I learned from the reception desk that John had been shot and rushed down to try to help. The police and the emergency medical services (EMS) personnel had arrived at about the same time, but it was too late. It was unanimous among the residents that it was an awful tragedy—none of us had ever heard John say a single bad word about anyone or anything.

After the EMS took John away, the police returned in anticipation of a mob gathering in front of the building. It was evident to all that the Dakota's entrance would be swamped by mourners for the foreseeable future. We instituted a set of security measures that made coming home to our beloved building like arriving at an Army camp. We kept the gate shut and immediately issued photo IDs to the residents so they could pass through barriers being set up outside of the building. Nor would tradesmen, decorators, or visitors be permitted entry until the crowds dispersed. The police manned barricades in front of the building to keep the crowds back. People, many of whom were too young to have ever seen John perform, brought flowers or little cards, which the police let them put on the driveway's large iron gate. TV cameras were there 24/7.

The number of mourners swelled from the second day on, when they were joined by the Save the Whales people and many other unrelated social activist groups. By the end of the first week, it was clear that the crowds would remain until there was a cathartic event to celebrate John's life. Yoko was unresponsive because of her grief, but one resident knew music producer David Geffen, her great friend. We discussed with David the need for a funeral or some other event away from the building to signal the crowds to disperse. Geffen knew that John and Yoko loved Strawberry Fields in Central Park and convinced Yoko to convene a ceremony there. It worked. The crowd dissipated, but tour buses and crowds still gather around the Dakota every year on his birthday and on the anniversary of his assassination. In truth, John deserves it. He was not only a prodigious talent, but also a truly peace-loving person. I hope he has gone to his just reward in heaven.

Years later, when our children went away to school, I sold that large apartment and bought a smaller one from an elderly woman and her son. They had been tenants beginning back when the Dakota was rent-controlled, and thanks to some curious decisions made by a left-wing New York court, had outfoxed Freddy Victoria, the famous antique dealer, for ownership of the unit. When I went to view it, only her son and a large dalmatian sleeping on a pool table in the living room were present. The son took me through the apartment. The walls inside his dimly lit bedroom were covered with golden discs. Since the Dakota had so many musicians, I asked if those were his golden records. He said, "No, these are my golden Frisbees." He had just won the national Frisbee championship in Central Park. Where but the Dakota could you find such an amazing mix of unusual people?

I bought the apartment and chose Mario Buatta to decorate it. Mario was one of the most brilliant interior designers of the twentieth century, whom the media dubbed the "Prince of Chintz," for his colorful design aesthetic executed with dramatic aplomb. His private client list read like a combination of the *Social Register* and *Who's Who*. He and Mark Hampton even redecorated Blair House in Washington—America's ceremonial diplomatic reception venue. I had originally hired Mario to decorate my first apartment in the Dakota, but he blew through my entire budget in the first room, so I fired him. Nonetheless, Mario is so good-natured that we remained friendly, and one year he even came to my daughter's birthday party. This was one of the earliest times when I saw Mario demonstrate his flair for practical jokes. Mario came with a large Tiffany bag, a gesture that would delight any young girl. As Amanda reached out for it, he dropped it to the floor with a great sound of breaking glass. She looked into the bag and saw that he had filled it with already broken window glass. He then gave her the real present.

Mario also carried around a pet plastic cockroach named Harold, who made an appearance at the most inappropriate moments. Mario loved to slip Harold onto a dinner partner's plate, provoking a squeal of horror. He then would pretend to squash it with his hand, while actually palming it up into his sleeve. Harold's most celebrated appearance came on a guided tour of the Opus One winery in California. In a gleaming stainless-steel production room, while the vintner explained how sanitary the winery process was, Mario placed Harold atop a vat and in a strangely high-pitched voice asked, "If you are so careful, why is there a cockroach here?" The vintner's head was beginning to explode until Mario covertly pulled the transparent string attached to Harold and put it back in his pocket. Everyone except the Opus One official found it amusing.

Buatta was also the greatest fan of the Australian female impersonator Barry Humphries, who performed as Dame Edna Everage. Buatta went to one hundred consecutive performances in New York, always taking along two clients and sitting in the same front-row center seats. After the eightieth performance, Humphries installed under Mario's habitual seat a fart-sounding machine activated by a button in Dame Edna's purse and activated it repeatedly during the show, to Mario's great embarrassment. Afterward, Mario, as usual, took his clients backstage to meet Edna. This time, Mario was livid and demanded that Humphries stop using the machine. Thereafter, Humphries confined it to two fart bursts per night. Mario never told me this story, but the late Humphries did at a dinner party in Greece a few years ago. He said that now that Mario had passed on (he died in 2018) he could reveal the story to good friends.

Studio 54

No one would ever accuse me of having Saturday Night Fever—I'm not a night owl, and I rarely ventured out to nightclubs. But I had enough exposure to the industry from friends involved in it that I learned quite a bit about how the concept of scarcity drove consumer-facing businesses.

In the early 1970s, FDS brought to the public markets Steak 'N Brew, a chain of steak and beer restaurants run by a Dakota neighbor, Larry Ellman. Despite his beefsteak empire, Larry was a vegetarian who relied on carnivorous friends like me to judge the quality of his red meat. Larry wanted to acquire a nightclub business, so I asked him to think about a place in midtown Manhattan that was on its way to becoming the most famous dance club of all-time: Studio 54.

Much has been written about the Studio 54 scene, but from a business standpoint the club had all the ingredients for a profitable nightclub: loud decorations, flashing lights, booming music, a high cover charge, and expensive drinks and food. Studio 54 had also benefited from a reputation as a hedonist's paradise for the drug use and sexual exploits that purportedly took place in the restrooms. People waited in line for hours hoping to be admitted, and paparazzi swarmed all over the place. The club really didn't get going until late at night and continued well into the next morning.

I never spent much time at Studio 54, but I did know one of the proprietors, Steve Rubell. We agreed to meet for lunch in the Plaza Hotel Oak Bar. Steve and his business partner, Ian Schrager, disguised themselves with very conventional suits and ties and insisted we meet when the restaurant opened at 11:30 a.m. They knew none of their clientele would be up that early or at such a staid place.

The chemistry between the two impresarios and Larry was pretty solid, and after some chitchatting Larry said to Steve, "You redecorate the place frequently. Isn't that very expensive?"

"Yes, but we have to do it every couple of months. You must remember our customers have relatively limited attention spans!"

"How do you decide who to admit?"

"We give the bouncers a list of our regulars, and they get right in. As for the rest, we have a formula. We want certain percentages of movie stars, of models, of politicians, of Asians, of Europeans, of gays, of sailors, etc. And we keep the grays below 5 percent."

"The grays? What are grays?"

He pointed to me. "People like him."

The story of Studio 54 shows that certain consumer businesses thrive on offering uniquely differentiated products. Studio 54 wasn't going to compete on price with other clubs. But its ultra-restrictive admittance policy let it charge absurd prices because people felt they were entering an exclusive world once they passed to the other side of the velvet rope. Similarly, Hermès's systematic rationing of the Birkin Bag has kept the prices for them insanely high, even though repeated auctions of used bags makes one question the actual scarcity.

Joel A. Rosenthal, also known as JAR, has built a splendid jewelry business by imposing brilliant design on relatively inexpensive materials. You need an introduction and an appointment to gain initial access to his unmarked and unadvertised store across from the Ritz Hotel in Paris. Once admitted, you only gain full access to his unique creations if he decides that he likes you. If you ever resell something you bought from him, especially at auction, you become persona non grata. The few pieces that do come up at auction usually sell for twice or more than JAR charges, because so few people have direct access to his creations. This phenomenon was exacerbated a few years ago when the Metropolitan Museum of Art mounted an exhibition of his work—the first time the Met ever exhibited a living jeweler in the main museum, as opposed to the costume department. My wife Hilary lent some pieces, and I supported the cost of the show. JAR, however, does not like to talk with the press, so when the *New York Times* called to ask if I would help them get an interview with him, he demurred and said I should just talk with them. Joel's anonymity added additional mystique to his products.

The cases of Studio 54, Hermès products, and JAR illustrate that everyone lusts for things that are just out of reach, and scarcity of a product—real or imagined—can help elevate its desirability. To the extent one considers buying a property, piece of art, or entertainment-related business, it would be wise to keep this in mind.

Daughters' Escapades

The late 1960s and early 1970s were a memorable time in my life as my daughters grew toward adulthood. I am prohibited by nondisclosure agreements from talking about either of my two marriages prior to my union with Hilary. But I can share some stories related to my two lovely daughters, Jessica and Amanda. They taught me as much about life as I taught them.

At age eleven, my younger daughter Amanda had a pet gerbil whom she loved. Freddie lived in a large cage that had a Ferris wheel–like apparatus in which he would run repeatedly and spin it. Freddie's chateau also had a food bar, water, and a resting place. Amanda would watch him for hours on end and occasionally take him out to play with him. She also had a smaller travel case, but it was too easy for him to get out of it, and when he did he would hide somewhere. In one hotel room we found him snarled in the bed's box spring, a dangerous place.

Therefore, when we went to a Florida hotel one year for Christmas vacation, we checked Freddie into a pet shop for safekeeping. Unfortunately, when we returned to New York after New Year's, he was shriveled and weak, having evidently caught a disease from another animal. My wife and daughter took the gerbil to the animal medical center, while I went home to the Dakota to do some work. Several hours later someone called and spoke in grave tones.

"Mr. Ross, I have sad news for you. We tried our best, but Freddie has died. You have my condolences."

I was alarmed, but having forgotten the gerbil's name, I asked, "Freddie who?"

"Your pet gerbil. I suggest that you authorize us to perform an autopsy."

"Autopsy? Why? Was there any indication of foul play?"

"Mr. Ross, this is a serious matter. Wouldn't you like to know what caused his untimely death?"

I declined. I could only imagine what an autopsy might cost relative to a $50 gerbil. In a way, that moment was a lesson to my children about money—don't throw good money at dumb ideas.

As I continued to have success on Wall Street, my conviction grew that children in affluent families should learn about money, work, and capitalism. All too often, the first generation makes some money and the next couple of generations dissipate it through indolence. I did not want that to happen to my family.

When my elder daughter Jessica turned seventeen, we had to decide how she and her sister would have summer jobs. It was not acceptable that they just loll around on the beach all day, so I bid on and won the fast-food concession for Flying Point Beach in Water Mill, a village near Southampton. There was one other bidder, a Brooklynite who had other Long Island beach concessions. But my spokesperson explained that I was a long-term resident of Southampton and chaired the local museum, and my girls had spent all their summers there, so the concession should not go to an out-of-towner. This xenophobic argument carried the day.

The girls were at their respective boarding schools when the concession was awarded, so I set up a conference call. This was the first time they learned about it.

"Girls, I have great news. We have solved your summer transportation and job needs. You two will be operating the fast food concession at Flying Point Beach, and a stainless-steel van will be exclusively your transportation and place of business!"

Silence was the response from these image-conscious young ladies. Then, "What if someone recognizes us?"

"Undoubtedly, they will. Lots of people here know you."

"Can we talk it over?"

Their self-image was not one of flipping hamburgers, but my girls finally agreed. We named the enterprise Tavern on the Beach in honor of our Dakota neighbor, Warner LeRoy, who owned Tavern on the Green in Central Park.

The next debate was the menu. The girls wanted to serve healthy, macrobiotic food. I convinced them also to have hamburgers, hot dogs, French fries, and other junk food. Guess what sold best? By the second week their sales were so good that their hot dog supplier, Sabrett, gave them logoed awnings to put over the chairs around the food wagon. Soon the van became the social center of the beach. Lifeguards and lots of others hung around, so we had to put out more beach chairs.

But, like any business, Tavern on the Beach faced competition.

One day I received a phone call from one of my daughters, "The Good Humor man has parked next to us and is taking our customers!"

I swooped in, and told the Good Humor Man in no uncertain terms, "We own the exclusive concession for this beach. If you don't leave, I'll have you arrested for trespassing." It was a far cry from my college days, when we petitioned to have the Good Humor Man restored to campus.

In the end, the Good Humor Man bailed, but that evening the girls were sad. They felt that he was selling ice cream to make a living, while they were simply in business to earn spending money. I explained about property rights, and they calmed down. It was a good lesson in the competitive nature of business.

Tavern on the Beach continued to thrive that summer. On the Fourth of July, they grossed $12,000—a lot of cash for two teenagers! When they got home that night, we went into the kitchen and divided it as usual: one-third for supplies, one-third to pay for the truck, and one-third for them. They were thrilled to get $2,000 each, even if the bills were stained with ketchup and mustard. They also were thrilled to have a vehicle in which they could drive their teenage friends around in the evening (even if the dinner bell clanged the whole time). Then, in mid-August, Amanda said she was quitting. I told her that she would have no allowance for the rest of the summer if she did. She flashed a bankbook and said, "I've saved $1,500, so I don't need an allowance!" Her sister immediately accused her of stealing from the truck. They gradually calmed down and both went back to work. Even though the girls did not share my dream of the food truck being the start of a global food service business, I was proud that they had learned a bit about business instead of lounging around.

As a teenager, Amanda rode horses in Central Park after school. When she went to Sarah Lawrence College, she rode a very good Dutch Warmblood gelding named LB in hunter-jumper competitions. Initially, we leased LB from a stable which soon filed for bankruptcy, an event to which I took personal offense, given my role in advising global companies on the brink of bankruptcy. I appeared personally in the U.S. Bankruptcy Court on Long Island and settled my claim for the large security deposit by gaining title to the horse. It made sense to own LB outright, since Amanda was consistently Sarah Lawrence's high point rider and continued competing with him after graduation. Then she decided to move to Paris with her French boyfriend, Arnot. That ended her interest in riding, so I put the beast up for sale. Month after month, no bids, just news flashes about LB winning this or that event. The stable was happy to collect my rent money for the stable and rent out LB to other riders.

In owning LB, I learned that horses are in the same category as boats—be prepared for the bills to come rolling in. The breaking point came while I was about to go to Florida for the holidays. Amanda called from Paris to specify what Christmas presents had to be taken to LB. I acceded to her wishes, but said, "Amanda, enough with the horse. I'm going to donate him to West Point and get a tax deduction instead of bill after bill."

She got hysterical. "No, you can't do that! I rode against those Cadets. They override their horses and don't take proper care of them!"

"I will give you until January 31st to find a home for LB. If not, off he goes to West Point."

On January 28th Amanda called back and said, "Dartmouth! They have a new indoor riding ring and they know the horse because I rode against them. They will pick LB up next week."

They did, and soon there came a thank-you note from the president of Dartmouth College for this valuable animal. He also started sending me all sorts of material promoting Dartmouth, not realizing I really didn't give a hoot about the college. My contribution was just a way to get rid of the horse bills.

A few weeks later, Amanda said her Parisian boyfriend had applied for admission to Dartmouth's Tuck School of Business and asked for a letter of recommendation. I wrote to my new pen pal, the president, and quickly got a thank-you note for the recommendation. He thought that he now had a new donor really on the hook. That fall, Amanda and Arnot went to Dartmouth, but soon broke up. I wrote the president to inform him that I now had two unwanted geldings at Dartmouth, so there was no point pitching me anymore.

Upon returning to the Hamptons, Amanda started a charity using retired show horses to provide therapy to children with autism and ADHD. The motion of the horse, and perhaps the child feeling for the first time in control of something, helped them. One day, she called, happily tearful that a ten-year-old autistic boy took one ride around the ring, and as he hopped off the horse, shouted, "Hi Mom!" They were the first words he had ever spoken.

––––––––––

Over the years I have learned that buying a few objects of really high quality is ultimately far more satisfying than buying large quantities of lesser things. Once lower-quality items lose the shine of newness, their appeal fades rapidly while the better ones continue to appeal, no matter how long you own them.

In the case of jewelry, items signed by well-known craftsmen typically hold their value better than anonymous pieces. Buyers in the resale market seem comforted by the label. A famous provenance also helps, especially with lesser objects. This is why single-owner sales usually fetch high prices at auctions.

With real estate, the three most important keys are, as one great property magnate often said, "Location, location, location." Location is the one factor the new owner cannot change. I have noticed over the years that even the worst house in the best location tends to appreciate more rapidly than the best house in the worst location. The most notable exception is when a neighborhood gentrifies, because that means that the location value has improved. "Patience, patience, patience," is also a wise saying—meaning that if the property is well-capitalized you can ride out the recurring cyclical downturns and benefit from the ultimate recoveries. But the most important determination of change in real estate values, in my view, is population migration. If your location is enjoying significant inbound migration you are likely to do well, but woe betide you if there is outbound migration.

Houses. Boats. Helicopters. Horses. I owned them all in the 1970s. Some turned out to be wiser purchases than others (and I will have much more to say about collecting art later in this book). Overall, factors such as scarcity, fixed costs, and expected frequency of use should be weighed carefully while deciding on any major purchase. But sometimes—as in the case of LB—the happiness that an item brings to someone else outweighs the financial costs. In the end, those closest to you are the personal assets that matter the most.

CHAPTER 5

The King of Bankruptcy

In the early 1970s, Weeden & Company, a block trading firm that was not a member of the NYSE, lobbied to abolish the exchange's traditional commission structure for trades. Weeden argued that the commissions on any given trade should be negotiated between the customer and the broker, not set arbitrarily by the exchange. The SEC welcomed the suggestions, and invited testimony from several Wall Street firms, including Faulkner, Dawkins, & Sullivan. I was the partner designated to argue against the change at an SEC hearing.

At the hearing, I made several points. First, at that point no institutional customer had ever complained to the SEC about the current structure. Second, a small individual investor would have no bargaining power against a behemoth like Merrill Lynch, and even institutional brokerages like ours would have no bargaining power against a giant securities-purchasing institution such as Fidelity. Firms would simply announce the commission rate and that would be it. Therefore, a change to negotiated rates meant that subsidies for FDS research coming from big institutional investors would end. I was feeling good about my argument.

Then the SEC put me on the defensive.

The SEC official leading the session thanked me for my testimony and said, "I now offer into evidence the financial statements your firm files with the SEC. I assume, Mr. Ross, that the copy I just handed you is correct."

I gulped, "Yes, sir," knowing what was coming next.

He said, "Mr. Ross, your firm mainly handles large trades and has net profits of 50 percent on revenues and 100 percent on your equity capital. Isn't that the real reason you want to keep the commissions at fixed rates?"

I responded, "We are so profitable because institutions reward us for providing superior research that improves the returns they can achieve for pensioners and the public investors in mutual funds. If commissions are cut, we won't be able to afford such good research, and neither will anyone else."

"Thank you, Mr. Ross. You are free to go."

Our argument did not carry the day. Six months later, negotiated commissions were the law of the land, and our average commission per share dropped by 40 percent. FDS remained profitable, but far less so than before, so we decided to start dealing with prosperous retail customers who would be attracted to our strong stock-picking record. We hired a sales manager from EF Hutton who brought in high-net-worth individuals to our New York office and to a branch we opened in Madison, New Jersey, a wealthy area. The new sales team produced large revenues, but was stocked with wild characters. One, who lived on a houseboat at Manhattan's 78th Street Boat Basin, had a strange way of getting through to the CEOs he was cold-calling. If they did not return his initial calls he would call again and say to the secretary, "Tell your boss I am his wife's divorce lawyer!" He generally got a very quick return call. Most of his targets became angry at the gambit and hung up, but a surprising number found his bravado sufficiently interesting that they started trading with him.

These big producers helped generate solid rates of return for the firm, but their antics also created headaches for our compliance team. Therefore, to limit the bad consequences of roguish behavior, we decided to buy a retail brokerage that was properly organized. Several senior executives of H. Hentz & Co. wanted to retire and were happy to sell us their controlling interest. Hentz was both a retail stockbroker and a midsize commodity trading business, so purchasing it would give us an opportunity to diversify our trading operation. Dwight Faulkner and I made a handshake deal with them, but as the word of the imminent sale got out, Sandy Weill's Shearson, Hayden & Stone swooped in and paid a much higher price. Sandy was on an acquisition binge in those days, and H. Hentz & Co. was not his final target. In 1977, he also bought FDS. Not wanting to be part of a major retail firm, I made my next move.

The Rothschild Legacy

In the late eighteenth century, Mayer Amschel Rothschild founded his first bank in Frankfurt, Germany. His five sons expanded it throughout Europe, each setting up shop in a different country. One of the Rothschild family's many noteworthy financings was a loan for the construction of the Suez Canal, which enabled the British government to become the canal's major shareholder. The bank's storied history has bequeathed many traditions to posterity, the most unique of which occurred inside a certain conference room at the firm's headquarters in London, known as New Court. Since 1919, the room had been used to fix the global price of gold twice each day. It had a table with five seats, one for each of the traditional firms dealing in gold bullion. In front of each seat was a small, lead-weighted British flag. The Rothschild chairman would call out gradually ascending prices. When the chairman got to a price favored by a participant, he (and it was always a he) would tip over the flag to signal its acceptability. When the last flag tipped and the price was set, everyone had a celebratory sherry and returned to their respective firms. Today, the world price of gold is based on actual orders received. The room, however, remains as it was, flags and all.

The story of the bank's expansion to the United States is fascinating. G. Peter Fleck was a Dutch partner of the Rothschild enterprise. During the early days of World War II, Peter fled Europe for the United States, smuggling with him a large amount of gold (one ton, as legend has it). He subsequently formed a business under the relatively anonymous name Amsterdam Overseas Corporation (AOC), and set out to win U.S. business for the venerable house of Rothschild. Peter was not only an investment banker, but also later in life became an ordained and practicing Unitarian Universalist minister, a unique combination for a smuggler.

AOC became a commercial finance company, lending at premium rates to companies turned down by banks. By the early 1950s, AOC was substantial, but still not big enough to borrow in the low-cost commercial paper market, so Peter sold it to Aetna Insurance, which had access to that market. They renamed it Aetna Business Credit. The proceeds went to start a venture capital and investment banking operation controlled jointly by the British and French Rothschild families. In a clever "inside baseball" move, they named it

New Court Securities Corporation. New Court was the name of Rothschild's London location, so only au courant Wall Streeters understood the provenance of the New Court Securities name. New Court in the United States would go on to provide the original financing for companies such as FedEx and Texas Instruments.

My entry into Rothschild came from a personal connection—just one of the many times in my life that I benefited from knowing good people. Because our daughters went to school together, I had a minor relationship with John Birkelund, a president of New Court Securities, and FDS had also done a little bit of business with the firm. When John learned from the trade press that our deal to buy H. Hentz had fallen apart, he invited me to lunch at the Brook Club. It was then that he revealed some startling news: "We need a new head of investment banking at New Court. And I'd like you to take the job."

The offer was very attractive, for a few reasons. First, the Rothschild connection held lots of intrigue. Second, I liked the firm's business model. The firm was owned one-third by the English Rothschilds, one-third by the French branch, and one-third by the New York executives. Because it was the general partner of a venture capital fund, I would be awarded part of the carried interest, as well as part ownership of the firm itself. Third, there was boundless opportunity to grow the investment banking unit, which was smaller than what I had built at FDS. New Court Securities' investment banking activities in the United States were at the time mainly confined to merger assignments referred to them by Rothschild in London or Paris. I knew I could have a major impact on earnings, and that it probably wouldn't be too hard to bring over at least some of my present clients, as well as capture new ones. So, in 1976, I went to work for one of the most famous banking outfits of all time. And in time, my guesses proved to be correct.

By that point in time, whether because of envy, anti-Semitism, or misguided government economic policies, the Rothschild family had endured many hardships that transcended normal business competition. In the twentieth century, the French Rothschild leader, Baron Guy de Rothschild, faced nationalization of his businesses three times: his railroads by Communists in the 1930s, by the Nazis during World War II, and by President François Mitterrand in 1981. Mitterrand's all-out socialist assault on the company resulted in the French government paying less than the market value for the Rothschild headquarters building on the Rue Lafitte. Mitterrand even confiscated Banque Rothschild's name, so the family ran ads disavowing any connection with it and emigrated to the United States.

As a shrewd manager of his empire, Baron Guy Rothschild showed up to work every day at the firm's U.S. headquarters at One Rockefeller Plaza. Guy retained both a gravitas and eccentricity that befit the head of a French banking family. He always arrived at the office accompanied by his beloved schnauzer. But this created a minor problem. Rockefeller Center was decidedly anti-dog, so we had to negotiate with the building's management on how the dog could come to work. Because Rothschild had recently represented the Rockefeller 1934 Trust in their sale of Rock Center to the Japanese firm Mitsubishi, we were not beloved by the Rockefeller Center executives. After some tough negotiating, the parties ultimately agreed that the dog's feet would not touch the ground between Guy's limo and our office floor, and that Guy would wear his dog pass on his breast pocket at all times. Guy himself thus carried the dog everywhere. Despite this favor, the schnauzer always snarled whenever I entered Guy's office. It did not respond to my commands in English, only in French, and only from Guy.

The Business of Bankruptcy

In the late 1970s and 1980s, Mike Milken and others proliferated the concept of high-yield bond financing, precipitating a boom in leveraged buyouts (LBOs) throughout U.S. markets. It was clear that more workouts would occur as a result, so I created a business at Rothschild of advising institutional lenders on their distressed loans. Over the years, I've been called a corporate raider, or, even more pejoratively, "the king of bankruptcy." I have some sharp rebuttals. For one thing, I reject being called a "corporate raider" in the way it is used to describe those who buy a company and immediately sell off anything of value to line their own pockets. My aim in advising on, investing in, or purchasing distressed assets was always to restore value (and earn a profit for me and my firm, of course). Largely because of my middle-class upbringing and, I confess, my Democratic politics, I was always sensitive to wanting to keep people employed and companies in business as I advised on bankruptcies. More often than not, I succeeded.

An unparalleled asset throughout my career was the U.S. bankruptcy code. It is by far the best in the world. Only America has a set of bankruptcy laws structured to help businesses stay alive through restructuring. When a company fails, there are only three alternatives: a government takeover, a liquidation, or a turnaround. A government takeover is not the optimal solution, because taxpayers should not be asked to finance bailouts, and a government receivership is no foundation for managing a company back to health. Liquidations aren't preferable because they tend to spell disaster for hundreds, if not thousands, of workers. A leveraged buyout of a failing company is the best way for society to responsibly address business failure. My work as a turnaround artist earned me the appellation "The King of Bankruptcy." To me, this title, first coined by *Fortune* magazine, is not slanderous. It is a golden third-party endorsement of what my teams and I were able to do to protect workers and creditors alike as we handled some of the largest bankruptcies in history.

One of our most interesting cases at Rothschild involved Federated Department Stores, the largest retailer bankruptcy in history. Federated owned Bloomingdale's and 220 other department stores in twenty-six states and had more than 56,000 employees. In 1990, Robert Campeau, a Canadian financier and shopping center developer, did a $6.5 billion hostile takeover with a leveraged buyout. He borrowed 97 percent of the purchase price, an extraordinary degree of debt that caused the company to fail within two years (paying rent turned out to be more difficult than collecting it). Campeau had been advised on the deal by an advisor at Credit Suisse First Boston named Bruce Wasserstein. Wasserstein had the nickname "Bid them up Bruce" because he recommended to buyers higher deal prices than many Wall Streeters believed were justified. Some hated Bruce out of pure jealousy for the huge fees he was able to earn, but Wall Street was correct in this case. Nevertheless, we at Rothschild, working on behalf of large institutional creditors, set to work to deliver Federated from bankruptcy on terms that were palatable to workers, management, and investors.

Because Federated's financial health had deteriorated in such a short amount of time, a House of Representatives committee scheduled investigative hearings and invited me to testify. As is usual, the witnesses were divided into three-person panels. The first speaker on mine was the president of the Federated union. He lamented the government's failure to prevent leveraged buyouts from endangering jobs. The second witness was a professor who argued that employees should own their companies. He was an expert on employee stock ownership programs, but had no insights into this particular situation. At the end of his testimony, the congressman chairing the hearing said, "Turning back to Federated, professor, what was the role of investment bankers in this and other failed LBOs?"

The professor, who was sitting in a wheelchair, waved an unlighted cigar and responded, "Mr. Chairman, investment bankers are to the financial systems what mud wrestlers are to the performing arts!"

The chair responded: "Thank you, Professor. Now we will hear from an investment banker involved in this case, Wilbur Ross." The chair of the hearing had really set me up!

To refute these ugly characterizations, I did what I have always done to win my arguments: invoke data-driven analysis. I told the committee, "The vast majority of LBOs perform well. And just as companies not acquired by an LBO occasionally fail, so too do some LBOs. Therefore, it makes no more sense to outlaw them than to outlaw cars because reckless drivers occasionally kill people."

As I completed these remarks, the professor murmured into the microphone loud enough for all to hear, "Another goddammed mud wrestler." While the room roared with laughter, the chairman said, "Thank you, Mr. Ross. This panel is dismissed."

I wasn't as charismatic as the professor, but no legislative proposal came out of these hearings. And I got an education on how congressional hearings usually work: The lawmakers opposing my side of the issue had gotten the sound bites they wanted, and could use them to pander to the unions and the anti–Wall Street folks. I remembered the PR purposes behind congressional hearings when I was called to testify before Congress multiple times while serving as Secretary of Commerce.

Despite the enmity coming from Capitol Hill, Federated slashed debt, ditched Campeau, and emerged from bankruptcy in 1992. Although the company did have to liquidate forty stores in the process, one writer hailed the outcome as "miraculous."[8] In 1994, the company acquired Macy's, and today Federated stores do billions in sales every year under the Macy's, Inc. brand.

Just as I saw lawyers come out of the woodwork to profit off the Sunasco merger years earlier, I also observed how National Gypsum became the target of dubious litigation that led to bankruptcy. Not long before unsecured creditors hired me to advise on proceedings, National Gypsum had been quite profitable. The problem was that the company had sold asbestos products decades before the dangers of the substance were known. Like sharks smelling blood, class action lawyers sued National Gypsum on behalf of the huge number of people previously exposed. The only way National Gypsum could survive the sheer volume of litigation was through a Chapter 11 bankruptcy. In bankruptcy, all claims are stayed until the case is resolved, normally by negotiation.

It was truly lowbrow how the lawyers ran their scheme. As is common in class action cases, trial lawyers often bring such cases on speculation. If they win, they recoup out-of-pocket expenses and a fee of up to one-third of what they collected from the target company. So, the lawyers find some willing plaintiffs, convince a court to certify the class, and sue on behalf of more than a million "victims."

This is exactly what happened in the National Gypsum case. During the proceedings, one of our staff learned that one lawyer was still actively recruiting clients for an unrelated asbestos case. That Friday, we sent someone undercover to the factory where the lawyers were recruiting, to generate a record of how they operated. It was a real eye-opener. They parked a big van just outside of the factory. A recruiter on a loudspeaker repeatedly barked out, "Come on into our van and have a beer! If you have ever been exposed to asbestos, sign up and tell us the story. We will represent you in court. You will not have to testify or pay any legal fees. And when the case ends, you will get some money. Come on in!"

We rushed into court the following Monday, brandishing the evidence. We asked the judge to throw the case out. He held a mini-hearing in camera—without any outsiders present. Ultimately, he ruled we could not put our finding into evidence because it might prejudice the case against the plaintiffs. The claimants prevailed and were awarded several billion dollars, partly in cash and partly in stock of the reorganized company. We don't know how many of those claims were legitimate, but current shareholders lost a fortune for events that happened decades before most of them even owned the stock. The same thing happened to Johns Manville Corporation and other building material companies.

The United States is the one jurisdiction in the world in which class action cases are prevalent, and the victims hardly ever see real money. It is rare that any individual claimant collects as much as $1,000 from a case, but the lawyers become wealthy. One can only wonder if there might be a better system for dealing with such matters. One thought is to limit the amount of time one has to file a claim after the discovery of the problem. Another would be random testing of the claimants by court-appointed examiners to determine if they have a serious malady consistent with the known effects of exposure to a substance. Either way, the U.S. Congress would do well to take up tort reform to stop trial lawyers from ruining perfectly honest businesses and causing managers to be fearful of doing anything that could produce a class action suit.

Airline Acrimony

More conventional than the National Gypsum case were the many airline workouts I handled as the industry deregulated. In the Pan Am case of 1991, my clients were the flight attendants and the Teamster unions. Pan Am was losing money and the workers feared that it would be liquidated. It was clear that a combination of labor concessions and exchange of debt for equity would not be enough to ensure stability. For one thing, Pan Am needed a major repositioning. For example, the Pan Am Building in Manhattan was so named because they were the lead tenant. Why did they need such a high-rent location?

This was one case in which the unions understood well the wounds management had inflicted on the company. To start with, executives had lavished on themselves unreasonable compensation and perks. Some high executives had houses in Bermuda, and the company ran many lossmaking flights from New York City to Bermuda to accommodate them. Unions accused management of under-scrutinizing these and other money-losing flights. The unions believed that margins could be improved if management were more thoughtful about the routes and how many first-class seats there were relative to business class and coach. Certain routes generally ran out of highly profitable first-class seats, so more should have been added. More significantly, there were hugely underfunded retirement funds and postretirement healthcare obligations.

Most of all, the unions hated Marty Shugrue, the CEO. I soon learned why. When I met with him to discuss a workout, prominently displayed on his desk was a riding crop that a British officer might have used to discipline a recalcitrant soldier. Shugrue was barely polite. He spent ten minutes excoriating me for representing the unions:

"You were educated at Yale and Harvard Business School. Surely you can find more appropriate clients than the skirts who are stewardesses and the thugs who are Teamsters." He continued, "You should be ashamed of yourself. You have some nerve coming in to tell me how to run an airline. We are Pan Am, America's flag carrier!"

"Mr. Shugrue, you are in terrible financial condition and need to make radical changes. That is the reality. You must face it." He then calmed down and asked to hear our proposal.

I pitched him on eliminating many unprofitable schedules, subletting the Pan Am building in New York, and moving the executive staff to less expensive space. His face got redder and redder, and I began to worry he might use the crop on me. He disliked every suggestion and only brightened a little when I said the unions would accept lower pay and more flexible work rules. He then asked, "Anything else?"

"Yes, sir. The unions feel you must retire to clear the air."

"This meeting is over."

We eventually convinced the board members that they had fiduciary duties at least to consider the proposal, but most were strongly in Shugrue's camp, so it was ultimately no use. Their recalcitrance led to the liquidation of Pan Am. It no longer exists, and it proves that a riding crop and a docile board are no solutions to real business problems.

An airline bankruptcy was also the cause of one of my earliest encounters with the legendary investor Carl Icahn. Carl had made one of his rare mistakes by buying all of TWA, which at that time was hurting badly. One of TWA's major problems was its underfunded pension fund. This was not necessarily prohibitive for an acquisition—you could usually make a good deal with the Pension Benefit Guaranty Corporation, the government agency that insured pension plans. However, just before I was preparing to negotiate with him on behalf of unsecured creditors, Carl's lawyers discovered an arcane pension law which deemed an owner of more than 90 percent of a failed company individually liable for the underfunding of a failed pension plan. This was a real problem, but Carl devised an ingenious solution. In return for contributing a huge sum to the pension fund, he convinced the management to give him a similarly huge amount of free airline tickets. He set up a wholesale travel agency managed by his then executive assistant and now wife, Gail. Ticket sales over a few years resulted in a net gain.

Later that summer, Carl had a housewarming party for his new oceanside mansion in East Hampton. While attending it, my longtime tennis partner Bob Nederlander and I noticed there were two tennis courts, so we arranged to play Carl and his partner the following Saturday at 2:00 p.m. During the week, Carl researched our skill level and learned that Bob had captained the University of Michigan team many years ago. That Saturday at about noon Carl called to say the TWA unions were arguing with him again, so we rescheduled our match to 4:00 p.m. When we got there, Carl and his partner had obviously been warming up for quite a while. Bob and

I only had the opportunity to hit a few balls back and forth before Carl demanded, "Let's get started."

His partner, a strapping twenty-one-year-old, was the captain of the Vanderbilt University tennis team. As you might imagine, he was all over the court covering for Carl. We did win a few games, but every time we did the college player really turned it on for the next game. That's Carl for you—winning is everything.

TWA endured two Chapter 11 bankruptcies in the 1990s, but went bankrupt for the final time in 2001 before it was acquired by American Airlines. It is sad that America's two leading international carriers failed. So did Eastern Air Lines, which had invented the Washington–New York–Boston shuttle service, but also had the poor sense to hire Marty Shugrue. He is the only man in aviation history to be CEO of two major airlines that went bankrupt. These carriers had flourished in the heavily regulated environment that existed prior to the Airline Deregulation Act of 1978. But they never really adapted to a new era of open market competition. Adapt or die: it's just another lesson that all businesspeople and investors must take to heart.

Unusual Cases

You do not normally think of electric utilities as candidates for bankruptcy, but in January 1988 the Public Service Company of New Hampshire (PSNH) became the first investor-owned utility to go bust since the Great Depression. Nuclear power cost overruns and regulatory disputes were the causes. In the early 1970s, when OPEC quintupled the price of oil, PSNH decided to build two 1,150-megawatt plants in a 50 percent–owned venture for an estimated $1.3

billion. However, protests, regulatory issues, and litigation caused numerous delays. The utility was prohibited from recovering any of its investment until it began to deliver electricity. These mounting "stranded costs" resulted in increased borrowings at ever higher rates. Ultimately, the commission forced PSNH to reduce its ownership in the plants to 35.6 percent. The second unit was canceled in 1984, and the first unit only became operational in 1990. Its final cost was $6.6 billion, more than five times the original estimate for both units. By 1988, the New Hampshire Supreme Court blocked a desperate request for emergency rate increases. Two days later, PSNH filed for Chapter 11, and I became the advisor for the Equity Holders Committee.

For PSNH, the first remedial step was to abandon state regulation and instead restructure under the auspices of the Federal Energy Regulatory Commission, which promptly granted 5.5 percent annual rate increases through 1996, to be followed by three years of no increases. The next step was to put the company up for sale because a buyer with a better credit rating could lower the financing costs and therefore pay more for the equity. This strategy infuriated New Hampshire Governor John Sununu. He wanted the auction criteria to be based on who would reduce the newly granted rate increases the most. He and I had very public arguments during which I accused him in the press of claiming to be a conservative, while acting like the dictator of a banana republic and trying to confiscate the shareholders' equity. Some at Rothschild were worried about me having such a public controversy with a man rumored to be a Republican presidential nominee, but the controversy continued until my favored bidder, Northeast Utilities, won and acquired PSNH.

This whole fracas was especially newsworthy within the utilities industry, normally a quiescent group. As a result,

I became a guest speaker at industry conferences and was hired by the Vermont Electric Cooperative for its restructuring. Later, I was hired by the Vermont Public Utility Commission as its financial advisor, and then by creditors of El Paso Electric in another nuclear energy bankruptcy. This was followed by engagements with several independent electric service providers and the mid-Atlantic grid operators. Within months, Rothschild's bankruptcy advisory practice transitioned swiftly from novices within the utilities sector to mainstream players. It was quite remarkable that this long-standing industry suddenly gravitated toward a firm with no real history with them, just a few benchmark cases. The reason for this shift was that the utilities' traditional investment bankers had an expertise mainly in underwriting the utilities' frequent bond and equity issuances, rather than giving them strategic advice.

This illustrates an important point. Many major investment banks have become commodity suppliers of capital rather than positioning themselves as thought leaders. That's why firms like Rothschild, Evercore, Lazard, Wasserstein Perella, Guggenheim Partners, Houlihan Lokey, Centerbridge Partners, Moelis & Co., and others, have prospered. As a few big financial services players become increasingly dominant in capital markets, there nimble specialist firms like these have found ample space between the big banks' vast concentric circles to carve out niches. Wall Street remains one of the last professional services meritocracies where there is substantial room for a clever and smaller specialist firm to thrive. The sustained existence of these creative-thinking firms is crucial, because if brawn always prevails over brains, innovative solutions will become rarer.

Utilities cases also provided a keen insight into how regulators and elected officials react to crises. Part of what made PSNH vulnerable to public criticism was its decision to site the plants on the beach at Seabrook. The decision to use seawater as a coolant was perhaps sound, but Seabrook's popularity with tourists made the project susceptible to attacks. Politicians and even judges succumbed to the rallying cry of "Not in my backyard!" instead of seeking a more reasonable solution. At the end of the day, the plant was built and has operated effectively and without incident for thirty-three years, so the main outcome of the protests was more expensive electricity for New Hampshire residents because of the delays in the plant's construction. Many extreme actions by today's climate change advocates seem similarly uneconomical and ill-founded. While reducing pollution is obviously a valid long-term goal, rushing the reduction of hydrocarbon production before adequate substitutes are available could cause significant and unnecessary economic disruptions.

Another surprising candidate for bankruptcy was A.H. Robins. For decades, the company prospered from selling basic over-the-counter pharmaceutical products like ChapStick and Robitussin. However, in 1970, it acquired the Dalkon Shield, a crab-shaped intrauterine device (IUD) made of high-tech nylon. By 1975, more than 2 million women had purchased the shield. But defects in the product caused many women to be severely injured, and others were even killed by it. The result was the largest class action suit in history to date (327,000 claimants) other than one related to asbestos. And unlike the asbestos cases, in this case, the victims were contemporary and readily identifiable.

The Robins family, which controlled the company, were a deeply religious clan and mainstays of society in Richmond, Virginia. Nonetheless, a federal judge in Minneapolis ruled that management knew of the health issues and covered them up. This ruling prompted Robins to file a petition in the Richmond bankruptcy court on August 22, 1985. The Equity Holders Committee retained me as its advisor. The debate centered on whether the company should be reorganized as a freestanding entity with the family remaining as the most important shareholders or if it should be sold to a larger company. The CEO, Edwin Robins, who had donated a record $60 million to the University of Richmond, strongly objected to selling. However, the committee concluded that selling was the best course both to maximize the value of the company on the open market and ensure better management oversight. Major bankruptcy decisions require the affirmative vote of holders of two-thirds of the impaired class of securities. In this case, the equity's view prevailed. Rothschild then managed the sale of Robins to American Home Products for $900 million, in addition to overseeing a $2.5 billion trust fund which had been established to pay out claims.

Having met key family members and executives associated with Robins, I struggle to understand how this tragedy unfolded. It's perplexing how such honorable individuals could continue selling a product if they were aware of its dangers, and it's even harder to fathom how they could overlook the deaths and injuries. This scenario vastly differs from the asbestos cases, where the products had been discontinued decades before litigation began. Perhaps it's evidence that greed always tugs at the human heart. It can be very difficult for even God-fearing people to resist its siren song. I have no way to know the real facts, but the courts found the company and its management culpable.

A Surprising Downfall

As I previously mentioned, in the late 1970s and early 1980s, high-yield bonds fueled many takeovers and led to numerous corporate defaults that I helped advise on. At the center of the junk-bond mania was Michael Milken's firm, Drexel Burnham

Lambert. Drexel had a storied history. From its origins as
Drexel Morgan, through various name changes, including
Drexel Harriman Ripley, DBL remained a prominent Wall
Street entity. At its zenith, it had the fifth-largest revenues on
Wall Street at $4.5 billion, the most significant profits at $545
million, $35.9 billion in highly leveraged assets, and ten thou-
sand employees. Fred Joseph, Drexel's CEO, was a classmate
at HBS. Still, it was Mike, never a director or officer, who was
the driving force of the operation.

My relationship with Drexel was intricate, and boosted
my career. Typically, Drexel, acting as the advocate for issu-
ers undergoing workouts, negotiated with the lenders on an
individual basis. This approach provided its underwriting clients with a significant advantage. To shift this dynamic, Bob
Miller, a tenacious bankruptcy lawyer from Berlack, Israels
& Liberman, and I reached out to junk-bond buyers. Our
proposition was that they should unite, thereby compelling
the company to cover our advisory fees for the bondholders.
The debtors had no choice but to acquiesce to this demand,
and as a result, the bondholders not only wielded the combined power of their numbers, but also had the expertise of a
seasoned investment banker and attorney advising them—all
without any cost. This concept spread rapidly because it presented a clearly superior alternative to the existing arrangement. Other advisors eventually adopted similar strategies,
but we benefited from our first-mover advantage. Moreover,
clients appreciated the improved recoveries we secured for
them, allowing us to capture a significant market share.
During the second half of the 1980s, other major firms began
underwriting junk bonds, reducing Drexel's market share
from more than 70 percent to 47 percent.

When the junk bond market crashed in 1989, with the
default rate jumping from 4 percent to 10 percent, DBL

reported its first loss: $54 million. Its commercial paper rating was downgraded twice by February 12, 1990, when the parent holding company defaulted on a $100 million loan. They sought a government bailout, but it was declined, allegedly because Treasury Secretary Nick Brady was displeased with the firm's support of T. Boone Pickens's raid on his former Dillon Read client, Standard Oil of California. The Department of Justice subsequently pursued several criminal actions against DBL under the Racketeer Influenced and Corrupt Organizations (RICO) statute. While a grand jury debated indictment, the firm pleaded guilty to various charges and paid a $650 million fine. If they hadn't, a $1 billion bond (which they couldn't have afforded) would have been necessary. Milken paid a hefty fine, and was rumored to have written out a check on the spot. He served twenty-two months in federal prison, but was later pardoned by President Trump.

My client in the Drexel case was the Unsecured Creditors Committee, the makeup of which ranged from some country's central bank, which loaned some of its gold reserves, without security, to traditional junk bond buyers. The case was unique for several reasons. When it filed Chapter 11, Drexel had balance sheet assets of $3.6 billion and consolidated debts of $3 billion. But many of the assets were highly illiquid securities while most of the liabilities were short term and/or had cross default provisions with other defaulted loans. Government and other new liability claims also poured in, and greatly exceeded the stated equity. In addition, many of the security assets were encumbered with debt that was less than their notional value, and even potentially more than liquidation value, especially since Drexel would no longer be the market maker, likely leaving nothing for the unsecured creditors. Finally, Drexel had laid off large numbers of highly paid people who now would have contract claims under their employment agreements.

In most bankruptcies, it is necessary to provide debtor-in-possession financing to keep the business going and preserve values, but Drexel was clearly about to liquidate under Chapter 11, so that would not be necessary. At our recommendation, the Judge created New Street Securities with just twenty employees and, at my suggestion, with Robert Shapiro, a former highly respected partner at Wertheim, as the chairman. The unsecured creditors I represented were awarded 100 percent of the stock but the former employees received warrants to purchase 20 percent once the cash recovered exceeded a certain level. After four years of working through the portfolio, they made the final distribution to unsecured creditors, representing 50 to 70 percent–plus recoveries, depending on their standing.

Drexel's remnants never regained their former glory. Still, its talented investment bankers went on to become billionaires by establishing firms like Apollo Global Management. Milken then dedicated his life to philanthropy, primarily through the Milken Institute. This think tank has had a significant global influence by funding health-care research and promoting capitalism. With thirty years of hindsight, high-yield bonds have proven to be a valid financial tool. Coupled with the Milken Institute's societal contributions, these achievements are outstanding. I hope Milken is remembered primarily for these accomplishments. I don't know anyone whose second act in life has produced such positive societal transformation.

New York Politics

My work at both FDS and Rothschild caused me to become friendly with plenty of New York–area politicians throughout the 1970s and 1980s. This was not, however, my first exposure to the political scene. My political involvement throughout most of my adult life was traceable to my parents' own participation. Mom had been a Democratic County Committeewoman in New Jersey for fifty years, and Dad was a local elected official, so I landed on the Democrat side of the aisle. When I was a boy, my parents were both supporters of Jersey City Mayor Frank Hague. Hague controlled the Democratic Party in New Jersey and dominated the state. There was a popular saying around my neighborhood: "There are two political groups here, Hague Democrats and unelectable candidates."

One day, Hague, who was friendly with my parents, suggested that they bring me to lunch, although I was only eleven years old (he believed in generational politics). His apartment was a duplex penthouse atop the newly constructed Jersey City Medical Center. On one side you could see Manhattan and on the other, all the way to Newark.

I asked him, "Mayor Hague, how did you get such a marvelous arrangement?"

He smiled and said, "It was a gift."

"A gift?"

"Yes, many people give me nice gifts. Your parents can explain that to you on the way home." They laughed.

In the 1970s, I decided to start fundraising for Manhattan candidates such as Bobby Wagner, the son of former New York mayor Robert Wagner. I managed to do well enough at it that in 1975, Joe Crangle, then the chairman of the State Democratic Committee, appointed me the State Committee Treasurer, a heady position for a twenty-seven-year-old. It wasn't just prestigious; it was also fraught with legal peril: I was responsible for certifying that each candidate's contributions were made in accordance with state and federal campaign laws.

Still, I did not let that deter me from working energeti-
cally to bring in money. We created a Chairman's Council,
to which each member gave $10,000. In return, he or she
received a free lunch or drinks with the many individual governors and senators from other states who had higher ambi-
tions and wanted to meet potential donors in the city. We
also organized auctions for a cocktail party at the Governor's
Executive Mansion in Albany, a U.S. flag that had hung over
the Capitol, various campaign memorabilia, and much more.
It worked well, but Crangle's preferred candidate in the 1974
gubernatorial primary, Howard Samuels, lost to Hugh Carey.
Carey replaced Crangle with Pat Cunningham, a Bronx leader
who had supported Carey's campaign.

After the election, Pat asked me, "Do you want to
stay on?"

"Only if you want me to."

"Okay, here's the drill. We're going to raise a lot more
money than before and your job will be to charge companies
$25,000 each to have a private lunch with the banking com-
missioners, the insurance commissioner, the utility commissioner, and so on."

I replied, "Mr. Chairman, that sounds too much like a
shakedown to me. You should find someone else."

He did. A few years later Pat went to jail for an unrelated corruption scandal. I guess that he was just a latter-day
Frank Hague.

Not every local pol was as slippery as Cunningham. Over
the years, I got to know Senator Pat Moynihan quite well.
From our first encounters, Senator Moynihan impressed me
as one of the most thoughtful political leaders I have ever
known. For example, his slender book *Beyond the Melting
Pot*, postulating that ethnic strife would remain a facet of
American life in coming decades, was both highly controversial

and prophetic. His report on the crisis of the Black family he issued while serving at the Department of Labor, *The Negro Family: The Case for National Action*, also forecast troubling trends. Pat was a real public servant, and it was my honor to be involved with the campaign to christen the new area of Penn Station the Moynihan Train Hall, which now serves more than 650,000 commuters each day.

At the core of Pat's thinking was his assessment that giving federal aid to able-bodied adults is not wrong, but recipients must be employed or looking for work to be eligible for it. This stance was and remains controversial among many members of his own Democratic Party, but, I believe, totally correct. In 2020, I saw how many recipients of COVID-19 assistance obtained more income from government payouts without working than they ever had earned while employed. This anomaly undoubtedly contributed to worker shortages, and, psychologically, has contributed to the widespread worker dissatisfaction that now plagues the business community. How overdoing federal support and decoupling it from any effort on the part of the recipient was considered an appropriate response to the pandemic is beyond me. It was both fiscally improvident and conceptually indefensible.

My experiences working with the Democrats of my early adult life confirmed to me that the Democratic Party of today has largely lost its way. In addition to a wrongheaded approach to welfare eligibility, immigration policy is the prime example of how many of its beliefs have become unmoored from facts.

The Democrats have always been, importantly, a party of immigrants. Many party leaders in the 1940s and 1950s were first-generation Americans. But never in my young adult life

did I hear them clamor for indiscriminately allowing in anyone who wanted to enter the country. The working assumption among liberal thinkers, as well as that of elected officials, was that meaningful borders define a country. Without
borders you are just a no-man's-land. Early in his career, my
father had a part-time job tutoring immigrants so that they
could pass the federal test required by the citizenship process.
In effect, this substituted for the civics and history courses
that natural citizens took in school. With open borders there
is no such civic education. (And as an aside, the collapse of
meaningful history and civics education means we are no longer teaching even *American-born* individuals to understand
what it means to live in this great country.)

Worse yet, these days hundreds of thousands of migrants
claim asylum from persecution as a rationale for entry each
year, but the numbers are so overwhelming and the immigration system so understaffed and backlogged that court dates
are set years into the future. Most applicants never show up
for their hearings, and instead depart for parts unknown
inside the United States. Meanwhile, the government loses
track of them, and they are rarely prosecuted when they fail
to show up for their hearings. Now, likely millions of new
residents are here knowingly in violation of the law.

"Catch and release" is another nonsensical policy that
fails to properly punish illegal entry. Many years ago, the
Rothschild family was considering buying a winery in
California. I researched vineyards for sale. The first one
was just outside Carmel. After a lovely dinner with generous samples of their wine, the next morning we followed the
entire winemaking process starting at 4:00 a.m. At that hour,
Hispanic workers with green sacks hanging from their necks
hunched over to remove seedlings from the sack and insert
them into small holes drilled into the soil. It was backbreaking

work. Months later, a tractor would harvest the plants which had been planted with precise spacing.

At about 5:15 a.m., a helicopter and trucks filled with heavily armed U.S. Marshals suddenly appeared. They arrested every worker. After the raid, I asked my host, "Is this why you are selling the business?"

"Not at all. Remember the tractor driver? That's his day job. At night he is a bus driver. The marshals always take them to Tijuana. They will be back before 4:00 a.m. tomorrow!"

I stayed over to check. He was correct. The immigration people must have known the routine. Re-expelling the same people over and over is no solution to illegal immigration.

President Trump, of course, adopted many uncommon tactics to stem the flow of illegals coming into the U.S. I was with him in the Oval Office one afternoon when he said, "Wilbur, I had a great session with Mexico's ambassador before lunch today. I've been pushing for them to put 28,000 troops at the border to reduce illegal immigration. At first the ambassador said they were not prepared to incur that expense. I told him that if they don't agree to it by Monday, I will announce a tariff of 25% on everything that they send to the U.S. and perhaps even make it higher than that. The ambassador asked for a few minutes to report the news to President Lopez Obrador. I said, 'OK, but make it quick. I have an important lunch date!' The ambassador then came back and said the Mexican government would be delighted to provide 28,000 troops on the border to give us time to build the wall."

Trump added with a smile, "It was true that I had an important lunch date it was with Melania! I don't often get to have lunch alone with her!"

Somehow, Trump had sensed that this was the right time to put pressure on Mexico. Prior presidents had apparently sought similar help through normal diplomatic channels but failed to obtain it. I am sure that no prior president was willing to be that confrontational with Mexico.

Under Joe Biden, illegal immigration has become far worse, as he effectively made the southern border wide open while enforcing border security at the boundary with Canada. Years of sanctuary city policies in metropolises such as New York and Los Angeles have also led to social breakdown and greatly exacerbated the homeless and drug problems in these cities. Even Democrat-run cities like New York are now begging the federal government to do something. Recently, Brooklyn high school students were displaced from their school so that it could serve as an illegal immigration shelter. Situations like these are disastrous for New York and the country.

Strangely, the Biden Administration has ignored these cities' pleas for help. Instead of seeing the morass he has helped create, Biden has attacked governors like Texas's Greg Abbott for sending illegal immigrants to major northern cities. Believe it or not, far fewer of these illegals than people think are coming here for jobs. For example, only 2 percent of the illegal immigrants who have come to New York City have filled out work authorization forms.[9] What's worse, we may not know until the next 9/11-type event how many terrorists have been let in. There are also massive quantities of drugs coming into the United States because of our porous border. This is an unnecessary mess that is directly due to a series of presidential decisions and will play a real role in the 2024 elections.

All this being said, it is still true that we also need legal immigrants to help generate economic growth and innovation. We should adopt a points system like Canada's and Australia's which prioritize the admission of immigrants with skills necessary for the economy. It is ridiculous to deport foreigners with high-tech graduate degrees from our universities, who then go on to create products that the United States ends up importing. Everyone knows this makes no sense, but left-wing members of Congress insist on combining a sensible approach to high-skilled, legal immigration with leniency for illegal immigrants with no special skills. This stance helps to cripple the prospects for immigration reform.

One of my greatest privileges as Secretary of Commerce was to attend a naturalization ceremony and swear in a new crop of Americans. For most of them, it was the emotional event of their lives, and I saw more than a few faces streaming with tears. These folks undoubtedly had waited patiently, followed the law, and desired to immigrate in the right way. It is important that America remain open to newcomers and strivers such as these. They are patriots who will help carry our torch of freedom forward.

By the 1990s, I was on the boards of several cultural institutions in New York City. As a former aspiring creative writer, and later art collector, I've always harbored a love for the creative arts, and it motivated me to get involved philanthropically. Arthur "Punch" Sulzberger, publisher of the *New York Times*; Marty Siegal, a financial consultant to labor unions; and I cochaired an initiative to force local politicians to include a cultural element in their campaign platform. None had ever done so, but as lovers of the arts, we believed they ought to.

The 1993 New York City mayoral race featured incumbent Democrat David Dinkins facing off against Republican Rudy Giuliani, who had come to prominence for helping deal a virtual death blow to the New York area Mafia as a federal prosecutor. In keeping with our insistence that the candidates maintain a cultural platform as part of their candidacy, Punch, Marty, and I organized an event at the Times Center auditorium in which both Mayor Dinkins and Giuliani participated. We also convinced the chairs of our respective boards and leaders of every cultural institution in the city to attend. Neither Punch nor Marty, as firm Democrats, wanted to brief Giuliani. I didn't really want to, either, because of how, as a federal prosecutor, he had overzealously pursued innocent Wall Streeters and made them do a perp walk in handcuffs. But it seemed unfair not to brief him, so I did. After he and his staff spent two hours with me, I said, "Mr. Giuliani, the cultural community is very liberal. Therefore, to get the Q and A off to a good start we'll make sure a softball question is asked first."

Rudy chuckled and said, "Ask me anything about the opera!"

"Anything?"

"Yes, anything. I know opera!"

When the event got started, an aggressive young left-winger asked him a highly technical question about some obscure opera, and Rudy hit that curveball for a home run. There was nothing but hushed silence among the crowd of artsy Manhattan liberals. Everyone was thoroughly impressed. That event may or may not have helped him win, but it did give me (and lots of others) new respect for him.

After winning handily, Rudy promptly initiated his promised cultural initiatives, so we saw him as someone we could work with. We proposed a new idea to him, the Cultural Challenge Grant, a mixture of public-private funding for more arts programs. The city and state each would contribute 25 percent to a program's costs, and the institutions' benefactors would chip in 50 percent. True to my mission of always coming to a discussion armed with the best data, I had extrapolated from a study conducted by the New York–New Jersey Port Authority concluding that increased state income tax, sales taxes, hotel taxes, restaurant taxes, etc. from the activities would fully repay the public funding. Mayor Giuliani, and his Deputy Mayor for Economic Development and Finance, John Dyson, who had been finance chair of the Democratic State Committee when I was the treasurer, both endorsed the program. So did Governor Mario Cuomo.

Soon thereafter, Dyson hired me as an external privatization advisor to the city, so I became a regular visitor to City Hall. We succeeded in privatizing one of the two TV stations owned by the city, WNYC, for $200 million, turning an unneeded money loser into a one-time gain. Several other deals followed, with the *New York Post* billing me as "Rudy's million-dollar man" because of the fees to my firm. This did not trouble me at all, because the city was obtaining enormous savings from my services, even with the hefty costs factored in. Among our successes was downsizing the municipal bureaucracy by offering people a lump sum of as much as $100,000 to take early retirement. Thousands did so because that extra money could pay off their mortgage or go toward a retirement home. The people with the greatest longevity were usually the highest-paid in each department, so we saved a fortune, and it gave the mayor more control over his departments.

My main disappointment from the privatization efforts was our effort to privatize LaGuardia Airport—one of the worst performing airports in the country back then—for $2.5 billion. Originally, the deal was coming together nicely: We lined up UK airports operator BAA, which managed Heathrow very successfully, to be the operator. Tax-exempt bonds backed by the airline gate fees, plus parking and retail concessions, would be the sources of funding under the reworked structure.

Then politics got in the way.

LaGuardia was not owned by the City, but by the Port Authority of New York and New Jersey, which used it to subsidize loss-making commuter buses and terminals. Consequently, they did not want to sell it. The mayor organized a press conference at which I presented charts attacking the Port Authority both for its mismanagement of the airport and its affairs in general. For example, the average Port Authority police officer was earning something like $100,000 per year for basically being a traffic cop, far more than New York City policemen, while their location could only be changed with thirty days prior notice. In fact, if an emergency developed at the World Trade Center and the Port Authority police had to come up from the PATH station below, they would be paid overtime. The Port Authority police group got so angry they ran full-page newspaper ads against us. Ultimately, we could not make them sell, so the project died.

As a resident of New York City for virtually all my adult life, it is clear that Rudy's biggest success was drastically reducing crime. His successor, Mike Bloomberg, could not have achieved what he did economically if Rudy hadn't first dealt with crime, which was rampant in the city in the 1980s and early 1990s. Rudy's example is also instructive for all big-city mayors who are today struggling with the unintended consequences of "defund the police." A secure city undergirds prosperity, jobs, tourism, and votes! Rudy also did an exemplary job steering the city through the aftermath of the 9/11 attacks, justly earning himself the title America's Mayor. Rudy's endorsement thus was very helpful to Mike Bloomberg in his first mayoral campaign. It is tragic that Rudy is more likely to be criticized in the history books for his role in contesting the 2020 presidential election than for all the good he did as the mayor of one of America's signature cities. His personal bankruptcy and legal problems are a terrible but self-inflicted ending for a politician who accomplished great things. It's not lost on me that his trajectory mirrors many of the busted companies I dealt with at Rothschild.

CHAPTER 6

A Bold Step

I spent a magnificent quarter-century at Rothschild advising clients on some of the most famous and challenging bankruptcies of the twentieth century. In 1997, Rothschild gave me the green light to start a $200 million fund to invest in distressed assets, and it produced high rates of return. But Rothschild was fundamentally more interested in the advisory side of the distressed asset business than the investment side. My enthusiasm was trending in the opposite direction. As the years went on, there were several changes of CEOs, and Rothschild finally brought in one with whom I was incompatible.

It was then, at age sixty-three, when most successful people are looking toward retirement, that I decided to take a bold new step.

One day I met with the board chairman, Ray Smith. My pitch was unambiguous: "I'd like to leave the firm and buy out Rothschild's share of the distressed assets fund."

He was nonplussed: "We're under no obligation to sell to you."

"I understand that. But the investors in these funds are there because of me. If I leave, they'll leave. And it will look bad for Rothschild. And you."

He thought about it for a moment.

"OK. But you must drop the Rothschild name from the fund, and you can't compete for the business of advising clients on bankruptcies."

"Sounds fine to me. Now, let's talk about the price. I will buy you out at your cost."

"You're joking!"

"No. You don't care about this business, and it will collapse if I leave. This is your best deal."

Some more thinking, and a sigh.

"You have a deal."

Thus, on April Fools' Day, 2000, WL Ross & Co. came into being, an appropriate date for a sixty-three-year-old to start up a business. I'm proud to say that the fund I started at Rothschild in 1997, and later carried with me to WL Ross & Co., had sufficiently good returns that we raised a new follow-on fund every eighteen to twenty-four months. I sold the firm to Invesco in 2006.

What was the secret, you may ask?

The truth is there is no secret to success but to pour all your effort into controlling the variables you can control. This is a habit that ought to characterize your whole life, so that a commitment to excellence of effort becomes standard in all you do. My successes on Wall Street began well before I ever worked for J.P. Morgan or FDS. It was the years of rifle practice that taught me the benefits of concentrating on the target. It was mentorship of men older and wiser than me, such as Horace Isleib and General Doriot, that helped me see opportunities with a critical eye. And when I finally did reach the "major leagues," preparation and hard

work—and a time-consuming mastery of bankruptcy law—
were my best friends in creating enough confidence to take
well-considered risks.

That tenacity continued at WL Ross. Fueled by endless
cups of coffee, my team and I spent every day analyzing
companies crumbling under the weight of high debt financing burdens, messy labor agreements, and competition from
rivals overseas. Every move we made was undergirded by
data: central bank reports, trade journals, and intelligence
from Washington, to name a few pieces. And, above all, we
showed discipline by not chasing opportunities outside our
area of focus. As Benjamin Graham wrote in *The Intelligent
Investor*, "Investing isn't about beating others at their game.
It's about controlling yourself at your own game."[10]

Successful investors are made, not born.

———————————

Starting WL Ross & Co. was exhilarating. For one thing,
I was fresh off the most intimate negotiation of my life in
buying the business from Rothschild. The structure of it was
favorable to my acquisition. I already owned one-third of the
general partnership interest in the fund, and the team had
another third, so I bought Rothschild's final third for just
$2 million. In addition, W L Ross & Co., wholly owned by
me, took over at no cost the advisory contract, which paid
an annual fee of 1.5 percent of the fund's assets. Initially, this
fee barely covered our costs. But we knew that if we could
keep adding more funds it would be very profitable since
the investment advisory business has considerable operating
leverage. The risk I took was that the investors might redeem
their gains rather than roll their interests from Rothschild
Recovery Fund into the new WL Ross & Co. Recovery Fund,

and I would be stuck with an embarrassing loss. As it turned out, all our investors stayed with us, and we were able to raise a new Asia Recovery Fund of $150 million while we transitioned to independence. Lest you think that Rothschild's pockets were picked, the fact that the fund's limited partners at Rothschild showed such strong support for the breakup confirms that each side viewed the transaction as a wise move for avoiding financial distress and embarrassment. Thus, from a senior-level personality clash was a happy ending written.

The entire staff of Rothschild's distressed asset business, including our driver and the mail room clerk, came over to WL Ross & Co. It was exhilarating to move into an office space of our own. As part of the deal, Rothschild gave me six months of free rent in space they had leased but were not occupying. Since we were a start-up, our next landlord made me put up a letter of credit as rolling security for twelve months' rent—a little ridiculous given our capitalization, but whatever. The odd thing we soon noticed after moving into our new location was that there were always the same well-built men hanging around in the lobby and a couple of SUVs with red lights outside. We later found out the Mossad had rented several floors. It was then that our perplexity turned to delight—we realized we were probably renting in the safest building in Manhattan! To decorate our reception area, I bought a large cow sculpture, one of several that Rudy Giuliani was auctioning off for charity. The "Dow Cow" was covered with stock symbols and prices. We called it our hedge fund cow because it had both horns and udders, unlike real bovines. It became well-known as our symbol.

Our office was near the old Four Seasons Restaurant on 49th Street, a Manhattan institution which is sadly now shuttered for good. It became our dining room. When Mom's next birthday came up, we took over the Rothko Room there and put on a dinner for family and friends after cocktails in our office. Mom became very confused and kept asking, "Who is going to pay the rent and the salaries of all these people?" In her world, you either were a doctor, a lawyer, or otherwise employed by a company. It was hard for her to conceive of her son owning a substantial business, but by the second dry Manhattan she had calmed down.

For a kid from North Bergen, of mostly modest means, I had come a long way. People sometimes ask me what drove me to work so hard at what I did. In truth, money was not the prime motivator (although growing up without much of it certainly fuels one's desire to make more). It's true that money is a way that competitive people keep score at some rudimentary level, and I was not entirely immune to that mentality. More than anything, my eagerness to seize opportunities and succeed at them was rooted in what was intellectually engaging and challenging to me. It's my assessment that very few people who are successful are motivated purely by money, especially at the outset. Steve Jobs, Bill Gates, and Elon Musk did not found their companies out of a desire to be trillionaires. It was the same way with me on a much smaller scale. The opportunities were there, and someone was going to do well. The only question was who? And why not me?

The Art of the Steel

One of WL Ross & Co.'s first investments was buying the conglomerate Ling-Temco-Vought's (LTV) steel subsidiaries in 2002. I had previously advised the unsecured creditors of LTV Corporation in its first bankruptcy in 1986. Now they were bankrupt again, and this time poised for liquidation. The steel mill was kept on "hot idle," with just enough molten metal running through it to prevent the mill's refractory bricks from imploding. That process was costing more than $1 million per week, so creditors were scrambling to auction off the mill. We studied the business and formed International Steel Group (ISG) in anticipation of submitting a bid for it. In the meantime, a bankruptcy court had already terminated the unfunded pension and retiree healthcare obligations, and the workers almost all had been let go. International Steel Group was optimistic about acquiring the mill, but a terrible labor contract had to be fixed before we could submit a bid.

I called Leo Gerard, the President of the United Steelworkers of America (USWA) union, and told him of our interest in purchasing LTV's steel operation. He and I soon met in Pittsburgh. ISG proposed to hire back most of the former workers, but do so on a "nonconforming" contract—meaning that it had more favorable terms than the other steel industry contracts. In exchange, we needed some tradeoffs. First, we needed to reduce the number of job classifications from thirty-two to five. The existing number of categories created artificial restrictions on who could do what, leading to gross inefficiencies. For example, the operators of a rolling mill and its maintenance team each knew how to do each other's jobs. But for weeks, maintenance men would sit around playing pinochle until the mill broke down. Then the operators would play pinochle for a few days while the maintenance guys went to work. This structure was simply too wasteful—we needed only one set of workers to both operate and maintain the mill.

As for wages, we left them unchanged, but cut out excess days off. Overtime pay would kick in after forty hours in a week, instead of beginning each day after eight hours of work. That let us offset overtime on one day with fewer hours on another day. Finally, only people who actually touched steel would be USWA members, not office workers. The quid pro quo for all this was that we set weekly targets for each shift on each machine and if the workers hit their production targets everyone involved would get a bonus, even if the company was losing money overall. I am a great believer in productivity bonuses for blue-collar workers. Unions dislike them because they prefer to be the exclusive intermediary between a worker and his paycheck.

At first Leo gagged on these radical proposals. But we broke for two hours and then met at his favorite Italian restaurant, up high on a hill overlooking Pittsburgh. There, while consuming gallons of red wine, we inked an agreement in longhand on a napkin. At the end, I had one more condition: The contract must be applicable to any other steel company we acquired. Leo was fine with it, but had another stipulation of his own: We must implement a plan to reduce the layers of management from factory floor to CEO office from eight to three. This reduction accelerated decision-making and gave the CEO better firsthand knowledge of what was going on. We also agreed that the CEO's base pay could not exceed 10 times what an experienced steelworker received, but there could be very large performance-based bonuses. Separately, WL Ross & Co. convinced Cleveland-Cliffs to supply iron ore not on a fixed price, but rather one that varied with the price of hot rolled sheet, our most basic product. This locked in our gross margins.

Not everyone in the steel industry looked favorably on the deal we had made with the unions. I soon received an unsolicited call from the CEO of U.S. Steel. The company historically has had a difficult relationship with the steelworkers' unions.

"Wilbur, I don't know you well, but I am calling to do you a real favor," the U.S. Steel CEO began. "You are making the biggest mistake of your life by trusting the steelworkers. If you buy LTV, they will f— you. Believe me, I have dealt with them for years. Don't do the deal."

I thanked him and hung up, convinced that, more than anything, he was worried that we might outcompete him. Indeed, our negotiation style was a competitive advantage. Typically, major industrial labor negotiations involve battalions of lawyers and public relations professionals hired by management. Unions then feel compelled to take up arms in the same way. There is little one-on-one negotiation, and the experts play head games with each other. Leo and I saved time and money by working out the key bullet points in one session and then tasking the lawyers to write out the details. I truly believe our ability to do this deal with the USWA saved as many as 100,000 jobs.

This situation was somewhat unique in our level of trust in one another. As I'd seen in other bankruptcies, I realized during our talks that the union understood the company better than the senior management. Hence, they had a realistic sense of why the operation was failing, and why they needed to give concessions toward a lower-cost operation. For my part, I won Leo's trust by showing him how cost savings could happen by streamlining job categories, and by demonstrating a good-faith interest in the welfare of his workers by promising productivity bonuses. Nor did I mind having a union representative on the board of directors. American companies actually get off easy if a single union rep is a voting board member—European companies often feature much greater union representation.

These talks reinforced that one of the most important relationships for any CEO must be with the head of his or her union. It should not just be a business relationship, but also have a social component. And it certainly should not be adversarial. This general posture also helped explain why the various auto parts businesses I was involved in never went on strike at the time I controlled them. In 2003, a *Slate* headline wondered "Is Wilbur Ross the Next Andrew Carnegie?"[11] The answer was no—at least where relations with the unions were concerned.

Three weeks later, in a blinding snowstorm, at Jones Day's Cleveland office, ISG was the only bidder for LTV, though U.S. Steel and others came to watch the proceeding. For $325 million, we bought $90 million in fixed assets, into which $2.5 billion had been invested just in the last five years. The deal also included $100 million of accounts receivable and inventory worth $50 million, which GE Capital financed 100 percent for us. But the best part was that the union fully honored the deal we had scrawled on napkins. We reduced the number of man-hours to make a ton of steel from close to six to one and a half. For years afterward, I kept up good relations with Leo and the United Steelworkers Union to let them know I truly regarded them as partners, and that we were mutually dependent on each other for prosperity—almost like we held each other hostage. Once, I went to a USWA picnic in a public park outside Pittsburgh. I showed up wearing my International Steel Group workman's jacket, blue jeans, and sneakers. U.S. Steel's two representatives wore Ralph Lauren blazers, Hermès ties, and Gucci loafers. The sartorial contrast symbolized a difference in attitude that was not lost on the union.

Not long after the LTV acquisition, several factors caused International Steel Group to begin to prosper. For one thing, China was in the throes of a building boom, pushing the price of steel higher. Second, the new labor contract had begun to return the mill to profitability. Third, U.S. automakers were pushing zero percent financing, goosing demand for vehicles. Finally, Leo Gerard and I successfully lobbied the Bush Administration to put a temporary tariff on imports so we would have time to requalify our newly reorganized mills with our big customers. I had in fact been closely monitoring the public communications from the International Trade Commission prior to the LTV acquisition, and was optimistic the administration would apply tariffs. They did, at a 30 percent clip, and LTV benefited immensely. This shows the virtue of paying strict attention to how policy decisions in Washington can impact your business.

The next year, 2003, the legacy steelmaker Bethlehem Steel filed for bankruptcy and was careening toward liquidation. Their lawyers soon realized that our contract with the union was applicable to any steel company we bought, and approached us about making a bid. This provides yet more evidence that good relations with the union were a net benefit: No one operating on the old contract could compete with us and Leo was not willing to give anyone else the same concession because he believed in ISG. We managed to buy Bethlehem by just paying the professional fees of the lawyers, accountants, and financial advisors involved in the deal, with no significant payments by us to unsecured creditors. The labor contract also needed the usual membership ratification, so we arranged for Bethlehem's shop stewards to visit counterparts at the mills ISG already owned. The result was an almost unprecedented 80 percent favorable vote to ratify a concessionary contract.

Two strange situations next developed. First, there were a few Bethlehem plant managers we wanted to retain, but most of them said they could not operate under the leaner management structure the labor contract called for. They quit. The thought of a forty-year-old executive preferring unemployment to accepting more responsibility is incomprehensible to me. The second weird thing was the board's insistence that we address its meeting when it considered our deal. It was a silly concept, because they really had no other option for a buyer. But our CEO Rodney Mott and I went to the board meeting at the Bethlehem, Pennsylvania, Country Club. Much to our surprise, we arrived to see not just the board, but top management, financial advisors, and lawyers—about fifty people in total. We went around and politely introduced ourselves. After a half hour, the CEO asked where the rest of our team was. Our response was, "They're busy making steel!"

Each director spoke for a few minutes to weigh in on what they thought about the deal. The most common suggestion regarding the transaction was that we keep the name Bethlehem for the newly merged company. Bethlehem was synonymous with the glory days of American steelmaking, having supplied the steel for the Lincoln Tunnel, the Empire State Building, and many of the U.S. Navy vessels for World War II. After all of them spoke, we responded, "Bethlehem is indeed an iconic name, but today's reality is that you have failed, and the name now has a pejorative connotation. So we can't use it." They grudgingly voted for the deal anyway. Had they not, Bethlehem would have been liquidated.

A few months later we took ISG public, with Goldman Sachs and UBS leading the IPO. Because of my appetite for purchasing money-losing steel mills, *BusinessWeek* published a cover story entitled, "Is Wilbur Ross Crazy?"[12] In the months and weeks to come, ISG stock subsequently traded above its issue price. My wife, Hilary, is still not 100 percent convinced that the question posed by *BusinessWeek* has yet been fully answered.

Negotiating Successfully

Having done thousands of business negotiations in my life, I think I've learned something about how the process works. Conceptually, a negotiation is primarily two people each trying to sell ideas to each other. You should not view this as a debate in which someone will win and someone else will lose. Instead, you should think of it as two friendly adults trying hard to accommodate each other's reasonable needs. Therefore, you should view yourself as a salesman, and adopt those qualities. Your task is to make the other party feel comfortable interacting with you. Your demeanor should be polite and attentive, and you should work hard at keeping the personal chemistry good. Aggressive behavior usually just makes the other person more defensive and belligerent—don't lose your temper. Bullying is also counterproductive, since most executives are sufficiently strong personalities to resist it. Avoid playing head games or being tricky.

A successful negotiation begins well before you even get to the negotiating table. Preparation is as essential to a negotiation as it is to any other aspect of business decision-making. An ill-prepared negotiator may well omit a key point early on and therefore be forced to return to it later. Doing so may cause contempt for you in the mind of the other side. Making a mistake, or worse yet, misrepresenting something, only does harm. You above all must be thoroughly prepared, not just about your side's desires but also about what are likely to be the fundamental needs of the other side. Once talks get underway, I like to begin negotiations with the topics likely to be the easiest to resolve. That creates a sense of momentum and possibly even goodwill. Establishing a deadline for concluding the talks is useful, but only if is truly a hard deadline.

Setting artificial deadlines is not useful. Violating them can create a sense that there is a lack of progress.

A good motto for corporate negotiators is that the to-and-fro should occur in the conference room, not the press room. It is rarely useful to be publicly critical of your counter party. Once people have taken a public position on a negotiation, it becomes twice as hard to make a deal. The one exception I have encountered is Donald Trump. He is so used to being attacked publicly and to counterattacking his adversaries in public that he doesn't care about it. He regards tumultuous statements as just part of the game. My negotiations with him over the Trump Taj Mahal bankruptcy, explored later in this book, proved the point.

Setting expectations for outcomes is also key. With professional negotiators involved, no one is going to crush the other one 90-10. The real question is how much can you marginally tilt the outcome to your benefit, perhaps 60-40? People who overplay their hand by insisting on unrealistic terms rarely achieve a satisfactory result. My motto is that if each side feels it gave a bit too much away, it is probably a reasonable deal. If you pay careful attention to the initial give and take, you can begin to estimate the other party's determination to get things their way, and react accordingly.

Consequently, tradeoffs are useful tools for negotiators. But deploy them sparingly, because they can have real financial and economic consequences. If you have gone back and forth repeatedly on the same topic without resolving it, introducing a tradeoff can jump start a path to agreement by making a lesser concession on a closely related topic that is within your tolerance. In some cases, noneconomic concessions like the company name or board representation for the acquiree can buy you tangible economic benefits. Describing a transaction as a merger of equals, as J.P. Morgan did with Guaranty

Trust, is often worth a lot, even if it may not be precisely accurate. You should be open to conceding such intangible matters in order to avoid sacrificing core interests.

Patience and polite persistence are virtues in negotiation. Part of your preparation should be developing multiple reasons why the other party should accept your request. Patiently reminding him how beneficial the deal is for his constituents is one of the best means of persuasion. But don't trot out every rationale right at the beginning. Wheel them out one by one so you can perhaps wear down his resistance by compounding one compelling reason on top of another. Similarly, preparing in advance your rationale for not granting a concession likely to be requested will lower the temperature. If the counterparty invokes many issues you were not expecting, one of you is missing the boat.

Appealing to precedent can be useful as a winning argument. If you can show that your requests are consistent with those that have been honored in lots of prior deals in a given industry, all the better. It is even better to show that you personally have gotten in prior deals what you are seeking now, or that another company has yielded the point in a prior transaction. When there is serious disagreement on the price of an asset, the way to bridge the gap may be to grant a higher price that only will be fully paid if the forecast results for the next few years have been achieved. In this way, the downstroke should be a bit less than you would have paid without any contingencies. That way you will have lowered your economic risk in the event of an operational shortfall. You also will want the triggering events to be measurable, simple, and difficult to manipulate. If stock is the earnout currency, you will need to make a value judgment whether to issue it at today's price or a future one. I tend to prefer today's price, largely to eliminate another uncontrollable variable.

There are a few other things to avoid in any negotiation. Accusing the counterparty of reneging is not useful. Simply repeating your argument about the merits of your original proposal in a calm manner is far better. If a negotiation is fraught with re-trades, it may be a signal of either party's insincerity, and perhaps foreshadow a contentious post-deal environment. It is, of course, a very bad idea for you yourself to renege. Being well prepared and careful should eliminate any need to re-trade on your part.

Next, sessions should not run late into the night. Tired people become grouchy, and that is not useful. Tiredness can also cause people to miss points of discussion. Similarly, there should be frequent breaks during the day for similar reasons, but there should not be long delays between sessions. Talks should be in person rather than by Zoom, to the extent possible, to make it easier for personal rapport to develop.

Unlike fine wine, negotiations do not get better with age. If they drag on, deal fatigue sets in, small issues assume outsized importance, and mutual distrust and even dislike can emerge. I also feel strongly that the fewer people in the negotiations room, the better. The presence of a big audience increases the risk of long speeches, less candor, and attempts at gamesmanship. Ultimately, a negotiation will be reduced to a question of who is more willing to walk away if his threshold demands are not met. If you are the one willing to walk—truly willing—and you handle yourself sensibly, the other party ultimately will realize he has a binary decision to make: Either yield to your core demands or lose the deal. Unfortunately, in many situations neither you nor your counterparty is really prepared to blow the deal, so neither is willing to walk away from a stalemate. Under those circumstances, the best approach may be to declare a moratorium on the discussion for a couple of days. During that time, either side may decide to yield or to walk away. If it ends, at least it will be after careful reconsideration.

The biggest mistake in negotiations is to set a formal redline, because if you do so and then go beyond it, you will have lost all credibility. In poker, bluffing can be a useful part of the game strategy, if it is not overused. But I have almost never seen it work in real life when serious and well-informed people are involved. Similarly, storming out of a room only works if the other side's approach is so unreasonable and filled with braggadocio that you need to show that you will not put up with it. Allowing yourself to lose your temper can do no good, only harm. Emotion is the mortal enemy of rational discussion. If you catch yourself starting to become emotional, call for a break until you can calm yourself. If the other party starts to flare up, a break again is useful.

These little tips do not guarantee success. But I can guarantee that if you do the opposite of each prescription, you will have a bumpier road and a lower probability of a successful outcome. Movies and television create larger than life stereotypes that make corporate negotiations seem more like hand-to-hand combat than they really are. If you want to succeed as a negotiator, cast these overly dramatic visualizations out of your mind. If you doubt my thinking, tell me the last time you convinced your spouse to do what you wanted by screaming at him or her. I rest my case.

The Worst Tragedy

Like the steel industry, the U.S. coal industry was also undergoing a hard time in the early 2000s. We created International Coal Group (ICG) by buying nonunion bankrupt mines, mainly in West Virginia, Kentucky, and Illinois. Months after we purchased them, they were turning around nicely, in large part because of the excellent management of Ben Hatfield, whom we had hired as CEO of ICG. We ran them responsibly, even honoring all of the environmental remediation obligations left after the bankruptcy, perhaps becoming the only coal company to do so.

Underground coal mining is inherently a difficult and dangerous occupation. Working eight hours in a cramped space thousands of feet below the surface is the ultimate claustrophobic task, and despite highly regulated safety precautions, any incident that occurs can destroy lives. When coal miners leave their wives to go to work, the goodbyes are almost as emotional as those from wives of fighter pilots going off on combat missions.

To help ensure the safest working environment possible, ICG specifically included a strong track record of mine safety as a determinant of our executive compensation packages. Ben had stressed in his job interview that no mine under his supervision had ever had a fatality, so we had confidence in his ability to adhere to the rules. The mine safety protocols held that prior to a whole shift going underground, one person would go down alone to look carefully for anything that might endanger his fellow workers as they joined him. This policy was followed meticulously and carefully recorded.

Nonetheless, before dawn on January 2, 2006, a day with powerful storms and lightning strikes, Ben called to say that an explosion at our Sago Mine in West Virginia had trapped thirteen men underground. Rescue efforts were underway, but the outcome was uncertain. I had owned the mine all of seven weeks, but still felt a responsibility to help. I volunteered to fly there to do what I could, but Ben admonished that since I had no technical skills to offer, I would just get in the way. We spoke repeatedly over the next hours and days, but an initially optimistic assessment tragically proved incorrect. All but one of the men were dead, and the sole survivor was close to death. This was the worst coal mining disaster in years. Accordingly, state and federal authorities carefully investigated it, and ultimately concluded that the probable cause was a freak lightning bolt igniting the methane gas typically present in the mine.

Nonetheless, some of our employees had died, and their families were inconsolable. I had lost my own father at age eighteen, so I knew the pain the children were going through. Compounding the grief of the families and the communities was that the media initially reported that twelve of the miners were found alive—something that had to be recanted later. We could not make up for their loss of loved ones, but at least we could provide financial support to relieve that aspect of the tragedy. I established and was the main contributor to a 501(c)(3) charity, the Sago Mine Fund, and asked the then-Governor of West Virginia, Joe Manchin, to appoint an independent board of trustees to allocate the fund's money. As a Democrat, Manchin could have made a huge political issue about a disaster at a nonunion mine owned by a private equity fund, but he knew that International Coal Group was a responsible company and chose not to do so. I was also grateful to Donald Trump in those days, who made an unsolicited and anonymous contribution to the fund, an especially generous act.

In the wake of the tragedy, our public relations experts had recommended that I make no public response to the vast amount of press coverage that ensued. But, as the head of the entire operation, I decided personally to face up to the media attacks and rebut the false accusations about ICG's malfeasance. Being reviled in TV and print interviews day after day was a harrowing experience, and it compounded my grief and sorrow in what I publicly described as "the worst week of my life."[13] Both the horrible event itself and the media attacks provided me with literal nightmares for a long time. Months later, when the inspectors made their report, there was little press interest. The tragedy was newsworthy. The fact that management was blameless was not.

Buffett and Burlington Mills

One of my other major acquisitions at WL Ross & Co. was Burlington Mills. Burlington was one of the leading textile mills in the United States but it and J.P. Stevens, another iconic mill, were suffering severely from foreign competition, mostly from Asia, as the apparel and other fabric-consuming industries moved there. Burlington had grown to eight thousand employees since its founding in 1923, but went bankrupt in 2001 with $800 million in debts and a mountain of unfunded pension liabilities. Those facts caused it to file for Chapter 11. Its unsecured bonds then collapsed, and we bought quite a few. I became chairman of the unsecured creditors committee, and prepared to bid for the company. Because Burlington was an established name in the industry, and had a reputation for producing high-quality products, we believed we could buy it and return it to profitability.

But as it turned out, someone else had a similar theory of the case: Warren Buffett, perhaps the most brilliant investor of all time.

Warren Buffett's experience in the textile industry ran deep: he had built Berkshire Hathaway from the remnants of a failed textile company, and he had recently bought Fruit of the Loom, so he knew the value of what he was acquiring, just as I did. But where we diverged was on *how* we would bid for the company. Warren's style is to decide on the value of something, bid it in cash, and if someone overbid, let it go. I and the other bondholders decided to outbid him using at par bonds in lieu of cash bonds that were trading at a steep discount.

In bankruptcy court, Warren tried to convince the judge that WL Ross & Co.'s bid should be disregarded, claiming cash was a more valuable currency than defaulted bonds. I was even put up for cross-examination. When his lawyer, a famous bankruptcy practitioner from Jones Day named Bill Hayman, questioned me, his line of attack was to argue that surely cash was a better bid than our equity proposal. My response was that the committee owned more than two thirds of the bonds, and we preferred to take the equity. Since it was our investments that were at risk, not Buffett's, the court should not impose an unwanted solution on us. In the end, the judge agreed: "If the unsecured creditors prefer stock to cash, I will not overrule them." We won.

Buffett is good-natured enough that this one victory did not preclude us from having a good relationship afterward. Sometime later, he and I were seated together at the White House Correspondents' Dinner. Someone wanted to photograph the two of us together. Warren said to me, "Let's give them a scene of you and me fighting over my wallet!" We staged a grappling match, and the press got their picture. Afterwards he confided to me, "Wilbur, it really wasn't worth fighting over. I only had one hundred dollars in it!"

Buffett's living habits reflect his general good nature. Unlike most billionaires, Buffett lives in the same modest house he bought in Omaha decades earlier. His food tastes are also unchanged: He favors steak and Coca-Cola. Every year he auctions off for a charity a private lunch. The first one in 2000 went for $20,000. The most recent one sold for $19 million. I don't know who has good enough clothes to wear to a $19 million lunch.

To return to Burlington, as part of our reorganization plan, we proposed a way we could buy the company just for the price of funding their pension liability. First, we would sell off the only truly profitable unit of their business, a leading carpet manufacturer (which we later did sell for twenty-plus times earnings to Mohawk Industries for $352 million). That would raise enough capital to deleverage the company to the point where its only real liability was the pension fund. We then would exchange the defaulted publicly traded bonds for 100 percent of the equity. The judge agreed with us, and that plan was put into motion. Soon, we merged Burlington with other assets we had acquired: Cone Mills, a leading denim producer, and Safety Components, a major auto seat belt manufacturer. No one can accuse us of being terribly creative in naming the new company International Textile Group (ITG), following in the footsteps of International Steel Group and International Coal Group.

The next step in making International Textile Group profitable involved internationalizing it.

We set up a joint venture in Mexico, allowing us to become a major producer there. We also started two joint ventures in China and in Vietnam. Sadly, the move to Vietnam proved to be one of the worst mistakes of my business career. As is common in Communist countries, including China, we were forced to rely on a state-run company as our business partner. State-run companies are dens of corruption and inefficiencies, and our Vietnamese "partner" made up the lost revenues by charging us seven times as much as they should have to run the business in Vietnam. The management was simply horrible. This was all my own fault—I should never have let my business be that dependent on a state-run company. As a result, we lost every penny we put in there.

Even though the company worked out well, we also under-achieved on a bad bet we had made on one of its proprietary technologies. Burlington had a scientific operation called NanoTex, which imparted chemicals into fabrics in a way that made them impervious to moisture. When they showed me how a tie could be resistant to a ketchup stain, I was hooked. We spun the NanoTex operation out of Burlington, and backed it with money from my own fund and other venture investors. At first, we convinced Brooks Brothers and other apparel retailers to buy NanoTex for its products, and things were going well. But two developments got in our way. First, another company, GoreTex, had developed a similar product that did as good a job, but was cheaper. This company had also figured out how to configure its formula so that it could be used on furniture and other fabrics. It would have taken serious money to compete with such a well-armed competitor, and that's not the business I was interested in. Eventually, we sold the NanoTex brand to our investors and it faded away. The lesson here is that technology is a risky area: You can never be sure you have the best mousetrap. Or if you do, how long will that be true?

Bankrupt Banks

I bought my first bank control position at age thirty—and it did not happen because of a crisis with the bank itself. The principal stockholder of the First New Haven National Bank in Connecticut also owned the major local department store. In 1977, downtown retailers in smaller cities were facing a crisis, as big suburban malls lured customers away from stores like the one in downtown New Haven. My group bought his 15 percent stake in the bank to provide the liquidity he needed to keep the store going. The financial analytics all pointed to a good decision: The stock was trading at a big discount from book value and with a high dividend yield, which supported a margin loan for the purchase. We then brought in a more sophisticated CEO and the bank prospered.

A few years later we sold First New Haven to Shawmut Bank, and soon went to the Federal Reserve Bank of Boston to approve the merger. In the lobby, a sign posted above the reception desk read: "The Federal Reserve Bank of Boston does not cash government checks." Below that notice someone had written in black magic marker ink, "What do they know that we don't know?" Curiously, no one had removed the graffiti. Disdain for the Federal Reserve still runs deep in American politics today. The Fed is burdened with two mutually contradictory mandates: maximization of employment and controlling inflation toward a 2 percent per annum target. Easy monetary policy fosters the first and tighter monetary policy the second. As has been repeatedly demonstrated, the way this ying and yang is balanced has huge political and economic consequences, but the agency is at least theoretically non-partisan.

At Rothschild, my earliest bank advisory assignments were the Bank of New England and a defunct savings bank in Philadelphia. Later, I advised the Italian government on restructuring Banco di Napoli. Like many Italian banks, it was owned by a local "foundation"— one heavily influenced by the Neapolitan Mafia. When word got out on our involvement, a local Naples newspaper, perhaps as a warning, ran an editorial questioning why the Italian government had hired an American "thug" to advise on the bank. Mafia bosses accusing me of being a thug—that was rich. Our investigation into the bank's finances showed an abysmal loan portfolio and many loan documents conveniently missing from the files. It was thus very difficult to evaluate them. I recommended that the government extract the tainted loans and divide the good loans, deposits, and related branches into segments that would complement the generally uneconomically small branches of the many foreign and Italian banks operating there. We obtained enough premiums from those sales to offset much of the government's losses embedded in the bad loans.

A far easier task was assisting the Mexican government on selling a small, failed bank to a major Spanish bank. When that went well, the government then invited Rothschild into a limited competition to advise them on the privatization of the Mexico City International Airport. Our presentation to the board went well until an old man sitting at the end of the table asked, "Señor Ross, how will you deal with the private aircraft fuel concession?" In other words, who got the contracts for refueling private planes, and how?

I responded, "These are best operated by specialists, so we would propose a separate competitive bid for this facility."

Little did I know then that our answer cost us the assignment. Rumor was that the question had been planted by the drug cartels, who did not want outsiders to know that their planes were secretly buying enough fuel from the facility to run narcotics into the United States. Our competitor either guessed right or was tipped off, because his answer was, "We would leave that facility alone."

In 2011, WL Ross & Co. had an opportunity to invest in the Bank of Ireland, our first European banking opportunity. At that time, the mortgage crisis was continuing to dominate that continent, and the Bank of Ireland was in dire straits. Larger private equity firms concluded that taking a piece of it in exchange for injecting liquidity and organizing a turnaround was too risky. Hence, there was no other bidder for the deal. But WL Ross went in at the invitation of my friend Prem Watsa, who is known as the Warren Buffett of Canada. Our decision was, as always, based on rigorous analysis. Most firms were wary of Ireland because they believed it was too dependent on friendly corporate tax rates for prosperity. They also regarded the Irish economy as similar to those of sclerotic Western European nations.

They had not done enough homework! Upon further examination, the Irish economy had many factors besides tax rates that augured a brighter economic future than other European countries could hope to enjoy. Ireland had excellent transportation and telecom facilities, and a young, well-educated, and diligent workforce. U.S. companies, mainly tech and pharmaceutical companies, had located production facilities there and often used Ireland as their base for European operations. (In fact, the little blue pills that give middle-aged men such pleasure are made in Ireland.) Also important were the government's extreme belt-tightening during the crisis and its fully funded national retirement system. Additionally, Ireland had the least restrictive of any European employment regulations. Laws making it very hard to release workers actually reduce employment, because employers are loath to hire workers whom they can't let go—a fact overlooked by EU and U.S. legislators. Ireland didn't have that problem. The fact that English was the spoken language was another plus. It was essential to understanding the economy, because when you buy the largest bank in a country you are really buying a warrant on that economy.

Upon sealing the deal, we made a few rapid moves. We took over part of the government's rights to subscribe to a third round of new capital. And, at our insistence, an existing Bank of Ireland executive, a South African named Richie Boucher, became our CEO. Two years later, the bank had been restored to health. This case was similar to the BankUnited situation (described later in this book): Because the government-imposed reserves were adequate and the underlying real estate was valuable, we thought Ireland would turn around rapidly. It was not a sure thing that the government board designees, one-third of the total, would adhere to the contractual agreement, but we took a risk that they would. They did, and the bank functioned in a commercially reasonable way. Things went so well that I sold my stake in 2014 at a nearly 300 percent return.

Part of the strategy for the bank's recovery involved me going on TV to repeatedly proclaim with confidence my belief in Ireland's "V-shaped recovery," and my conviction that the bank's problems were behind it. That helped convince other investors that Ireland was a place to be in the long run. A few years later, the Taoiseach (Prime Minister) of Ireland, Enda Kenny, went into great detail about my role in the bank's recovery in a speech to the American Ireland Fund at the Breakers hotel in Palm Beach. The Irish press also repeatedly referred to me as "the man who saved Ireland." It was of course, hyperbole, but it did boost my standing with my Irish American wife.

The successes I had at WL Ross & Co. brought my career to a new level. It is certain that I benefited from a network of personal and professional contacts who were as generous with their advice and invitations as they were skilled in financial dealmaking. But in truth, the victories were attributable to a continuation of habits adopted long before I first walked through the doors of Buckner and Co. A dedication to preparation, focus, and discipline—executing your strategy for a successful outcome despite any distraction or adversity—has made all the difference.

CHAPTER 7

International Adventures

In the 1980s, my daughter Jessica had been dating a young man from a mining family in Zimbabwe (formerly known as Rhodesia). One year, she went over there with him for his sister's wedding. When she came back, she announced that he and his parents would be in New York over Thanksgiving weekend, so we invited them to join our holiday dinner at the Dakota. While I was carving the turkey in the pantry, the young man came forward, knelt down, and asked for her hand in marriage. The following spring, they were wed at St. Thomas More Church, and the Forbes band of Scottish bag-pipers lead us two blocks to the reception, which Jessica had desired to have at her old school on East 91st St., Covenant of the Sacred Heart.

That December, we visited the in-laws in Harare (formerly Salisbury). When we arrived from our hotel at their residence, the father asked me to indulge the local custom and be introduced to the household staff. We went to the rear of the house and there, kneeling on a steep flight of stairs, were a dozen domestic workers. As I approached them, he introduced me and each one put a hand up to shake mine, but never looked up. It was a surprising expression of servitude, because apartheid was long gone.

The next day I had lunch with the CEO of the Merchant Bank of Central Africa. It had been 50 percent owned by N. M. Rothschild and 50 percent by American Metal Climax for almost one hundred years, but had never paid a dividend. Yet you have never seen an office with so many large gold and silver decorative objects. I remarked to one of the executives, "The bank has never returned cash to investors, but there's precious metals all over the walls."

He shook his head. "These are the only assets we have that can protect against the inflation here. It's between 50 and 100 percent each year."

On returning to the United States, I told this story to an investment manager friend of mine. He sent me a Zimbabwean $100 billion bill. Its value then was about 25 cents. Now it is probably less than 5 cents.

How did one of the richest countries in Africa, replete with natural resources and fertile soil, fall into the pit of economic ruin? Indeed, Zimbabwe can no longer even feed itself. Former Prime Minister Robert Mugabe broke the huge, efficient farms into small, inefficient ones, which he then gave to farmworkers with poor sense of how to manage them properly. Where Zimbabwe had once been a major exporter of maize, the staple of the Zimbabwean diet, now the country must import this critical product into the country. The nation's rich diamond and mineral resources also have languished. The entire situation is reminiscent of Venezuela, one of the most oil-rich nations in the world, and formerly one of the wealthiest, which has now been reduced to a wasteland. South Africa is not far behind these nations on its descent into poverty and societal breakdown.

My trip to Zimbabwe was one of my earliest exposures to a country plagued by corruption, instability, and socialism. The lesson for me was to minimize my investments in places characterized by these ills. By contrast, when investment opportunities arose in prosperous and stable foreign countries, I made little distinction between those places and the United States.

———————————

My time in Zimbabwe was not confined to Merchant Bank's offices. That same day, my new relatives took us on a tour of the capital. As we approached the presidential palace, there were huge signs, in English and the local native languages, prohibiting cars or pedestrian traffic on those streets from 6:00 p.m. until 8:00 a.m. There were also many security guards. When I asked what would happen if someone violated the rule, I received a nonchalant answer: "They would shoot them dead!"

That evening, we had the same driver as the night before, but as we approached the car he explained, "Bwana! Something terrible has happened! I can't take you there again!" Our hearts sank in fear that there might have been violence. He then added, "A rival tribe changed all the street signs last night so I can't find my way."

"But the streets are still the same, why can't you just repeat last night's route?"

He reiterated that he could not find his way, so I had the concierge draw a map which we Scotch-taped to the steering wheel. That solved the problem. But when we left the house, he had the same difficulty. So, I took the map and turned it upside down and we got back to the hotel.

We spent the weekend in the family's cabin on a bluff high above the Zambesi River, on the other side of which was

Zambia. In the evening, the only lights on the Zambian side were campfires. It seemed like a Stone Age country. Along the way we noticed a witch doctor performing a ceremony in a nearby field. He did not bother us, which my wife regarded as a professional courtesy to me.

The next morning, Ken, my new son-in-law, volunteered to gather water by taking a bucket a few steps into the river. Since there was always some danger from crocodiles, we tied a rope around his waist, because, in the case of an attack, crocodiles drown their prey prior to eating it. His father held the rope tightly. Fortunately, Ken emerged unscathed. We later boarded a small boat and cruised downstream, careful not to get between the hippopotamus families and the nearest shore. Had we done so, they would have attacked the boat and knocked us into the crocodile-ridden waters.

We next drove into the veldt—the wild grasslands of Africa. Every several hundred yards there were large white squares with a black circle in the middle. The black was a chemical that attracted and killed the male tsetse flies that endangered cattle. It was fascinating that the government put a greater premium on protecting cattle than providing for their own people.

Suddenly, we came upon a pack of wild dogs with huge square jaws. Four of them stationed themselves near the car. The rest hunkered down in a marsh. We soon saw a herd of zebra being driven by other dogs from the pack into the swamp. It was a total coordinated ambush—the hiding dogs jumped up to bite the zebras to death. Most remarkable was the dogs' speed—they were so fast that they could keep up with the zebra while jumping up to bite at the midsection over and over until the zebra died.

It was a fascinating thing to see the wildlife of the African continent, but I was more distressed at Zimbabwe's condition.

Sadly, the country has continued to deteriorate. The severe economic problems have caused large emigration. The professional class has dispersed across many countries and the impoverished tribal members have mostly gone to South Africa. Unfortunately, they do not get along with the local tribes there, so there are violent conflicts between them. Optimists point out that much of the world's future population growth will come from sub-Saharan Africa and that by providing development money the world could trigger huge economic growth there. However, I have watched military coup after military coup and the corruption and incompetence of the dictatorships, so I am skeptical—at best—that these nations will be able to pull themselves together. As Secretary of Commerce, I led a U.S. trade mission to sub-Saharan Africa, and during the first night of my visit someone threw a hand grenade at the President of Ethiopia. The government of the second country we visited fell two days after our trip. When one considers such instability, combined with the poverty, illiteracy, and poor physical health of the citizenry, I find it hard to make a bullish case for sub-Saharan Africa. The major capital needs run into the trillions of dollars, which would be a very heavy lift even if other investors do not share my pessimism. That doesn't mean we should not provide aid, but we must be realistic in our expectations for progress.

Russia

Russia was another country rife with problems. Early in the 1990s, Russian President Boris Yeltsin privatized many Russian state-owned companies and tried hard to remold the country's economy. President Bill Clinton was highly supportive of Yeltsin and created a U.S.–Russia Investment Fund to provide capital and advice to assist the privatization process. At the suggestion of Senator Pat Moynihan, President Clinton appointed me to the board. It was during this period I first met Vladimir Putin at a cocktail party, when he was vice mayor of St. Petersburg. The only reason I remember the meeting after all these years is that he had the most frightening visage of any person I have ever met. When he looks at you, you think his gaze is going right through your head. He could play the villain in any James Bond movie. Meeting him more recently at bilateral meetings with President Trump did not change my opinion.

Helping privatize Russia was a fascinating set of responsibilities, but one that often left me disappointed. A Western-prescribed set of "shock therapy" economic policies, while necessary, had caused the devaluation of the ruble and disrupted the rhythms of Russian life. One of the fund's most strategic initiatives was solving the problem of inadequate healthcare in Moscow. Russia wanted to bring in American companies, but few American managers wanted to relocate there because of the poor healthcare facilities, especially if their wives were of childbearing age or if they already had young children.

The fund joined with PepsiCo, a U.S. company well-established in Russia, and the Hermitage Hospital in St. Petersburg, to create the first health maintenance organization (HMO) in Russia. The authorities promptly granted approval for this novel healthcare delivery mechanism, provided that any Russian could pay the monthly fee for service and join. We believed that few Russians would pay close to the $1,000 per month fee. However, we overlooked one constituency that needed lots of medical services and whose members could well afford it: the Russian Mafia. American companies understandably worried about having a wounded gangster in the bed next to one of their executives, so the project never realized its full potential. Nonetheless, I keep on a shelf the miniature model ambulance that memorializes the project.

The Russian Mafia figures prominently in another anecdote from this period. A neighbor of mine in the Dakota, Peter Terian, owned a major Rolls-Royce dealership in Glen Cove, New York. Rolls-Royce management convinced Peter to open its first dealership in Moscow in 1993, just a few weeks before the tanks rolled up to parliament as part of a constitutional crisis in October of that year. I ran into Peter at an airport soon thereafter and asked if that hurt his sales.

"Not at all," he replied. "The Mafia have adopted the Rolls as their off-duty vehicle of choice, so sales are booming. But they still make me pay protection money each week. I told them that this is pointless, because I just add it to the cars' prices. They told me that it was a matter of principle."

The Russian domestic car industry was very weak, so much so that a joke was circulating around Moscow. A Russian had saved enough money to buy a domestically produced car, so he negotiated a price with a dealer. The car salesman then suggested, "Your delivery will be February 22nd, five years from now, at 10:00 a.m. Does that work for you?" The car buyer looked through his datebook and said, "No. The plumber is coming that day." Another great joke I heard revolved around Soviet propaganda. A Ford and a Russian car had a race. The Ford won easily, but the state-run newspaper *Izvestia* covered the race. Their article the next day proclaimed, "Great news about the international auto race! Our car came in second, but the Ford was next to last."

Even before Putin's invasion of Ukraine, doing business in Russia meant taking the risk of operating in a lawless environment. In the early 2000s, one of my company's private equity funds owned VTG, Europe's largest railcar leasing company.

VTG had decided to capture a share of the freight moving between Russia and Europe by solving a long-standing problem: Russian track beds were not the same gauges as European ones. Therefore, freight had to be unloaded at the border in each direction and reloaded onto cars with the appropriate gauge. The original intent had been to block European nations, e.g., Germany, from invading by means of rail. VTG developed a system where the cars had two sets of wheels each, of which could be extended or retracted, thereby reducing delay at the Russian border.

As part of entering the Russian market, VTG's customers put up security deposits in dollars to minimize currency and credit risks and took in a Russian partner to help deal with local issues. For a year or so VTG did well, until the local partner stole the company. I do not mean he pulled off a mere financial swindle on paper. He took over VTG's Russia office with armed guards, switched bank accounts, and started to confiscate VTG's fleet. Fortunately, our CEO had been active in Christian Democratic Union politics in Hamburg, and so he contacted Chancellor Angela Merkel, who a few weeks later was to meet with Putin, and asked her to solve the problem. We never learned whether the Chancellor herself had intervened or whether the staff handled it, but VTG came out all right.

I have never since invested in Russia. That nation is the ultimate example of a one distinguished by the law of the ruler rather than the rule of law. Most dictatorships and their courts tend to be inhospitable to foreign companies, especially if well-connected local businessmen are the adversaries, but this was an especially severe case. Other tales of how things are done in Russia should discourage any reasonable person. Some years ago, my friend Bob Kraft, a paper magnate, who owns the New England Patriots football team, was in Moscow on a trade mission, and seated next to Putin at a dinner. Putin admired Bob's Super Bowl ring and asked to try it on. Bob gave it to him, and it was a perfect fit. Putin then took it off and put it in his pocket and turned away from Bob. When Bob asked the State Department to get it back, his contact said, "We don't want a big row with Putin over a ring. You can afford to buy a replacement." Bob spent $30,000 on one and has been dining out on the story ever since.

Putin's bully tactics make Russia seem formidable as a world power. But the truth is that Russia is far less potent than its dictator-leader would have the world think. Despite being geographically the largest nation in the world in size, its gross domestic product (GDP) is about the same size as Italy's, and only about half the size of California's. Natural resources are the center of its economy, and there are no Russian multinational manufacturing companies of any true renown. Militarily, while Russia does have nuclear weapons, many are more than fifty years old, and, judging from Russia's inadequate maintenance of fighter planes and tanks, you have to wonder if its nuclear arsenal is even fully operable. Nonetheless, Russia plays a significant role in the Middle East, in Africa, and in Latin America. Worse yet, Putin has strategic relationships with China, Iran, and even North Korea, a deadly trio bent on displacing American power. The conflict between Israel and Hamas in Gaza, which has polarized the Democratic Party, has pushed the war in Ukraine off the front page. I am not a conspiracy theorist, but given the rapport among Russia, Iran, and China, I can't help but wonder if Hamas might have chosen to launch its attack against Israel on October 7, which is Putin's birthday, to symbolize that it was in part a gift to him.

Russia's prosecution of the war in Ukraine is yet another example of how it is largely an impotent country. Putin miscalculated that Ukrainian and Western resistance would be as feeble as it had been previously when Russia first went into Crimea, and Russia has suffered more than 300,000 casualties two years into the war.[14] Still, Russia could achieve victory if it is willing to continue absorbing such high levels of killed and wounded. The most unfortunate part of the present war is American ineptitude. I believe that the invasion was precipitated by President Joe Biden's amateurish handling of the withdrawal from Afghanistan and, more precisely, by his announcement that Ukraine would eventually be admitted to NATO. Had he instead initiated its immediate accession, the war would not have started six months later. Worse yet, he went on TV daily for weeks suggesting the invasion was imminent, but did not provide any weapons until thirty days after the incursion. Had he properly armed Ukraine, it is likely that Russia would have been repelled quickly, and with far less loss of lives and property.

Now that the war there has dragged on for so long without a Ukrainian victory clearly in sight, American political leaders and the public are beginning to lose interest in it, especially with the Hamas-Israel war taking up so much attention and money. EU countries have been filling part of the gap. Many of them know that their individual security will be at risk if we let Putin win. Too bad America has not, by and large, learned the same lesson.

Italy

In any professional services relationship, it is essential to make yourself readily accessible to your clients or investors. Nothing is more frustrating to them than to be unable to reach a trusted advisor when faced with a problem. In the days before cell phones, when there were pay phones on virtually every street, I kept a roll of quarters in my briefcase so I could always keep in touch wherever I was traveling. On one occasion, however, the challenge of getting to a phone was far more complex.

During August one year, I rented a house in northern Italy for two weeks. It was in a vineyard on the land surrounding Castle Brolio, midway between Florence and Sienna. The broker promised me that there would be a phone in the house, but when we arrived, the house lady, Signora Fedora, informed me, "There has never been a phone—the nearest telephone line is three miles away. The castle has one line—maybe the count would let you pay to use his sometimes."

That evening we went to a cute place for dinner in the nearby small town, a combination restaurant and bodega. I noticed a gleaming, nickel-plated phone in a small booth at the bodega. I inquired of the owner, "Is that handsome young man who is helping you by any chance your son?"

"Yes," he replied, looking befuddled. "Why do you ask?"

"I have a business proposition for the two of you. My rental house has no phone. If my office needs to reach me, I will have them call me collect at your number. You will refuse the charge and ask them to call back in thirty minutes. Meanwhile, your son will pick me up so I can take the call here. I will pay him 10,000 lira each time."

"Signore, you have a deal!"

The boy's car was a tiny Fiat whose whirring engine sounded like a giant sewing machine. Whenever it came down the mile of dirt road leading to our house one of the girls would hear it and cry out, "Daddy has a phone call!"

Aside from the telecom issue, my family had a great time wandering through the other Tuscan hillside villages. Each had its own cuisine and its own local wine and many had churches which contained art from the fifteenth century or thereabouts. You had to insert a few lira into a slot to turn the lights on so you could see the art—a practice I took to calling "illuminairis." I concluded from this trip and others to Italy that Italians, rich or poor, know better how to have fun than any other nationality. In contrast, I never have been able to make a business deal there, save for the tortured exercise in helping the government restructure Banco di Napoli. I think the various men with whom I was negotiating must have read and reread Machiavelli every year since the first grade. Things got so complicated every time, and their stories were self-contradictory and constantly shifting. Nonetheless, I will keep trying!

A Trusted Partner

About a year after the International Steel Group (ISG) IPO in 2003, Robert Pilkington, a UBS vice chairman, called to say that Lakshmi Mittal and his son Aditya wanted to meet. Lakshmi was an Indian emigrant to London who had built an original tiny mill in Indonesia into a major steel company spanning several developing countries. But his small U.S. operation was struggling. Aditya, his son, was a graduate of the Wharton School and one of the brightest young men I have ever met.

The Mittals had made many low-cost acquisitions, such as buying a major mill in Kazakhstan just by providing the next month's payroll. The mill was so bad off that it was paying workers with its own worthless scrip. The Mittals later modernized it at a cost of more than $1 billion and were now generating more than that amount each year in cash flow. In effect, they were doing outside the United States what ISG was doing inside of it.

What had been proposed as a courtesy meeting went so well that it lasted for a couple of hours. We realized that we had more in common with each other than either of us had with the rest of the steel industry. Combining the two companies would result in one of the world's largest and most geographically diverse steel companies. By the end of our time together, we had negotiated a deal to merge the two entities. ISG would get $26 per share, half in cash and half in stock. I would go on their board and our CEO, Rodney Mott, would run the combined U.S. operations.

The Mittals were staying at the Palace Hotel in New York, so they invited Hilary and me for a celebratory dinner that night at the famous Le Cirque restaurant, located there at the time. We agreed to go to Pittsburgh prior to making any announcement to introduce the Mittals to Leo Gerard, and assure him that the merged company would work as closely with the steelworkers' union as ISG had. We also planned to tell Leo that the union representative on our board, Lewis Kaden, a partner at Davis Polk & Wardwell, would remain. Leo was satisfied so all was well. As is true of most personal interactions, blindsiding the union with important public announcements can destroy the trust that is essential to a good mutual relationship. When Nippon Steel made its recent takeover bid for U.S. Steel, the company, possibly worrying about leaks of insider information, failed to consult with the union before announcing the deal. This was a huge mistake that inflamed the union and created a lot of political fodder and controversy in an election year.

About a year later, Lakshmi thought about acquiring Arcelor, the major European Union steel company. It made total commercial sense, but the CEO, Guy Dollé, likely would not agree. I had met Dollé a few times at industry functions and regarded him as an arrogant egomaniac. For example, at a World Steel Dynamics conference in Paris, I was the luncheon speaker and Dollé was at the same table. The speech went well and got a few rounds of applause, after which Dollé leaned toward me and said in a loud voice, "Mr. Ross, that was a pretty good speech for someone who knows so little about the steel industry." He clearly would oppose a takeover by non-European upstarts.

Lakshmi and Aditya decided the only option was to submit a hostile bid. Our board appointed them and me as the subcommittee to handle the fight. Since they would have to live with Arcelor management after the deal, I became the company's voice responding to whatever public criticisms Dollé would make. He was vicious, at one point announcing that he opposed Arcelor shareholders being offered "monkey paper." I responded that ethnic slurs were not a valid financial argument. Meanwhile, Aditya went around to each of the major Arcelor shareholders and got proxies from most of them, including the governments in Belgium, France, and Luxembourg. He had to make some commitments about continued levels of employment to them, but none that had a meaningful impact on operations. Sure enough, Dollé resigned in protest, but his number two stayed on, and the deal closed.

ArcelorMittal was now the world's largest steel company, and Aditya delivered on his promise to reduce the combined company's costs by €400 million per year. When we had our first post-closing board meeting at Arcelor's headquarters in Luxembourg, we went down to the wine cellar. It had something like ten thousand bottles of expensive wine, the contents of which were served daily in their opulent dining rooms. We promptly auctioned off the wine. The Mittals were dedicated to efficiency and that divestiture sent a clear message to the staff that times had changed.

Yet, even as Lakshmi was parsimonious with company money, he did not mind luxury if the company didn't pay for it. Some years after, he bought a house in the Kensington Palace Gardens section of London, often called Billionaires' Row. It was at the time one of the highest prices ever paid for a home anywhere. The house included an indoor pool, a beauty parlor with three stations, and underground parking for twenty-three cars. He and Aditya each have country estates in England, a chalet in St. Moritz in the Swiss Alps, and a major yacht.

But for as much as they spend, the Mittals are also very charitable. In 2005, the Mittals donated $10 million to the India Hurricane Relief Fund and asked me to set up the joint press conference among the three of us, President George H. W. Bush, and President Bill Clinton, who were also involved in the relief efforts. The two presidents did not usually get along well with each other, but very successfully cochaired this cause. It would be wonderful if such bipartisan comity were more common than the present enmity. Included in the photo section is one of Lakshmi, Aditya, and me with the two presidents in Washington, D.C.

Asian Opportunities

WL Ross & Co.'s Asia Recovery Fund invested in Japan and Korea during the Asian financial crisis, which began in 1997 after the devaluation of the Thai baht currency. Japan and Korea share many similarities. Both are heavily pro-American, are net exporters to the United States, and have U.S. military forces permanently stationed in their countries. Both have strong research and development skills, and both tend to rotate executives through the United States on a three-year cycle. Critically, both countries are relationship-based societies. Executives from both nations will live up to the letter of their contract, but not go one inch beyond its bounds. As a result, they tend to argue over every word in the document. On balance, both are excellent to deal with, but you can't act like a sharp-elbowed American with a "wham, bam, thank you ma'am" approach to doing business.

Despite their commonalities, Japan and Korea have significant differences. The main one is a degree of overt aggressiveness. Japanese are firm but polite, always demonstrating a respect for decorum and honor. In South Korea, there is a harder edge. Labor strikes, even violent ones, are commonplace. The South Korean court system will frequently send a high-ranking public official or chaebol (conglomerate) executive to prison (but he will reemerge in a high position). The South Korean media, too, are more like the big British tabloid newspapers, where the Japanese ones are more constrained. There are also national security differences: South Korea's military, owing to the threat of North Korea, has long been robust, while the Japanese constitution has limited the size of Japan's own military until recently.

My team at Rothschild advised many Japanese institutions regarding their holdings of distressed U.S. assets. This experience led to an assignment for Daiwa Securities, the second-largest Japanese investment bank. Its debt was rated BAA, the lowest investment-grade rating, but was on credit watch for another possible downgrade. Downgrading the bank to junk bond status would have destroyed its business. Daiwa hired me to advise them how to restructure the firm and to convince the rating agencies not to take precipitous action. The project gave me insight into every aspect of the firm, and we successfully maintained the rating until they merged into Sumitomo Mitsui Banking Corp, a company from the same keiretsu (network of interrelated companies). One senior Daiwa executive generously commented that I knew as much about Daiwa as its senior executives did.

This relationship made it natural for Rothschild's new private equity fund (which later became my fund at WL Ross & Co.) to create a joint venture with them to buy distressed Japanese mortgage debt. We established an office in Tokyo, and Sumitomo Mitsui Bank permitted me to hire Tatsuo Kubota, who had run its retail business prior to the merger with Daiwa. The idea that I was "permitted" to hire an executive from another company may seem strange to an American reader. But in Japan, if you poach a senior executive without the bank's consent, the aggrieved company will never do business with you again. Kubota was unusual in that Sumitomo had recruited him from the presidency of the successful Citi Private Bank in Japan. Very few Japanese executives had become senior officials of American banks and then joined a Japanese institution at the board level.

Kubota soon proposed that we buy Kofuku, an Osaka-based bank the government took over because of bad real-estate loans. I commuted several times to Japan to analyze the bank and to seek the government's approval of us as buyers. By the time they approved the deal, I was separating from Rothschild and had to convince the government to sell to us, even though the buyer was affiliated with a famous investment bank. They agreed.

We reopened as Kansai Sawayaka Ginko: Kansai for the region; Sawayaka for rebirth; and Ginko for bank. We were closing twelve branches, but did not want our first announcement to be laying off a thousand employees. The government hired them to oversee the disposition of loans we rejected and to take over the leases. We also hired attractive young women to solicit accounts from local businesses and

to collect our loans. They proved excellent at both tasks, so
we promoted three of them to be branch managers to prove
they could have real careers with our bank. But there was no
assurance our belief was correct. No Osaka bank had ever
had a female executive, and this did not sit well with some
quarters of the banking establishment—the Osaka Bankers
Association even threatened to expel us. The ubiquitous
Japan Post Bank, however, rewarded our competence-driven
results by accepting our credit and debit cards. Our customers loved that their debit and credit card from a regional
bank was usable throughout Japan—previously, the card
was only useful regionally. We also stopped lending at 1.5
percent as part of a major company syndication. Instead,
we lent to small and medium-sized enterprises (SMEs) and
households at rates above 8 percent, albeit with a bit more
in the way of write-offs. In two years, we sold the bank to
Sumitomo Mitsui's Kansai regional bank. But we didn't want
to embarrass the government with our gain, so we never
announced the price. We made one announcement that we
were negotiating the sale and a second that the acquisition
was completed.

The closing dinner was in Kyoto at a geisha restaurant. One geisha stood behind each chair and literally
fed us each mouthful. Others played traditional Japanese
stringed instruments, sang, and performed regional
dances. (Those were the only services they offered.) This
extravagant evening was only one of my many culinary
experiences in Japan, all of which reaffirmed the intense
Japanese focus on food. At one point, there were more
Michelin-starred restaurants in Tokyo than in Paris.
Many of these were small places where only a dozen
people ate at the food bar. At another business dinner in
Tokyo, I tried fugu, a type of blowfish with a thin lining of

poisonous material around the belly. Only eleven chefs in all of Japan are licensed to cut fugu because of the danger involved, and partly because of this mystique, a fugu meal is the most expensive in all of Japan. This restaurant's entire menu was fugu: fugu ceviche as an appetizer, roast fugu the entrée, fugu flavored ice cream for dessert, and fugu-based saki. The danger associated with fugu gives the fish a reputation as an aphrodisiac in buttoned-down Japanese society.

More opportunities in Japan soon arose on the strength of the Kansai Sawayaka Ginko deal. In total, I made eighty-four trips to Japan during my business career. With all this Japanese activity, the Japan Society in New York invited me to join its board of directors. Founded in 1907, the Japan Society flourished after World War II under the leadership of John D. Rockefeller III and his successor, Jim McDonald, the president and CEO of Rockefeller & Co. Jim recruited me to the board, and when he died I became chairman. Motoatsu Sakurai, the former Japanese Consul General in New York and CEO of Mitsubishi, became president. Strange as it seems, he was the first Japanese CEO of the society. Previously, both the pro bono chairman and the paid president had always been Americans. The combination worked well. We added board members, expanded the membership, opened an alumni chapter in Tokyo, and regularly hosted senior Japanese businessmen and government officials. Prime Minister Shinzo Abe actually sang one of his favorite songs for us shortly after the photo you see included in the photo section was taken. Years later Abe and I met again when President Trump sent Vice President Mike Pence and me on a bilateral mission to Japan. I was heartbroken to hear of his assassination in 2022.

A key moment for the Japan Society came in 2011 with the Fukushima nuclear disaster. At my suggestion, the society created a website that raised over $10 million from forty thousand Americans for the victims. The region was so rural that we had a challenging time finding any local NGOs to which we could give grants, but in the end the aid was delivered. As a gesture of appreciation, in 2015 Emperor Akihito of Japan awarded me the Order of the Rising Sun, Gold and Silver Star, which the *Wall Street Journal* generously speculated in its headline was similar to a British knighthood.[15] (I just wish there were more occasions when I could show it off.) At the ceremony in the Japanese consulate, Mike Bloomberg made some nice remarks, and my friend Richard LeFrak read an English-language version of traditional haiku, a highly stylized poetic form with just three lines and a limited number of syllables on each line.

My experiences in Japan taught me that Japanese business society is highly structured and filled with symbols. For example, the major companies have various waiting rooms so that you don't wait in a big lobby for your appointment. The art on the walls of the room assigned to you hints at whether the meeting will succeed or is going to be an exploratory session. If your room has valuable original French impressionist paintings, you are in good shape, but if there are just reproductions, it is a bad omen. The most dramatic displayer of art was the insurance group Nippon Life. It had bought Van Gogh's *Sunflowers* for a record auction price. To view it at its headquarters you had to make an appointment to go to a totally dark ground-floor room with the painting brightly illuminated at the far end. The exit door let you into a large area filled with life insurance salesmen, setting up a great soft-sell sales pitch. If you were Japanese and had just seen this most beautiful and valuable work, how could you resist buying life insurance?

Republic of Korea

As our Japanese business began to flourish, South Korea came into the picture. The former head of Hyundai Motors U.S. introduced me to Chairman Chung of the Hyundai chaebol in South Korea. His nephew had a separate chaebol, the Halla Group, that became overextended during the Asian crisis in 1997–98. The South Koreans knew that during the crisis my fund had bought huge amounts of Korea Development Bank bonds at steep discounts, and soon cashed them out at par. We did this because we knew that South Korea didn't have too much debt overall, just too much short-term debt. This was easy money, because soon the International Monetary Fund bailed out South Korea out at no loss to creditors. Our bond buying during the crisis made us popular with the South Korean government. So Chairman Chung, sensing that a restructuring would need political sign-off, hired us to help restructure the Halla Group.

The Halla account required opening an office in Seoul with a local staff. As was true in Japan and later in India, I only hired local nationals abroad. That helped us to avoid political, commercial, and social mistakes. But it also created a significant travel burden and the need for teleconferences at least once a week. A hastily assembled staff in a remote location needs lots of interaction with the headquarters, so that they understand the strategy. Intercontinental communication is easier today with Zoom, but back then, on teleconference, a speaker's lips would move a few seconds before you heard each word and hand motions were rather jerky. For insurance that things were going according to plan, we brought the key Seoul staffer to New York periodically, and all our staff made an investment in and received carried interests in the fund for which they worked. It helped them to think like principals, not just employees. It also fostered symmetry between them and our limited partners. To help the strongly upwardly mobile ones, I arranged for them to borrow 50 percent of their investments by guaranteeing the loans, while making them maintain their primary exposures.

Later, WL Ross & Co. decided to buy out of bankruptcy Halla Cement, the largest and lowest-cost South Korean producer and the most automated cement company in the world. Two parallel mile-long conveyors connected its mill to a private deepwater seaport. One conveyor brought in the imported limestone, a key ingredient, and the other took the finished product out. At the time, South Korea was building infrastructure so rapidly that its per capita consumption of cement was among the highest in the world. But Halla overall was over-indebted, so the cement operation had to be sold.

We brought Carl Icahn into the deal as part of a plan to repay the Halla Group's bad loans by buying newly issued shares of the company for cash and canceling the remainder of the debt. Since it was a big bite for us, we approached major foreign cement companies as potential partners. French group Lafarge was interested, but didn't want the complexity of a South Korean bankruptcy proceeding. Based on the prices they had paid for other Asian cement companies, we expected to double our investment in one year once we exited bankruptcy. Carl loved the deal—a cheaply priced, basic asset was right in his sweet spot. It worked well, and Lafarge did buy it a year later. Carl often tells this story at dinner parties, but embellishes it a bit.

Separately, the World Bank funded the South Korean government's hiring of advisors to help the banks modernize their lending practices. We won the contract to modernize Chohung Bank, one of the oldest banks in the country. For a year, we held weekly seminars on lending policies for the benefit of the bank's officers. Chohung, like many Asian banks, made loan decisions mainly based on relationships and asset collateralization. Cash flow-based lending was new to them, but by the end of the year they were proficient.

One of my trips to Korea involved a humorous interaction with Donald Trump, years after we had once been at loggerheads over the terms of his casino bankruptcy (more on that later). As I was booking one particular trip to Seoul, I learned Korean Air's first-class section was fully booked. This seemed impossible, because I was normally the only passenger flying first class to Korea during the Asian financial crisis. It turned out that Donald Trump had booked the whole first-class cabin in anticipation of flying to Seoul to open a luxury apartment building named after him.

I called Donald and asked him to bump one of his staff to coach so I could fly in comfort. He said, "No problem. We will turn over a seat to you. It will just be Melania and me, anyway."

"Then why did you book the whole first class?"

"You'll see when we land!"

Trump knew that booking the whole first-class cabin would be a hook for attracting the media, and give him a great chance to promote his real estate deal. Sure enough, the whole South Korean press corps was at the gate and gave him enthusiastic coverage. The Seoul daily paper even ran a front-page photo captioned "Donald J. Trump, Melania, and an unknown American arrived today." I was the unknown American. It was another indication of Trump's lifelong knack for salesmanship. Few people recognize even today that Trump is the only real-estate developer in history to create exceedingly high values for properties globally just by attaching his universally known name to a project.

South Korea provided two additional anecdotes. To com-
memorate its restructuring, Halla Shipyard gave me a small
silver model of a "turtle ship." In centuries past, turtle ships
were oar-powered armored vessels, atop of which were two
long steel poles with huge axes affixed. The turtle ship's
armor protected it as it pulled up alongside a sailing war ship
and the poles were swung into the enemy's sails, ripping them
and stopping the vessel. The turtle ship then would ram the
ship's hull until it sank. In two years, the turtle ships sank the
entire Japanese invasion fleet. The plaque on the model ship
was dated 1592, the year of the Battle of Sacheon, a landmark South Korean naval victory over Japan in which the
turtle ship was first used. The long history of Japanese-South
Korean warfare explains a lot about the relationship between
the two countries today. Only recently, because of China's
increased aggressiveness, have the two begun to collaborate.

Just as the Irish would later do, South Korean President
Kim Dae-Jung paid tribute to me for helping them during
their time of crisis by awarding me a medal. Kim was an
inspired leader who invented the "Sunshine Policy" to reduce
tensions between South and North Korea. The United States
had thirty thousand troops in Seoul and provided billions of
dollars of military support, but President Kim had lined up
eight hundred Korean and Japanese companies to build factories in North Korea. He made one of the first state visits to
President Bush. He didn't need U.S. money, just our acceptance of the initiative. Bush turned him down because he
would not help a terrorist-supporting state like North Korea.
President Kim was brokenhearted, and I believe Bush's rejec-
tion was a huge mistake. A country that has both dangerous toys and a starving population (there were reports that
North Korean families were cannibalizing their own children
at that time)[16] needs economic vitalization. Also, while North

Korea is smaller in population than China, its very low labor costs could have provided a partial production alternative to China. "Sunshine" also would have fostered cooperation between South Korea and Japan.

The performance of Asian economies will continue to be integral to the overall performance of the global economy for years to come, but the three leading Asian economies each have widely divergent outlooks. India has grown at a 7 percent compounded rate annually for the last ten years and Jeffries recently forecast that by 2027 it will surpass both Germany and Japan to become the third-largest economy.[17] China's highly leveraged economy is suffering from the collapse of its housing boom, and Xi's increasing consolidation of power is not likely to help much, but its growth rate will continue to exceed that of the developed world. As of 2024, neither earnings per share nor dividends per share of the MSCI China Index have increased from the levels achieved thirteen years ago. Consequently, January 2024 was the sixth consecutive month of global investors being net sellers of Chinese equities. China's disappointing demographic forecasts are problematic, and the same can also be said for Japan. Japanese companies are worried about lackluster future domestic growth, and the Nikkei 225 index only recently surpassed its high met in 1989—a long wait, even by Japanese standards. Japan just recently abandoned its negative interest range, becoming the last country to do so. Japan's companies are currently using their strong balance sheets to pay high prices for overseas acquisitions, as demonstrated by Nippon Steel's controversial high bid for U.S. Steel. Meanwhile, geopolitical issues are becoming ever more paramount for all three countries—as well as all other nations. The glittering emerging markets of yesteryear are no longer necessarily lined with gold. Finding value in overseas markets will become a more complex—and risky— decision for investors than previously imagined.

CHAPTER 8

The Many Faces
of Finance

The global investment banking firm Lazard Frères & Co. began in New Orleans in 1848 as dry goods merchants. When I first met representatives from the firm, Lazard was a global powerhouse with forty-one offices in twenty-six countries. Its New York office was just above Rothschild Inc. at One Rockefeller Plaza, and we did a lot of business together.

In the 1980s, Michel David-Weill ran Lazard globally. His daughter was just finishing her first year at Sarah Lawrence College, where I was a trustee. My main responsibility was to help President Alice Ilchman pitch parents for major contributions. Many wealthy women had graduated from Sarah Lawrence, but few gave significant sums, because the college neither held reunions nor solicited alumnae. They relied on the parents of current students for donations.

We asked Michel for lunch with us, earmarking him for a $1 million donation. He readily agreed to host us, and we were ushered quickly into his office upon arrival. He greeted us at the door and immediately handed over a check for $100,000 saying, "Wilbur, this will save you a lot of effort at lunch. Now we can talk about more interesting topics."

The clever old fox had outwitted us. He guessed that we were coming to ask for a much larger amount, and that his preemptive move would end that. We couldn't really hand the check back and say, "Well thank you, Michel, but we want much more." We had no choice but to thank him and enjoy a pleasant lunch. You could tell by the twinkle in his eyes that he knew he had outflanked us. To this day, I am embarrassed that we did not anticipate or escape his plot. True, $100,000 is a great gift by any normal standard, yet it still was a clever move that might have saved him $900,000. Of such cleverness are world-class investment bankers made. The upside of all this is that I learned to use the same gamesmanship to good effect when some politicians come seeking bigger campaign funds than I am prepared to provide.

Exposure to people like Michel David-Weill and a thousand other fascinating figures over the years gave me an opportunity to study how they operated, the businesses they built, and, in some cases, what they do with their money. Observing how they ran their firms—including how they built their boards of directors—provided sharp insights on what to do and not do in managing a company.

Board to Death

In 1984, Pennzoil, a Houston-based oil company, announced a deal to acquire Getty Oil, but Texaco stepped in and bid it away from them. Pennzoil hired Joe Jamail, a famed Texas personal injury litigator, to sue for damages for "tortious

BusinessWeek cover story.

With Senator Moynihan and President Clinton.

At Gracie Mansion with Mayor Bloomberg.

With Presidents Bush and Clinton and Lakshmi and Aditya Mittal.

Dinner with Gorbachev.

Play-working
on horseback in
Southampton.

On the White House
front lawn.

At Bedminster, after privately learning of my nomination.

Vice President Pence administering the Oath of Office.

With Vice President Pence on Air Force Two.

Well-guarded with our ambassador to India at the Embassy.

Signing a treaty
with India.

Oval Office
signing of the
Clean Oceans
Bill.

Launching a weather balloon before a hurricane.

Bilateral meeting with the UK.

In Beijing, signing a part of my $70 billion of concessions from China.

Working in my Department of Commerce office.

With Reince Priebus, Ivanka Trump, and Jared Kushner at POTUS's Riyadh speech.

With President Trump and "Mad Dog" Mattis at a Cabinet meeting.

Walking with POTUS from the Oval Office to the Rose Garden.

Partying with Prince Charles.

With Australian Prime Minister Morrison, Mrs. Morrison, the Trumps, and Hilary.

Mar-a-Lago SCIF
meeting to launch
missiles at Syria.

Canadian Trade Minister
Chrystia Freeland.

Speaking at the
India Economic
Summit.

With Secretaries Mnuchin and Azar testifying at a House Budget Committee hearing.

Washington Post cartoon, appearing January 26, 2019 (originally illustrated by Bagley for the *Salt Lake Tribune*).

Dinner in Honor of
Chinese Vice Premier Liu He

January 30, 2019

MENU

Classic Caesar Salad
Hearts of Romaine, Herbed Croutons
Freshly Grated Parmesan Cheese
Matanzas Creek Winery Sauvignon Blanc, Sonoma County 2017

Beef Tenderloin & Jumbo Lump Crab Cake
Wilted Spinach, Roasted Garlic Mashed Potatoes
Broccoli Florets, Acorn Squash
Rosemary Demi-Glace, Tarragon Butter
Averaen Pinot Noir, Willamette Valley, Oregon, 2017

Trio of Desserts
Flourless Chocolate Cake, Panna Cotta with Blueberries
Raspberry Tart in a Chocolate Cup
-and-
Metropolitan Club Cookies
Assortment of Almond Macaroons & Chocolate Chip Cookies

Coffee, Decaffeinated Coffee or Hot Tea

Dinner menu signed by the participants in the China trade talks.

Tussling over Warren Buffet's wallet at the White House
Correspondents' Dinner.

Clowning in front of a favorite Magritte, *Hegel's Holiday*.

Part of my shoe collection.

Some of my challenge coins.

interference" with a contract, a relatively arcane concept. The law held that it was illegal for someone to interfere uninvited with a pending contractual agreement between two other parties. Jamail was a physically impressive, big Texan with a pronounced drawl, a large silver belt buckle, lizard-skinned boots with zippers on both sides and one in the heels, a leather bolo tie, and a wide-brimmed leather hat. He famously had several martinis at lunch, but remained stone cold sober.

Texaco hired an equally famous litigator, David Boies. In contrast to Jamail, David was diminutive in size, and typically appeared in court wearing a gray sweater rather than a jacket. He was soft-spoken, but a deadly cross-examiner. He would start by asking one softball question after another, gradually putting the witness at ease. Then he would suddenly tie it all together with a torrent of very pointed questions, often destroying the credibility of his target.

Boies was extremely confident of winning the case, and displayed that confidence by not putting on an expert witness to testify what the damages should be if Texaco lost the case. Jamail did put on an expert, who claimed the lost deal cost Pennzoil more than $10 billion. Jamail won the case in the lower court after testimony filling 24,000 transcript pages, and also prevailed before the Texas Supreme Court. Texaco's last hope was an appeal to the U.S. Supreme Court, but that process would take a year or so, and it was hard to predict the court's decision. Meanwhile, interest rates were rising, and Texaco could not afford to pay the necessary $10.53 billion owed to Pennzoil while it continued to litigate the matter at the Supreme Court. So, despite being a very profitable, dividend-paying company, Texaco filed for bankruptcy, solely because bankruptcy automatically stops any litigation.

To recover what they could from the company, Texaco equity holders formed a committee with a colorful chairman, the grandson of the famous wildcatter and founder of Texaco, "Bet a Million" John Warne Gates. In his youth, this gentleman had become famous himself as a Marlboro Man in cigarette ads. More significantly, he was Texaco's largest individual shareholder. The committee retained me as its financial advisor. Meanwhile, Carl Icahn bought the stock as it plummeted in bankruptcy. Carl did not join the committee because he didn't want fiduciary responsibilities to anyone else, but, Carl being Carl, he was making his presence felt.

Our analysis showed that the Supreme Court only takes about 15 percent of the cases that are appealed to it. That frightened me, because the accrued interest on outstanding bonds would run the total up to around $12 billion by the time the case was decided. If we didn't settle, there was an 85 percent chance we would lose by default and that would mean vast dilution for the shareholders. And even if the Supreme Court accepted the case, there was no assurance we would win it. We recommended that the case be settled for around $3 billion, instead of the court-decreed $10.53 billion, but Jim Kinnear, the president and CEO of Texaco, was convinced he was in the right and insisted on continuing it. He wanted vindication, so Texaco's shareholders decided to take matters into our own hands.

I arranged for us to meet J. Hugh Liedtke, the Pennzoil CEO, in Houston. The chairman, the committee lawyer, and I went to the airport together to fly down but we almost missed the flight because the chairman of the equity holders committee had a huge hunting knife in a scabbard on his belt, causing a ruckus with airport security. Once we made it to Houston, the negotiations went on for a few hours and we finally got to our limit of $3 billion. Leidke said, "I have to get more than $3 billion." Our chairman said "Okay. $3 billion, 1 million. Deal?"

"Deal!"

We shook hands, went back to the airport, and called Kinnear, Texaco's CEO, to tell him what we had done. He furiously insisted that we go directly to Texaco's headquarters for a hastily convened board meeting. The room was set up like a real star chamber, with thirty or so advisors and executives in big chairs arranged in a semicircle around two little folding chairs in the middle. Kinnear spent ten minutes introducing all his big-name associates to impress and frighten us and said they unanimously disapproved of the settlement and said they also would ask the court to sanction us.

We explained our reasoning. With only a 15 percent statistical probability of Supreme Court acceptance, and perhaps a 50 percent chance of winning if they did accept it, the odds were overwhelming that we would lose far more than $3 billion. We saw no rationale for optimism, and the Texaco executives did not refute our math. But they could not countenance our argument, saying, effectively, "This is such a miscarriage of justice that we are certain to win on appeal."

We retorted, "That is an emotional argument, not a rational one." We ended the meeting by saying, "We're willing to take our chances. We believe our settlement will be well received by the court and that the shareholders will vote for it. After all, the money belongs to the shareholders, not to the executives or the board."

We were never sanctioned. The shareholders overwhelmingly approved the deal and the stock more than doubled.

A major problem in this situation was that Texaco's board seemed captive to the CEO. In this case, disaster was averted, but the point remains: It is extremely difficult to convince the boards of bankrupt companies to disavow or even criticize the CEO who led them (or is leading them) into insolvency. This problem most often has roots in the fact that the

CEO of most large companies usually handpicks his CEO friends as board members, and they are loath to criticize him. Moreover, directors, most of whom spend lots of time on their own firms, often leave too little time to properly execute their directorships. As one of my associates quipped, "There is only one way to transform ten successful CEOs into incompetents. That is to appoint them as outside directors."

Another problem is that directors are typically compensated in cash plus stock options or grants. It would be more symmetrical to shareholder interest if they were solely paid in restricted stock that vested over several years. In addition, if they had to buy more than a minimal number of shares with their own money, they would have some skin in the game. That combination would align their interests far more closely to those of the public shareholders. It also would be good to limit the number of concurrent directorships to four and to preclude them from an executive position at any company. These rules would ensure that they had enough time to devote to each board membership. Finally, staggered term limits for directors might be a good idea. The longer you are associated with the CEO, the more likely you are to be co-opted by him or her, but staggered terms will assure a high degree of continuity combined with a constantly refreshed board membership.

It also might be better to create a special class of retired executives who would be nominated as board members by the institutions holding most of a company's stock. These directors would only be beholden to shareholders. That could create some new problems, because some institutions still have social policies that are inimical to shareholder values, but it is probably worth trying. Retirees would have the time to spend on their directorships and would know that if they didn't do a good job, they would no longer be chosen as directors by the institutions. While it's true that many people decline physically in their seventies, many remain sharp for many years thereafter. Henry Kissinger, for example, was sharper at age one hundred than most men half his age. The common age limit of seventy for a directorship is shortsighted.

Entrepreneurs

Entrepreneurs come in all different shapes and sizes, but they all have a few characteristics in common. First is an abiding self-confidence, even exceeding that of powerful CEOs. Second is a gambler's instinct. The third is resilience. Most serial entrepreneurs have experienced both notable failure and notable success. Strange as it may seem, many of them had to overcome dyslexia or ADD in their youth. That may explain why they developed their other unique characteristics.

Few entrepreneurs have overcome challenges like my friend Steve Wynn. Steve has been afflicted with the eye disease retinitis pigmentosa since roughly age thirty, and was legally blind in the years when he built four hugely successful Las Vegas casinos and one in Macau that alone generated $1 billion per year in cash flow. This would be a staggering level of success for anyone, but for a blind person like Steve to accomplish a fraction of this is mind boggling. He is a natural entrepreneur who remembers everything he hears or touches. He is also the only person I know who has flipped both a big boat and a big airplane at profit.

In addition, Steve has accumulated a vast collection of Picassos and other works of art and constantly wheels and deals in the art market, mostly on the advice of the famous art dealer Bill Acquavella. Steve also parlayed a personal setback into a financial gain some years ago, when he and his longtime first wife divorced. She got half of his stock in Wynn

Resorts, effectively ending his regime there. But this had a great benefit to Steve. Since he was out, he had legitimate grounds to liquify billions of dollars' worth of Wynn stock at more than 30 percent above its present price. If he were still CEO of the casino group, he could not have sold that much.

Steve and his darling new wife, Andrea, have been friends with Hilary and me for years. When they were deciding where to live, they stayed with us in Palm Beach for a while to decide whether to move here. They did, and we helped them to decide on the house they bought. It had "good bones," and while being situated mainly on the inland waterway, also had a view of the ocean from upstairs. The house had been decorated in a dark, heavy European style by Victor Vargas, allegedly the banker for the Venezuelan dictator Hugo Chávez. Victor's divorced wife was the seller, therefore we thought it was selling at a discount from its real value. Andrea has now brightened the décor, and with the addition of their art, the house has taken a place among the great showplaces of Palm Beach. Steve and Andrea are now selling their Beverly Hills mansion, their spectacular Central Park South duplex in New York, and their property in the Adirondacks, all the while buying, fixing up, and flipping houses in Palm Beach. He and Andrea are forces of nature, and big reasons why Palm Beach keeps getting more and more interesting.

One more unexpected example of dogged entrepreneurship I encountered in my career was the government of Qatar. Shortly before Ramadan in 2017, Saudi Arabia instituted an economic blockade against Qatar. This created serious economic problems, particularly regarding the import of milk. The Saudis had previously supplied 80 percent of Qatar's milk, a product that figures prominently in Islamic holiday menus. To fill the shortfall, the Emir of Qatar purchased 4,500 dairy cows for immediate delivery via cargo plane and several thousand more to be delivered by ship. But there was still one hurdle: Deserts are not hospitable environments for cows. So, the Qataris built an air-conditioned indoor dairy farm just outside their capital, Doha. They proudly had me tour this farm—probably the most highly automated dairy operation in the world—while I was there on a trade mission as Secretary of Commerce. While impressive, there is something a bit dystopian about it. The cows don't go outside. They are kept motionless in two rows of stalls with the cows' rear-ends facing each other. In the middle, a sluice disposes of their fecal matter. Grain is brought to the individual stalls, so the bovines move very little. Then, at a prearranged signal, the animals go down a corridor, at the end of which they step onto a slowly turning circular platform where suction cups attach automatically to their udders. The rotation lasts ten minutes, just enough time to collect the milk into a pipe which takes it directly to the processing facility.

This setup doesn't exactly call to mind a traditional Wisconsin dairy farm, but it is admirable. Not only did it solve Qatar's milk needs, but the Qataris' fresh milk tasted better than the Saudi condensed milk, so it became a strong export product. The company subsequently diversified into fruit drinks, and while I was there it had a highly successful IPO. This is a classic example of turning adversity into a commercial success. Kudos to the Qataris!

Elsewhere in the world, few people have an entrepreneurial spirit like the Chinese. Whether in mainland China, Hong Kong, Taiwan, or even in the United States, they are a people who seize opportunities like few other. I first met Hong Kong billionaire Silas Chou at a Manhattan dinner party, and we immediately hit it off so well that we soon partnered in a denim factory in China. Silas's father had been a major industrialist in Shanghai, making cathode ray tubes for early versions of televisions. When the Communists took over, the Chou family moved to Hong Kong. As a young man, Silas developed an exporting business selling sweaters, and gradually expanded from there. Eventually he became wealthy enough to buy the second house down from Hong Kong's famous Victoria Peak. Over the course of his career, Silas bought and sold Tommy Hilfiger (twice), Michael Kors, and the iconic luxury brand Asprey. He is now an investor in a Formula One racing team.

Silas was a great business partner in part because he was so well-connected in China. His father was among the first capitalists to move back to Shanghai, so the government liked him. The Chinese government had a policy of restricting the amount of the superior American cotton Chinese companies could buy to mix with the lower-quality Chinese cotton. Whenever we had a problem with the quotas, Silas usually fixed it. Later, a relative became the Speaker of the Assembly in Macau.

Sadly, winning the favor of communists can often be the difference between business success and failure in China. The night before the opening of our Chinese mill, Silas put on an elaborate dinner at the China Club in Hong Kong. My dinner partner was a thirty-five-year-old who was born poor but now owned most of the toll roads outside Hong Kong. I asked, "How did you manage to buy all of the toll roads?" He replied, "I had a boyhood friend in the Communist Party who helped me." The following morning, our party left the Peninsula Hotel in a five-car motorcade. As we went onto the main highway, there was no traffic. Silas's friend had blocked off the entire road.

The factory opening was a typical Chinese ritual. Young girls in high-cut red skirts escorted us to our seats and then the ceremony started. Acrobats performed to drumbeats. There was a great cloth lion's head atop a few performers hidden in the bright red body of the faux lion. They did a few dances to the very loud sounds of cymbals clashing to ward off the evil spirits. Then Silas and I cut the red ribbon and we were in business.

Just before the Olympics in China in 2008, a Chinese developer using the name Morgan was building a luxury condominium building directly across from the stadium in Beijing. He ran out of money, so Silas financed the remaining construction. Part of his reward was the penthouse apartment. In typical Chinese fashion, the roof was flat, but Silas hired BMW to design a metal roof covering with two halves, each of which would retract on command so he could have open-air parties, one of which he put on in our honor. To this day Silas remains a great friend and a savvy operator.

Perhaps the most memorable of all the entrepreneurs I've been privileged to know is Sir Richard Branson. In 2007–08, the UK bank Northern Rock was failing. WL Ross & Co. went in with Sir Richard to buy it and fix it up. Richard is of course one of the most active and aggressive entrepreneurs ever. His first big success was Virgin Music, but he also had the Virgin Atlantic airline and founded Virgin Money, a credit card company in the UK. It was effectively the private label of an American Express product, but that was not widely known, and it became one of the most respected UK brands.

The UK government had cleaned up Northern Rock's bad loans, so our main task was to create a business plan with a high rate of return for a retail bank in rural England. We believed that if we could migrate Virgin Money customers to bank with Northern Rock, and convince Northern

Rock customers to obtain Virgin Money credit cards, then we would have a unique and highly differentiated offering within the UK banking sector. We beat the only real competitor in the bidding and recapitalized the bank with a strong equity position.

We could not imagine a serial adventurer like Richard running a bank's day-to-day operations, or even going to monthly board meetings. So, we arranged that neither he nor I would be directors ourselves, and that a majority of the board members would be independent. My designee was Jim Lockhart, the former CEO of the Pension Benefit Guaranty Corp., and a partner at WL Ross & Co. Our CEO was Jayne-Anne Gadhia, who had run the mortgage business at Royal Bank of Scotland. She did so well that the Queen named her a Dame of the British Empire, the female equivalent of Commander of the British Empire. Besides his capital, Richard did bring value to the operation. Right after we closed, he made a huge PR splash by rappelling up the walls of the Northern Rock headquarters building in Newcastle. Ultimately, Virgin Money merged into Clydesdale Bank in October 2019, long after we sold our shares in an underwriting.

After we closed the Northern Rock deal, Richard invited the board and me to spend a weekend at his private resort, Necker Island in the British Virgin Islands (BVI), about forty minutes by boat from Tortola, the largest of the BVI. Shortly after arriving, he took us on a tour of Necker's seventy-four acres. As we walked up one hillside, there was a sudden sharp pain in the sole of my left foot, so we stopped and took the sneaker off to find that a cactus spine had punctured it. Richard immediately took the sneaker, bit the wide end of the spine, and pulled it out with his teeth, a scene worthy of the old *Crocodile Dundee* movie. We then visited the flamingos and flying lemurs that he maintained elsewhere on the island.

Along the way, Richard described how he came to buy the island. In his younger years, he fell in love with the woman who remains his wife decades later, Joan Templeman. He wanted to show her a good time, but had no money. So, he cunningly called the leading property broker in the BVI, saying he wanted to buy an island. The broker arranged first-class tickets for him and his fiancée, put them up at a five-star hotel, and spent two days helicoptering them around to see all the islands that were for sale. The third day brought the denouement. The broker said, "Now you've seen all the available islands. Which one are you going to buy?" Necker had the lowest price, €250,000, but Richard knew he had to make a bid that would never be accepted. He bid only €10,000 (which he actually did not have) so his bid was summarily rejected. The broker realized he had been scammed, and promptly canceled their hotel and their return flight. Richard somehow hitched a ride for them back to London on someone's private plane.

A couple of years later, the broker called Richard, who by then had had some success. He pitched Richard: "Mr. Branson, that island you liked is still for sale. They won't take €10,000, but the price has been reduced to €100,000." Richard bought it and has since put €30 million into developing it, to spectacular effect! His cunning in this case also shows how gifted entrepreneurs never stop wheeling and dealing, whether or not they have money.

His showmanship during my visit continued that evening with a candlelit chicken barbeque on the beach. At one point he threw several chicken breasts from a pier into the sea. When he came back, we asked why. He said, "Every evening at this time I toss out meat for my favorite great white shark."

We asked incredulously, "And you want us to swim in these waters!?"

Richard laughed and said, "We swim on the other side of the island. He never comes over there! He hangs around here waiting for his daily feeding. You may not know it, but sharks are pretty lazy."

He was right. There was never any sign of a shark where we swam. Entrepreneurs like Richard try to take only calculated risks. In this case, he succeeded.

True entrepreneurs never stop finding new adventures, and Sir Richard has proven that over and over in his life. While I was serving in government, Richard founded two space companies, Virgin Orbit and Virgin Galactic. While both have run into a few hopefully short-term problems, entrepreneurs like Richard are gifted at maximizing their returns, and it would not surprise me a bit if these two eventually prospered. Similarly, Elon Musk and Jeff Bezos, for whom more wealth is quite irrelevant, have also founded companies dedicated to space exploration. I believe that both men ultimately will make more from their space ventures than from their original core businesses. But it is not the money that is important to these men—it is the challenge.

Even more importantly, their entrepreneurial spirit has caused America to recapture the lead in the space race. Until 2010, the U.S. was the unquestioned leader, but President Obama effectively put us out of the game by canceling all our launches. Instead, we paid the Russians as much as $82 million per seat to carry our astronauts to the International Space Station.[18] Our reward is that now Russia and China have hypersonic missiles going twenty times the speed of sound and we do not. President Trump strongly supported reinvigorating our space launch efforts, but at the first meeting of the Biden Administration National Space Council, its chair, Kamala Harris, directed its focus to be on cleaning up space debris and other environmental issues.

Money in the Mundane

Not everyone has to be Richard Branson to be a successful entrepreneur. American history is littered with examples of people who have gotten rich from less flashy businesses. A 2022 *New York Times* study of the 140,000 Americans who earn more than $1.58 million per year found that many of them ran mundane businesses like auto dealerships, beverage distributorships, and gas stations.[19] One outstanding performing stock on the NASDAQ over the past ten years has been Cintas, a company that provides essential products to businesses such as uniforms and cleaning supplies. There is exciting money in mundane enterprises.

In my career, I saw how people got rich from ordinary products time and time again. One of my clients was one of the two manufacturers of the little green wires used to hold corsages. They only sell for a few pennies, but are a very high-margin product. When I asked why he decided to go into that business, he answered, "I really wanted to make coat hangers. But it was too difficult, so I decided to try this." He earns millions of dollars a year from being a member of the duopoly. Another duopolistic business I became aware of was a manufacturer of envelopes with clear openings that eliminate the need to print the address a second time on the envelope. This simple idea earned him hundreds of millions of dollars.

Another of my clients was Harold Snyder, who inherited a small amount of money while he was working as a biochemist. He quit and started a laundromat. It promptly failed, so Harold took what was left and created the generic equivalent of penicillin, which had just come off-patent. It was an immediate success, and he used the cash flow to reproduce other pharmaceuticals as their patents expired. Years later, I pitched the Snyders on going public with their company,

Biocraft Laboratories. The facilities were in an undistinguished building in suburban New Jersey, inside of which was an immaculate factory. We met in their small executive office, whose only real decorations were a photo of Albert Einstein and a letter of his explaining that he used the same bar of soap for bathing, washing his hair, and shaving because it was too complicated to use multiple detergents. Einstein's genius ability to make complex things simple was Harold's abiding inspiration. He remarked, "That is what Biocraft does. We take complicated formulations and make them into simple, very inexpensive pills!" My firm and Lazard Frères brought Biocraft Laboratories public. And Harold went straight onto the Forbes 500 list.

Even more ordinary was a Texas client for whom we sold a huge carpet distribution business for $150 million. The celebratory party was at his ranch two hundred miles from Dallas. After dinner he invited me to tour his private museum. I was hoping for French impressionists, but that was not to be. This gentleman collected sixteen-foot-long strands of the barbed wire that restricts livestock to a certain area. Each strand was neatly bracketed on the wall and no two were the same. Some were a single heavy strand, while others were multistranded with smaller-gauge wire. He had 475 different examples, but also had empty brackets that could hold the thirty-eight other varieties he had not yet been able to acquire.

I asked, "Why is each strand sixteen feet? Did you just decide to cut them to that length or is there some reason for it?"

"That's a pretty good question from a city slicker. There's an engineering reason. If the distance between the two supporting posts is more than sixteen feet, the cattle can push against the wire and knock the posts down and run free."

I had another question. "Can you just buy a sixteen-foot section or do you have to buy more and dispose of the excess?"

"I usually have to buy the whole installation. Once I actually had to buy the whole ranch, take the wire, and sell the real estate."

This man remains the only barbed wire collector I have ever known. But now that auction houses sell used sneakers, handbags, and pens, one day we may see strands of barbed wire as a new collectible. Hopefully my friend will have amassed the few missing varieties before then and make another fortune selling to these future avant-garde collectors.

Business is ultimately a Darwinian environment in which only the fittest survive over the long term. Most companies that go bankrupt simply incur too much debt and/or make woefully incorrect business decisions. One example that has stuck with me for most of my life occurred in the early 1950s, when Montgomery Ward lost its big position in retailing. The company was one of the nation's signature department stores in the years following World War II. But management was worried the country would revert to a depression after the war, so they did not expand, while Sears Roebuck embraced a growth-centered strategy. Montgomery Ward lost market share and began a long decline that culminated in the cessation of operations in 2000. That story reinforced to me that you need to understand how the economy works if you are going to make business decisions—the wrong forecast can be fatal. Curiously, Sears later had to reorganize because it had accumulated too much debt. For large technology companies, the biggest risk is not to keep up with innovation. That is why

Polaroid and BlackBerry failed and why Intel lost its initial premier position in semiconductors.

I tried to notice patterns common to the successful executives, boards, and entrepreneurs with whom I worked. The ones which ran their companies well avoided a loser's mentality of blaming their misfortune on external forces outside of their control, like China, inflation, recession, or the unions. Replacing them with a more solution-oriented team usually improves results.

Many executives have difficulty admitting to a bad decision, especially over expansion. Pride and hefty sunk costs reinforce the instinct to double down on costly decisions instead of abandoning the trajectory of failure before it's too late. Overexpansion is among the most common causes of corporate distress, especially since it usually is funded with debt.

Very often, bad mistakes happen because C-suites of major companies are so thronged by staffers that it's easy for them to lose touch with the nitty-gritty of the business. When our International Steel Group bought Bethlehem, they had more executive staff in their headquarters than we had total executives in our whole company. They had eight layers of management between the factory floor and the CEO, while we had only three. Our CEO's office was in a very plain building in the midst of a steel mill. Theirs was in a fancy downtown office building. C-suite distance from day-to-day operations is exacerbated when CEOs take outside directorships. While there may be a commercial benefit from doing so, outside boards can consume a lot of an executive's time, which could be better dedicated to gaining more intimate direct knowledge of what is happening on the home playing field. Keep the main thing the main thing!

It is easy to become overstaffed but hard to escape the consequences. Too many cooks in the kitchen adds more steps than necessary before a decision reaches the CEO, thus killing off any advantage gained from speed. Staff also tend to insulate the CEO from important information, especially bad news. People also invent tasks for the CEO to do which do not actually add value. As the management critic C. Northcote Parkinson once said to me, "Executive workload expands until it consumes the time and money available." How true! Lastly, even major decisions too often are distilled into a few pages by staff and the words steer the CEO in the direction favored by the Praetorian Guard around him or her. This often results in unwanted surprises, and, as I have heard Warren Buffett say, "In business, if you are surprised by something, it is usually a bad surprise."

Business leaders too often act like lemmings heading to the sea, latching on to the latest business trends without considering whether an action is best for the company. Until recently the buzzword was "diversification," so every company wanted to become a conglomerate. My experience is that a majority of conglomerative acquisitions never achieve the projected results. The theory that a good manager can manage any kind of a business is enchanting but flawed. Industry knowledge and expertise are very important for even the most gifted manager. Similarly, it is a challenge for an executive with experience only in the United States to flourish in an emerging market. Such geographic or functional narrowness can be overcome, but mainly if the executive has a strong support team with local knowledge to help fill in the blanks.

On that note, the current geopolitical situation only exacerbates the importance of choosing good geographies. For decades, internationalizing operations was in vogue. It became common to manufacture or source components from several different low-cost countries and ship them to yet another country for assembly and final shipment to customers. This can save money, but there are two inherent problems with this model. First, each extra geography adds to managerial complexity. Second, as we learned in the pandemic, each overseas location also adds a point of vulnerability. The emerging paradigms surrounding locating operations overseas are likely to emphasize proximity to market and simplification of supply chains.

Another observation is that it is dangerous to get too enamored with the brilliance of the concept, rather than focusing on whether the team can really implement it. It is far better to back a brilliantly executed average concept than a poorly executed brilliant concept. The home run, of course, is if both the concept and the execution are outstanding.

Ultimately, a big personality like Steve Wynn's or Richard Branson's isn't necessary for winning in business. Nor do you have to be the most ruthless negotiator or slickest salesman. Study. Have a plan. Stick to it. Follow through on what you say you will do. And never stop surrounding yourself with people you trust will tell you the truth.

CHAPTER 9

Washington Calls

On April 12, 1990, Merrill Lynch and Bear Stearns underwrote an $800 million mortgage bond to finance the construction of the new Trump Taj Mahal casino in Atlantic City, New Jersey. Within months, the casino quickly defaulted without making a single interest payment.

Soon the call came in from the bondholders: Would I act as their financial advisor?

I agreed. My first task was to negotiate with the Taj Mahal's owner: Donald Trump.

On the Thursday before Labor Day weekend of 1990, Trump called me to insist I fly on his helicopter to Atlantic City the next day to begin our negotiations. That was the last way I wanted to start my holiday weekend, but as a matter of business, I could not decline. At 4:00 p.m. on Friday, at the East 63rd Street heliport, I boarded a chopper whose sides were emblazoned with four-foot-tall letters in nail-polish red: TRUMP.

Thirty minutes later we landed on the Atlantic City boardwalk helipad. The Donald met me in a stretch Cadillac limo with two flags on the front bumper, the Stars and Stripes and a Trump crest. Riding with him through the streets of Atlantic City was like riding with a Latin American dictator. As we made our way through mobs of tourists they screamed, "The Donald! He's here!" and pressed against the car in a total frenzy. It took twenty minutes to transit the two hundred yards to the casino. On arrival, we did not enter from the front. Instead, we drove around to the rear, where hundreds of people were alighting from chartered buses with palpable excitement. We entered the jam-packed casino, where the patrons continued to flock to him. People were desperate for his autograph, and one woman even had him sign her bare back!

Trump led a detailed private tour of his new crown jewel property, even pointing out the overhead panels through which security monitored table games. We then went to his office to negotiate.

"The bondholders will be lucky to get 25 percent of par," he said. That was the price at which the bonds were then trading.

"No. They want 100 percent plus accrued interest, a majority of the common stock, and a revised board of directors and management."

He then played what you could call a trump card. He proclaimed, "The bondholders don't have the license or the name as collateral, just the building. A big, empty, anonymous building on the boardwalk is not worth much!"

I responded, "You are the managing partner of the partnership that issued the bonds. We will come after you personally for any deficiency." I thanked him for the tour and walked out on him. To this day he repeats, most recently at my eighty-fifth birthday party, how shocked he was at my blunt style.

In truth, the pageantry surrounding Trump had convinced me that the casino would be worth more with his star power there than if we kicked him out. He also had good points about the weaknesses in the collateral position. In retrospect, it is hard to understand why insurance companies bought bonds in a start-up without better covenants. It very well may have had to do with Trump's powers of persuasion.

Soon, the New Jersey Casino Control Commission held a hearing to determine his financial fitness to continue controlling his three casinos, including the Taj. He was the only party in town to own more than one, and all three were struggling: Trump was $3 billion underwater. The Taj itself had gone well over its construction budget—its final price tag was around $1 billion—and ultimately gave its trade creditors essentially nothing. Carl Icahn (the largest bondholder) and I sat in the front row, aware that this same commission recently had turned down Hilton Hotel's application for a license. The bondholders had two separate worries. First, we obviously wanted Trump's gaming licenses to continue so that the casinos could take in revenue. Our other worry was that Trump might convince the commission to take actions that would hurt the bondholders' claims in a forthcoming bankruptcy tussle. No such issues arose at the hearing. After about one hour of discussion, they voted unanimously in Trump's favor. They too seemed to realize that the Trump name and persona helped draw people to Atlantic City, although how that could translate into financial fitness remained a mystery.

Weeks of very public bickering between Trump and me ensued. He claimed he would have the bondholders fire me for being irrational, and after other claims and counterclaims, he announced a somewhat better offer to the media. My comment was something like "Donald has gotten his seasons mixed up. You only get gifts at Christmas, and it's not yet Halloween, so it's also too early for trick-or-treating." Such public sniping continued for days until Bob Miller (the bond-holders' lawyer) and I decided to unleash our nuclear weapon. We went to his office in Trump Tower and gave him our best and final offer. He would reinstate the full par value of the bonds, pay the accrued interest, and give our investors 49 percent ownership. He would keep 51 percent and would run the casino for a mutually agreed level of compensation, but a majority of the board would be independent. Otherwise, we would put the Taj into bankruptcy. He immediately rejected the proposal, so we said, "We will see you in court."

We had the strength to make this offer because we knew that the last thing Trump wanted was a bankruptcy. He had recently just lost the Plaza Hotel to its lenders, but disguised his loss by giving an impressionable young *Wall Street Journal* reporter an exclusive interview announcing he had sold it for $350 million and kept a 10 percent inter-est. In reality, the foreclosing lenders gave him the 10 per-cent to avoid protracted litigation and the $350 million was the amount of debt he escaped. Trump knew that the bank lenders would not respond to inquiries to verify his claims. In total, thanks to his usual PR brilliance, he turned a disas-ter into a coup. A Taj bankruptcy, however, would be even more publicly damaging to his reputation and probably the Taj's business as well. Nonetheless, he immediately rejected the proposal.

We promptly put out a press statement that the Taj Mahal mortgage holders committee would have a major press con-ference at 5:30 p.m. that afternoon at the Marriott Marquis. When it hit the wires, Trump called me and asked heatedly, "What is this press conference at the Marriott?"

"Donald, we told you that if you rejected our final offer, we would put the Taj in bankruptcy. We will announce it at 5:30." We hung up and worked on the script.

A few minutes later, he called back to negotiate a few technical changes to our final offer. We canceled the Marriott session and instead held a joint 5:30 p.m. conference in the Grand Ballroom of the Plaza Hotel. It was packed with media. Donald spoke first, saying that he had agreed to a deal that was good for his customers and his employees and that, contrary to rumors, he would retain management of the Taj. I announced the details, confirming it had been unanimously approved by the committee and by Carl Icahn, the largest bondholder. I then got to the tricky part: "To be sure that no one can upset the deal, the technical form of our transaction will be a consensual, prepackaged Chapter 11 proceeding. It should be very quick and have no impact on operations. We all believe that the property will be more valuable with Donald Trump remaining in charge." Trump wasn't thrilled about having his name attached to Chapter 11, but attacking it publicly would have only drawn more attention to it. I didn't hear any more from him.

After the press conference, I wearily headed home in the limo. Then the phone rang.

"Wilbur, this is your mother calling! Have you lost all self-respect? How could you make a deal with that man after all the mean things he said about you? I was playing mah-jongg with my friends and they all agree this is a disgrace. If you had become a lawyer like I wanted you to, you wouldn't be in such a mess!"

"Mom, I'm sorry you don't like it, but our clients got a fair deal."

"Well, I am still appalled!" She hung up.

The oddity of this whole thing was that Trump and I became friendly as a result. He respected my tough-nosed negotiations with him, and we rubbed elbows in the same New York circles enough to see one another socially. Little did I know at the time what this transaction would lead to.

New Directions

Around the middle of the 2000s, life changed a good bit for me. I'd made all the money I'd ever wanted or needed, and with the WL Ross & Co. fund being successful, I decided to cash out a bit. In 2006, Invesco, a trillion-dollar asset manager, bought our future stream of recurring management fees, although the team and I kept the carried interest embedded in the funds. Invesco made money on the deal and treated me well, supplementing my contractual earnout with restricted stock and bonuses. But the buyout taught me a few new lessons. First and foremost, an entrepreneurial firm acquired by an entity one hundred times its size cannot change the larger firm's corporate culture, and may have trouble blending its own culture with that of the new owner. This was reflected in Invesco's relatively unsuccessful effort to raise funds for its new acquisition. Invesco's products and marketing were geared toward the buying and selling of relatively conventional open-market securities: stocks, bonds, exchange traded funds, etc. We had hoped that since WL Ross & Co. charged advisory fees that were three to five times higher per million of assets than what our new parent company charged, Invesco's seven-hundred-strong sales team would eagerly market our funds and broaden our one-hundred-institution investor base. But very few did. Invesco's relationships were with different parts of major institutions from the ones that invested in limited partnerships. It did add some smaller institutions, but did not transform us into a major asset builder like Apollo,

KKR, or the Carlyle Group. They built their private equity marketing internally and Blackstone spun off BlackRock, a company similar to Invesco, so each of their entities built a separate sales force tailored to its needs.

Shortly after our acquisition, WL Ross & Co. began the transition to the next generation of management by creating the office of the chairman, which I shared with a couple of younger partners. I later gave up the CEO title and instead became chairman and chief strategy officer. As I prepared to go into government, Invesco appointed Stephen Toy, who had been with me since 1997, and a longtime Invesco executive to be co-CEOs. I remained chairman until I sold my holdings altogether when I joined the Trump Administration. But the new configuration did not raise meaningful amounts of new funds, so Invesco ultimately decided to wind down the operation, leaving two of my former partners to create a new firm to run off the assets. The aforementioned Dow Cow is now in the lobby of Oppenheimer & Co., one of Invesco's more recent acquisitions.

The other major development in my life in this decade was meeting my wife, Hilary. Hilary Geary and I initially knew one another a bit from New York and Southampton, but one day in 2002 a mutual friend named Amanda Haynes-Dale was putting on a birthday party at which we both sat together. We hit it off, and started going out every night until we got married. One of the best memories of our dating period was from our first date. On this particular day, I went to pick up Hilary in a new Porsche that I was quite proud of. I pulled up with the top down, looking cool, and she got in. We had gone about one block when a house's sprinklers suddenly turned on and drenched her. Despite being soaking wet, she kept her cool as I helped her dry off. Her poise and even temper really impressed me. I'm proud to say her sense of humor when things go awry continues to this day. She's not dramatic—thank goodness—and it's unusual how rarely we disagree. Lucky me!

Hilary and I were married on October 9, 2004, in an intimate ceremony at St. Andrew's Dune Church in Southampton. We later had a much larger reception at the Rainbow Room at Rockefeller Center, where the great cabaret singer Bobby Short played his piano and sang. Over the years, I had spent many cocktail hours listening to him at the Café Carlyle. By the time of our wedding, Bobby was crippled and in very bad health. His performance was flawless, but he insisted that the lights would be turned off as he entered and again while he left the stage. He didn't want anyone to see his bad physical condition. A few months later he died, a sad postscript to a happy event and a great performer.

At the time I met Hilary, the thirty-first floor in the Sherry-Netherland apartment hotel, at 59th Street and Fifth Avenue, was my bachelor pad after a divorce. Situated diagonally across from the Plaza Hotel and fronting the southeastern end of Central Park, it was a wonderful location. As my courtship with Hilary progressed, we decided that Mario Buatta would return as the decorator. This apartment was smaller than my original in the Dakota, and I was now more prosperous, so he was more or less affordable.

One day I came in from a business trip in the late afternoon to inspect the progress. To my horror, the living room on the Fifth Avenue side was painted bright pink. Nothing could have been worse, so I called Hilary's cell phone in a panic. She and Mario were in a cab coming back from a shopping trip. I screamed at her, "Have you lost your mind?

A goddamned pink living room?!" They burst into laughter. The pink was just the undercoating for what was to become deep red Venetian marble painted walls. The apartment was eventually featured on the cover of *Architectural Digest*[20] and in the *New York Times*.[21]

Living in the Sherry-Netherland had some complications. Diana Ross was a couple of floors above us and building security occasionally sent her guests to us and ours to her by mistake. Charlie Rose was another resident. Each one's mail also sometimes went astray, and it was embarrassing to see how many more glamorous invitations they got than we did.

The Sherry was fun, but there really was no big entertainment space, so after our wedding we began to consider selling it. One night, we were having dinner at Cipriani on the ground floor, when a former Sherry neighbor, Bob Meister, vice chairman of Aon Insurance, came in and had a drink with us. He looked distraught so we got him a dry martini and asked what was wrong. He replied, "I'm going to marry my girlfriend, and we want to live in the Sherry Tower, but there is nothing decent for sale. I want an apartment like yours."

It was a great stroke of luck. I said, "Bob, if you are really serious, we are thinking about moving to a bigger apartment. If you meet our price with no broker, we will sell you ours." After another martini, we had a deal at $13 million, which in those days was a big price for the Sherry.

Hilary and I then bought the duplex penthouse in the Briarcliff on West 57th Street in 2007. It was a great space, but needed redecorating, so once again Mario Buatta came to the rescue. A large terrace area faced across 57th Street to Carnegie Hall, so Mario had us put a pagoda there with a fireplace for use on chilly evenings. Its approval required six months of fighting with the New York City Department of

Buildings, which viewed it as a fire hazard. We finally convinced them that flames typically go up, not down, and that if they somehow did go down it would be our floor that got burned, not someone else's apartment.

By 2015, Hilary and I were spending much more time in Palm Beach, so we sold the penthouse at the Briarcliff and bought a pied-à-terre in River House. River House—and its companion social club River Club—were founded in 1931 at the east end of 52nd Street by the East River in Manhattan. Before FDR Drive was built, wealthy Long Islanders would dock their yachts there, play squash or tennis at the club in the morning, and then change to go to work in the city. Its early membership included Whitneys, Vanderbilts, Roosevelts, and other illustrious names. Even today, River House is among the most prestigious residential buildings in New York, with Henry Kissinger, Evelyn de Rothschild, Peter Grace, Ambassador Don Blinken, Arne Glimcher, and Uma Thurman among the more famous recent residents. On the day we bought there, we had no idea that we would soon move to Washington. By the time Mario Buatta refurbished the apartment, I had become Secretary of Commerce, so for the next four years we were mainly there just for the United Nations General Assembly week each September.

With so many strong-willed and wealthy personalities in residence there, there naturally arose multiple controversies between neighbors over the years. One such dustup occurred when John Gutfreund, then CEO of Salomon Brothers, hired a gigantic crane to lift a Christmas tree up to his penthouse. This obstruction infuriated one of his neighbors, the CEO of PepsiCo. In apparent retaliation, he erected a massive red neon Pepsi-Cola sign in Queens smack in the middle of the view from the Gutfreunds' living room. Whatever the reason for its existence, the sign remains visible there today, long after the tree and the Gutfreunds have departed.

The sale of WL Ross & Co. also gave me new philanthropic opportunities. In gratitude both for the student aid Yale provided me when my father died and for the way it helped shape my mind, in 2010 I contributed $10 million to pay for the new library designed by Sir Norman Foster situated at the very front of the new Yale School of Management campus. At the opening ceremony, Norman posed a question to our group: "What is unique about this library?" Neither I nor the other adults figured out the answer, but my then-teenaged grandson did. He said, "There are no books!" Only someone of his generation could grasp that ink on paper was becoming an archaic form of communication, as everything has moved to being digitized or stored on microfiche. That also explained why as little as $10 million could create a substantial business library for a major graduate school.

Membership on the Yale School of Management's Advisory Board was fascinating because Dean Ted Snyder developed the Global Network for Advanced Management, GNAM, a network of more than thirty schools around the world which, instead of neatly packaged cases, provided students with raw data from a variety of sources which students then organized and analyzed. This method struck me as much more closely resembling how the real world asks people to solve problems than the prepacked nature of HBS's offerings. Not only are the cases international, but often the class discussion of a case is conducted simultaneously over videoconferences among students at various geographies. That comes a lot closer to the way that international enterprises really function. The HBS approach is much more an academic exercise than a practical one. It will be fascinating to see over time which approach creates better execution.

American Home Mortgage Services

Even as I scaled back my management of WL Ross & Co. after Invesco purchased it, I still stayed active in scouting opportunities. Staying hungry and engaged in work is key to a long life and preserving one's mental sharpness. It wasn't long before foolish investment strategies and destructive government housing policies combined to produce a new class of distressed assets, the scope of which even I had a hard time imagining.

In the early 2000s, investment banks had gone wild purchasing mortgage-backed securities. Very often the mortgages in the portfolios were ones that no bank would issue had it properly evaluated the homebuyers' ability to repay them. "Liar loans"—loans made without proper declarations of income and employment—abounded. Nevertheless, many investment banks bought these mortgages, bundled them together as a security, and offered them for sale.

I had cautioned about the perils inherent in subprime mortgage securitizations at a mortgage-backed security buyers conference a year before the crash. I reasoned that collateralizing a portfolio of 90 to 95 percent loan-to-value mortgages with multiple tranches, the total of which exceeded the principal amount of the underlying mortgages by 5 percent, eliminated any equity value because of the commission and legal fees on resale. And since the borrowers had low credit scores, there would likely be lots of defaults, which would impinge upon the lower tranches and perhaps even some of the more senior layers. No one wanted to hear more, so the conference sponsor whisked me off the stage without holding the usual fifteen-minute question-and-answer session.

Within a year, as the economy soured, default rates began to soar. When the crash came, it was clear that mortgage originators would be unable to repay the warehousing loans they incurred to build up inventory for securitization, and would therefore go bust. But the servicing fees which they retained from the securitization would still have to be paid regardless of the loans defaulted. This was a specific requirement of the servicing agreement. In effect, the interest on the performing loans subsidized the fees on the non-performers.

To meet the total value of the syndication, the resale price of the defaulted property would have to recoup the premium plus the commission and legal fees on the sale. Therefore, if the whole portfolio defaulted there would have to be substantial appreciation for the lenders to recoup their cost. Therefore, my firm decided we should buy the servicing contracts. The challenge was how to obtain them at a low price. I decided to create our own opportunities by approaching firms that were not yet bankrupt. We offered them a debtor-in-possession loan at an abnormally low rate if they collateralized it with the servicing contract and a commitment approved by the bankruptcy court to auction off that contract within sixty days. That would repay part of the warehousing loan and let them reorganize quickly.

We selected American Home Mortgage as our target. It was the nation's third-largest mortgage servicer and not yet in bankruptcy. I knew the CEO and main shareholder slightly because he had a summer home in Southampton. I called him and said, "I hope that your company will not go bankrupt, but in case it does, my fund will commit to make you a debtor-in-possession loan at a low rate, secured by your servicing. The proceeds from selling the servicing fees will repay your loan."

A few weeks later, American Home Mortgage filed for bankruptcy. We made the loan and managed to take over the servicing by extinguishing the loan. No one else bid, probably because we were already so thoroughly embedded in the company and supported by management. Bank of America, the major pre-bankruptcy lender, tried to appeal the bankruptcy court's approval, but a federal circuit court ruled against their late intervention. It is unclear to me why they did not make a bid themselves, but their decision to ask the court to force us to buy the remaining part of the company was doomed to failure. What was unique about this transaction was using bankruptcy as an offensive weapon wielded by investors with no prior connection to the company. The process now has become sufficiently popular that it has a title: "Loan to own." Overall, this transaction demonstrates the lengths to which private equity investors sometimes must go to create values. We eventually sold American Home Mortgage to yet another large servicer, so it proved to be a worthwhile experiment.

Switching Parties

In the wake of the subprime mortgage meltdown, the federal government started the Consumer Financial Protection Bureau (CFPB). My tangling with the CFPB was another dramatic demonstration of the left wing pursuing a fundamentally worthy objective—consumer protection—through overzealous bureaucratic meddling. The experience also helped trigger my political metamorphosis from a Democrat to a Republican.

In 2009, my private equity fund joined with Blackstone and Carlyle Group to back John Kanas in buying Florida's BankUnited from the Federal Deposit Insurance Corp (FDIC). John was one of the most impressive business figures anywhere. At age twenty-five, he had become CEO of North Fork Bank in Mattituck, Long Island, a tiny bank with just $25 million in deposits. Over the course of thirty years, he transformed it into a an institution with $35 billion in deposits, even successfully penetrating the Manhattan market with this incongruously named bank. Eventually, Capital One Bank bought North Fork for $14.6 billion, about three times its then-book value.

By 2009, John had served out his noncompete period after the Capital One acquisition, so he was ready for a new challenge. He found just the thing in Florida-based BankUnited. BankUnited had specialized in the worst types of loans: adjustable-rate mortgages at higher than 90 percent loan-to-value ratios, mainly given to noncitizen Latin Americans buying second homes in Miami. The bank, the largest in Florida, was going under during the financial crisis. At the time, people feared that Florida's economy would collapse and the state would become like the lost continent of Atlantis. We believed that if we bought and fixed up BankUnited it could recover quickly, and Florida would remain the de facto capital of Latin America. WL Ross and our partners pooled $935 million and bought it from the FDIC. There was only one other bidder, Toronto Dominion Bank, whose proposal would have cost the FDIC another billion dollars in losses.

Eighteen months later, after some restructuring, we took FirstUnited public in the largest bank IPO ever. Around the same time, the Consumer Financial Protection Bureau, which imposed new regulatory supervision on banks, came into existence, largely through the advocacy of future Massachusetts Senator Elizabeth Warren. BankUnited was among the first to be inspected under the new CFPB regime.

On the day of our very first board meeting, eight newly hired CFPB officials showed up to headquarters, two of whom were from the enforcement division. We asked why there were enforcement people at our very first gathering. The answer was, "You bankers have taken advantage of the public for too long, but those days are over with. You better get used to enforcement people being all over you."

Our inquisitors then requested to see the complaint book which all banks were required to maintain. Our book was very thin because we had very few complaints. One enforcement officer thumbed through the book and asked, "Where are your credit card complaints?"

We responded, "We don't issue credit cards. We're too small a bank to do so."

The other compliance officer shouted, "You mean you are denying your customers access to credit cards?!"

"Perhaps you are not aware, but everyone in the United States is inundated daily with credit card offerings. There is no shortage of credit cards."

They next complained about the fees we charged for mortgages, so we asked, "Is there anyone else in this market offering mortgages?"

"No, no one else is making mortgage loans."

"So, would you prefer we offered lower fees, but actually made no loans?"

"Your fees are just too high."

This adversarial give-and-take went on for an hour and a half. Then, one of the enforcement officers said, "We just came from another bank about your size and they have twice as many compliance officers as you do. You must hire more."

We asked, "Did they have more complaints than we did?"

"Yes, many more."

"Shouldn't there be a correlation between the number of complaints and the level of staff to deal with them?"

"All I can say is that you better have more compliance people when we come back next time."

BankUnited's stock ran up before the next visit, so all three funds sold their shares and we resigned from the board.

We did hear later a rumor that two of the CFPB officials who visited us were recently retired police officers who had been walking beats and two others were former elementary school teachers.

Eventually, the CFPB succeeded in bullying the banks into hiring more compliance staff. Many smaller ones now have more compliance officers than loan officers, an unworkable business model. The CFPB seems to be unaware that its overbearing regulation produces the very thing it hates—consolidation of the banking industry. The total number of banks in the United States has declined from about 7,400 in 2006 to just over 4,100 in 2022.[22] Much of that decline reflects how community banks are being absorbed into bigger ones. These community banks are the most common funders of local small businesses, and the disappearance of local lenders is one outcome that I am sure Senator Warren neither anticipated nor desired. Someone once said, "The power to tax is the power to destroy." The same could be said of the power of overregulation. There is little doubt that some of the big banks and big nonbank financial institutions had contributed to the financial crisis. But instead of precisely punishing and reforming these entities, the Obama Administration fired a blunderbuss at the whole industry.

Perhaps more notably, the CFPB, sixteen years after it was created, did not prevent two of the largest bank failures in history in 2023. After the subprime mortgage crisis, rulemakers encouraged banks to buy safe government bonds. They ignored the market risk inherent in long-term bonds and permitted banks (other than the five systemically important ones) to buy bonds and not mark them down for regulatory purposes if the market price declined. They just had to list the securities as "held to maturity" rather than "available for sale." This fiction is what caused Silicon Valley Bank and

First Republic Bank to fail. As too many depositors withdrew funds simultaneously, these banks had to sell bonds to raise cash and every sale was at a loss since interest rates had been increased by the Federal Reserve Board. Silicon Valley Bank actually had more assets listed as "held to maturity" than the total amount of loans they had made! This ended the regulatory fiction of carrying them at cost, but many other midsize banks remain in the same position. Thus, regulation intended to help banks literally caused two of the largest bank failures in history. A simple precaution would have been to limit the percentage of assets designated as "held to maturity" so that it was not disproportionately large. We don't really need banks to be huge buyers of government bonds, but we do need them to make loans.

The CFPB's mindless persecution of the financial services industry also happened shortly before Bill de Blasio was elected mayor of New York City in 2013. His left-wing governance brought greater crime and disorder to a city that Rudy Giuliani and Mike Bloomberg had worked hard to restore from its nadir in the 1970s and 1980s. In one speech addressing the Partnership for New York City, on whose executive committee I then served, de Blasio asserted something to the effect of, "There is no empirical evidence that the local tax policies affect business decisions." The air went out of the room. All of the leading businessmen there were astonished that he could be so ill-informed. The subsequent emigration of businesses and private citizens from the Big Apple proved how wrong he was.

Upon hearing this, Hilary and I didn't want to leave as valuable an asset as the Briarcliff penthouse in his left-ist hands, so we sold it to the ex-wife of the famous shale developer Howard Hamm. She reportedly waited a week to cash the check Harold cut her—almost $1 billion—because she wasn't sure it was enough. Similarly, in our transaction with her, her lawyer demanded a trivial reduction in the purchase price because her home inspector found a couple of electric outlets that did not work. We gave the small concession to get rid of the problem. That is probably how Harold Hamm felt when he wrote that check.

In many ways, the de Blasio era marked the end of an era for commonsense Democrats in New York City. Although Rudy and Mike were great Republican mayors, I remained a Democrat the whole time I was a New York City resident. In most of my years living in the city, it was pointless to vote in the Republican Party because the Democrats normally won the general election. Therefore, the real election was the Democratic primaries. Voting in them gave me a chance to have a voice, however small, in the key local and state races. But as the Democrats drifted leftward locally and nationally, I couldn't take it anymore. In the years prior to Trump's run for President, I began to fundraise for a few Republican candidates and stopped giving money to Democrats. I did not formally switch parties until Trump ran, but I had good reason for not doing so. Declaring myself a Republican would have broken the heart of my mother, a lifelong Democratic operative, so I waited until well after her death.

How to Become Secretary of Commerce

Though I had been friends with Trump for many years since our bankruptcy dealings, and had heard him muse about running for President before, nothing could have prepared me for the phenomenon that was Trump's 2016 campaign. Besides being

Donald Trump's friend, I supported his run on the merits. His goals of cutting taxes and regulations, sealing up the southern border, rebalancing trade relationships, and strengthening the military sounded good to me. I also perceived that, of all the Republican candidates, only Trump understood how upset working-class Americans were, and especially at how inflation had outpaced wages for many years.

I was among the first well-known Wall Streeters to endorse Trump as the Republican nominee. Just prior to the debates in the summer of 2015, the host of CNBC's TV show *Squawk Box* asked me something to the effect of, "If Donald Trump were to be the Republican nominee, would you support him? I responded, "Yes, I would!" The hosts—mostly "Never Trumpers"—were dumbfounded at my response. Subsequently, Hilary and I put on a major fundraiser at our home in Southampton. I also wrote several editorials, mostly in regional newspapers; debated publicly with left-leaning think tankers; acted as a surrogate for the Iowa primaries and elsewhere; and participated in many policy discussions at Trump Tower.

It was clear people in the top echelons of business and politics refused to take Trump's appeal seriously. Months before the election, the British ambassador, Sir Kim Darroch, convened a dozen American business executives who, like me, were members of the BritishAmerican Business group. Everyone else thought Hillary Clinton would win. I alone forecast the Trump victory, explaining that he was the only one who understood that middle-class Americans were furious that inflation consistently outpaced their salary gains and that they were upset with illegal immigration. The Ambassador was an engaging personality, but a few years later resigned because he had sent the Foreign Office cables criticizing President Trump. His successor was Karen Pierce, whom Hilary and I got to know before leaving office.

Election night 2016 was thrilling. I spent most of the evening sitting with Carl Icahn, another Trump supporter, at the campaign watch party at the Hilton Midtown. Once it was clear Trump would win, Carl said, "I'm not sitting around here anymore. I've had enough martinis. I'm going to buy stock futures."

In the spring of 2016, Trump had designated former New Jersey Governor Chris Christie to lead the transition team and make recommendations on candidates for positions in the new administration. Days after Trump's electoral victory, Christie was sacked, apparently because he proposed too many names from his own team and too many lobbyists. Bill Hagerty, later U.S. Ambassador to Japan, continued as part of the team tasked with recommending Cabinet members. Prior to the election, I had not really thought about a post-election role, but he and I held discussions on my possible interests. I told him my first choice would be Treasury if the President didn't pick Steve Mnuchin, as I guessed he would. If he did, then my preference would be Commerce.

Two weeks after the election, the President-Elect's office called, inviting me to his Bedminster Country Club in New Jersey at 1:30 p.m. on the Friday after Thanksgiving. The young lady on the other end of the line didn't say what it was about, but I could guess.

I began to consider the idea that I would be the next Secretary of Commerce. Getting your head around the gargantuan agency is a job unto itself. Commerce is one of the more complex Cabinet departments. It includes a raft of government agencies, including the National Oceanic Atmospheric Administration (NOAA), the Census Bureau, the Patent and Trademark Office, the National Institute of Standards and Technology, Bureau of Industry and Security, the U.S. Foreign Commercial Service, Office of Space Commerce, National

Weather Service, the National Travel and Tourism Office, the Bureau of Economic Analysis, Economic Development Administration, International Trade Administration, Minority Business Development Agency, the National Marine Fisheries Service, and the National Environmental Satellite Data and Information Service. The Secretary of Commerce is also the designated advisor to the President regarding telecoms. It has more than forty thousand employees, more than two hundred domestic offices, and seventy-two teams in embassies around the world, plus sixteen satellites to manage. It would have to hire and manage more than 400,000 part-time, temporary census takers for the 2020 Census. In short, it was a large conglomerate that posed real management challenges. That opportunity intrigued me.

But even as I mulled over the vast new responsibilities I might soon have, I didn't take it for granted that I'd be chosen. Just as I'd done before every big meeting in my life, I prepared intensely for the meeting with Trump. I put together a hundred-day plan to serve as my opening remarks. To make sure I was on time, Hilary and I helicoptered the night before out to a motel near Bedminster and had dinner at the very good local steakhouse. We had never been there before, but the maître d' greeted me by name and wished me good luck. He clearly had some idea what was going on.

The next day, a limo took me to the club through several security checkpoints along the ten-mile route. The driveway itself was three miles of curving roads through a beautifully manicured golf course and up a hill to the clubhouse, the former estate of the automobile executive John DeLorean.

Upon arrival, there were one hundred media people in a roped-off area on the far side of the parking lot at the front entrance. One of Trump's aides told me to stay in the car and drive around to the back door. We went up a flight of wooden stairs to the club's cocktail lounge. Sitting there having cold cuts and drinks were Rudy Giuliani and other applicants for various posts. Most notable was Jonathan Gray, then the head of Blackstone's real estate group. He was the only one who seemed likely to be a rival candidate for Commerce.

Ultimately, I was called into a large living room at the other end of the corridor. It had about a dozen chairs in a large semicircle facing a single chair in the middle. The President-Elect and Vice President-Elect, Mike Pence, were there, as were Steve Bannon, Steven Miller, Reince Priebus, Kellyanne Conway, Jason Miller, and a few others whom I don't remember.

I sat down and started to take out the sales pitch. Trump said, "Wilbur, no need for that. We've decided to give you Commerce!"

I thanked them and Reince, the Chief of Staff–designate, explained the next steps. An FBI background check would take a couple of weeks, during which the FBI also would check on Steve Mnuchin for Treasury. We would be announced together as the "economic team." Until then, no one was to know, although Trump added with a big smile, "Except Hilary, of course." That was it. Trump and Pence escorted me to the downstairs door and the three of us smiled at the press. The President gave his thumbs-up to hint I was getting a Cabinet post. A few days later, on November 30, it was official.

In the first week of January, I reported to the Presidential Transition Office at a General Services Administration building in Washington. I spent half of each day prepping for the confirmation hearing and the other half being briefed by experts from various parts of the Commerce Department. The hearing prep was in a room that re-created the actual committee hearing room. There were a dozen or so seats set up high and my chair was below them. One staffer acted as each of the committee members, even imitating their accents and mannerisms and the questions each was likely to ask. They also mimicked the comings and goings of senators that are always a part of hearings.

Once the nomination was submitted to the Senate, I made courtesy calls to the senators who would control my fate in the Senate Committee on Commerce, Science, and Transportation. The first was to South Dakota Senator John Thune, the Commerce Committee chair, and the second was to Florida Senator Bill Nelson, the ranking member. I knew Nelson already because my Palm Beach tennis partner was among his supporters. Meanwhile, on rechecking our household staff credentials we found that one had initially falsified her ID. We had made all the proper deductions, but she was an illegal immigrant. The two senators pre-agreed how to defuse the issue. After the opening statements, the chairman would describe the maid situation and say he was content with my explanation and Nelson would concur. It worked. Not a single member brought it up again.

The meeting with Senate Majority Leader Chuck Schumer was less satisfactory. Back when I was a Democrat, I had hosted one of his first fundraisers and we had been cordial ever since. After about a half hour of chitchat I asked, "Senator Schumer, may I count on your support for my confirmation?" He immediately replied with a grin, "Not a chance, Wilbur. I am the loyal opposition."

After a three-hour hearing on January 18, 2017, the Committee forwarded my nomination to the full Senate with a favorable "voice vote" recommendation, meaning that no Committee member objected. The strongly bipartisan confirmation vote ultimately was seventy-two yeas and twenty-seven nays, including Schumer's. That marked the high point of my relations with the Democrats in my Secretary of Commerce years. A few years later, at another hearing, a woman dressed as Marie Antoinette stood up and threw pieces of cake around the room. The Capitol Police escorted her out. I then said to great laughter, "As you can appreciate, she was not part of my prepared remarks."

My relationship with Donald Trump—and his high regard for my negotiating skills—certainly was an advantage to my candidacy for a Cabinet post. But our bond was only one part of landing it. Over my many years in business and philanthropy, my ability to focus closely on my assignments and deliver value for my clients and causes gave me a reputation as a trustworthy and competent manager. Even the most solicitous individuals cannot obtain a Cabinet spot simply through flattery or an ability to toe the party line. My success in business had proven my command of financial and economic matters, so much so that I was deemed fit to run a Cabinet agency. Based on my track record, the President-elect and his team had confidence that I would be able to achieve the same successes in government. This time, my "clients" would be my fellow Americans.

CHAPTER 10

How Washington Works

"Barron, come to the conference room! I have to talk with you!"

President Trump's stern voice boomed over the Air Force One intercom, summoning his teenage son to the presidential sitting area. Each weekend during the winter, the President usually asked Hilary and me to join him on Air Force One to Palm Beach. The world's most famous aircraft would usually leave Washington on a Friday and return on Sunday. So it was with this trip.

Barron, like his father, is a tall and self-confident man. But the tone of his father's voice was enough to rattle even him. As he shuffled down the corridor toward the President's quarters, he was naturally worried that he was about to be rebuked for something.

Instead, as Barron entered the room, the President and the rest of the traveling party burst out in a chorus of "Happy Birthday" and unveiled an elaborate cake. A relieved smile covered the young man's face. Surprising? Sure. But then again, lots of things in the Trump Administration were.

A fair number of American cities are the national hubs of certain industries. For finance, it's New York. Tech, San Francisco. Entertainment, Los Angeles. For Washington, politics is the "industry" around which the town revolves. For Washingtonians, having power (or being in very close proximity to it) is a massive determinant of one's professional status. Everything depends on your standing in the hierarchy. As a result, everyone you meet—even your political rivals—can be unfailingly polite, in hopes of accumulating more power and influence (and the most polite ones are usually the most duplicitous). Even as Democrats and members of the media disdained President Trump and our Administration, they knew that their ability to achieve their own goals depended in great part on a good relationship with people like me. And I, in turn, recognized their value.

For all my years living on the East Coast, I was not terribly familiar with Washington when Hilary and I moved there in 2017. I had been the chairman of the Smithsonian Institution's National Board of Directors years before, but my visits to town were limited to quick trips for meetings. Consequently, one of the first steps I took even prior to moving to Washington was to begin building relationships with everyone who could help me advance the Trump Administration's policy objectives, or potentially cover them favorably in the press. Thus, even before my Senate confirmation, Hilary and I bought a house suitable for entertaining overlooking Rock Creek Park. The seller, Adrienne Arsht, was most gracious. When I met her at a party in New

York not long before the deal closed, she gave Hilary and me each a key to the house, saying we were free to use it even before the deal was done. The house purchase also signaled to Commerce Department staff that I intended to stay in the job for the long term. The Secretary of Commerce gig was no bit of policy tourism.

Hilary and I hired a brilliant Palm Beach decorator named Scott Snyder to decorate the house. The morning after the sale closed, he had twenty-five workmen there, causing a shortage of contractors that other Cabinet members were hoping to use for their own renovations. Five weeks later we had a housewarming party. Our invitations simply said the party was "In Honor of Scott Snyder," a detail which caused some confusion. Some recipients thought we were having a party for a famous comic-book author of the same name. Others mistakenly believed it was a bash in honor of Rick Snyder, the Governor of Michigan. Either way, it was well-attended by high-profile Democrats and Republicans, including Senators Richard Blumenthal, John Cornyn, Ted Cruz, Amy Klobuchar, Joe Manchin, Ed Markey, Mitch McConnell, Bill Nelson, Marco Rubio, Tim Scott, John Thune, and Roger Wicker. Many members of the House of Representatives were also present. For entertainment, we hired the singer Christopher Mason.

Hilary and I have always been tremendously social people, but now socializing meant much more—it was key to my ability to attract new friends and connections who could help me in my work. Not long after our housewarming party, our friends Lally Weymouth and Don Graham of *Washington Post* fame, teamed up with the late Washington superlawyer and former Ambassador to the European Union C. Boyden Gray to host a major cocktail party to introduce us to the local swells and the embassy crowd. As befits their roles in the Washington permanent establishment, they did the same years later for my successor Gina Raimondo, and, with her gracious consent, had us join the event. Soon after the Weymouth-Graham-Gray party, we were flooded with invitations from ambassadors. We also became friendly with Washington mainstays such as the Albrittons, Folgers, Donnellys, Dubersteins, Bernsteins, Carls, Ryans, Lynda Carter (who played Wonder Woman), the Cafritzes, the Maleks, the Reynoldses, the Bermans, and the Ishams, to name a few.

The Ishams did us an especially nice favor one day when NetJets screwed up our flight. We normally flew to and from town via Reagan airport, but one day we arrived there to discover that NetJets had changed our point of departure to Dulles airport and failed to tell us about it. After a long wait the company revealed another error: They claimed they had mistakenly booked our flight from the Hamptons rather than to it. We were tired of fooling around, so we went back to Washington to a favorite restaurant, Masseria— just one of many jewels in Washington's flourishing restaurant scene. It was fully booked, but the Ishams, part owners of it, were hosting a dinner party there, and simply added us to the list. That converted a bad experience into a nice evening.

One of the strongest new friendships we made was with Amy and Bret Baier. Bret anchored the 6:00 p.m. Fox News newscast, and Amy was the Board Chair of the Children's National Hospital, where one of their sons had had multiple surgeries. After the Administration, the Baiers came to Palm Beach and bought a house from Tommy Hilfiger, whom they met at one of our dinners. We often dined at our respective homes and at Café Milano, the epicenter of political dining in Washington. Milano, emulating New York's old 21 Club, always gave us the same table, as they did with other regulars, such as President Clinton, current and former Cabinet members, ambassadors, members of Congress, and high-powered lobbyists. Milano embodied much of the pomp and ceremony on which Washington thrives, and which is highly infectious if you are in a high position. Within twenty-four hours of your confirmation, the doormen at hotels and the maître d's at the hottest restaurants suddenly know your identity and treat you the way the British treat their aristocracy. It becomes easy to forget that they are really honoring the position rather than the individual filling it for the time being.

Another impressive D.C. institution was the Chevy Chase Club in Maryland. It had a wide range of facilities and many of the members were present or former government officials. A humorous event happened right before Hilary and I went to the club for our membership interview. In honor of Egyptian Independence Day, the Egyptian embassy had hosted a reception with multiple stations offering food and handicrafts. One of these stations had a woman painting traditional Egyptian decorations in black henna on women's hands. Hilary cheerfully participated in getting a design. As we prepared to depart the reception, she tried to wash off the ink to no avail. Needless to say, it was not the look that the Chevy Chase Club's membership committee was prepared for! All we could do was to explain to them what had happened and how embarrassed we were. They had a good laugh and voted unanimously to accept us. We loved our time at the Club and met many luminaries there. One night, Governor Phil Bryant of Mississippi was there having drinks. I expressed my admiration for his boots adorned with his state's seal. A few weeks later, a pair emblazoned with the Secretary of Commerce symbol showed up.

Professional Ties

Building connections with my fellow Cabinet secretaries was also essential—after all, I would be collaborating with these men and women on any number of complicated topics. The intellectually robust Secretary of State, Mike Pompeo, and his wife Susan often hosted black-tie "Madison Dinners" at the State Department. These gatherings brought together private-sector thought leaders and a few of us from government for a robust exchange of ideas. The Madison Dinners were strictly off the record, and, unlike so many other meetings in Washington, there never was a leak as to the contents of the discussions—perhaps their convivial nature led the participants to honor their secrecy.

As for President Trump, he liked to entertain with movie nights at the fifty-seat White House theater, replete with popcorn and soda, and often followed by dinner at his hotel. I often had to pinch myself on these evenings. No matter the occasion, no matter what else you have done in life, every time you walk into the White House (in my case, often a couple of times a day), your heart beats a bit faster. You feel like a big shot when the security guard greets you by name. And every function held there is a thrill, whether it is an intimate dinner with the President in the Rose Room, or a formal state dinner. I'll never forget the visit of the Prime Minister of Australia, Scott Morrison. The weather was good, so we were seated outside in the Rose Garden, with two orchestras playing on the White House roof. This dramatic and dignified scene showed off the best of American hospitality. Even grander was the two-day state visit of France's President Emmanuel Macron and Mrs. Macron.

One perk of Cabinet posts is that you can invite friends to view the amazing White House Christmas decorations. First

Lady Melania pulled off a beautiful but very different design each year. We invited friends to the event and to dinner later. Many of them had not been to the White House or had been but had never seen the Christmas decorations. It made you feel like a big deal to have them invited, whether they came or not.

Even the small working lunches with the President and foreign leaders were quite elaborate. The White House has full-time calligraphers who help prepare place cards and menus. President Trump always invited everyone to keep the menus as mementos of the visit, and just about every guest did so. On some occasions we signed and passed them around for everyone else's signature the menu, making it an autographed bit of memorabilia. We are all tourists at heart.

But for all the ceremony attached to them, working lunches with the President were truly business affairs. Sometimes they turned a bit hostile. The first lunch with German Chancellor Angela Merkel—who is herself a strong personality—quickly became adversarial when the President asked some very direct questions.

"What is your trade surplus with the United States?" Trump inquired.

On hearing an answer of several hundred billion dollars, he grumbled about the tariff and nontariff trade barriers that the EU levied against the United States. Merkel didn't sidestep the complaint, claiming that Americans bought German auto and other manufactured products because of their high quality and reasonable price.

The President pushed back, saying, "You also are not good to our farmers."

She responded with something like, "Your farm products are largely genetically modified organisms, and do not comply with European standards."

After a brief interlude of chit chat, the President asked, "What percentage of your total budget is the military?"

She responded, "About 1 percent."

He said, "Do you think it is fair that we pay 4 percent and you don't even spend the 2 percent NATO target? You are a wealthy country and you should pay more."

She responded, "Mr. President, military spending is very unpopular in Germany, and I am soon up for reelection. Let's talk again after I am reelected." The conversation then became lighter and soon ended.

Some months later, Chancellor Merkel did return for lunch after she was reelected. The President's first question was, "When will Germany begin to pay 2 percent of their budget for defense?"

"Perhaps by 2030."

He became angry, saying, "2030!? I won't even be President then. You must do much better than that."

The relationship between the two leaders remained a bit sour for the rest of the four years. I have heard the President repeat this story on unclassified occasions, so I feel empowered to repeat it here.

A few months later, the CEO of one of my former German portfolio companies, VTG, arranged for me to discuss U.S. trade policy over Zoom during a convention held by Chancellor Merkel's political party. About halfway through it I was disconnected and never reconnected. When I met the CEO at another conference a few months later I asked why she had cut me off. Her response was, "I would never do that. There was a technical problem, and we were running late. By the time we fixed it we couldn't fit you back in." I have no comment.

Washington was also my first experience working with two key decision-makers in the President's orbit: Jared Kushner and Ivanka Trump. Hilary and I knew Jared and Ivanka slightly from New York social events, but we grew much closer through the campaign and the Administration. Both Ivanka and Jared made important contributions to the Administration. It was remarkable to see the energy with which these two young, talented dynamos approached their work, even while raising three young children. Jared's tirelessness was clear even before the inauguration. Not long after the election, Jared had the likely incoming Mexican Foreign Minister and Secretary of Commerce come repeatedly to my New York apartment to discuss ideas for revising NAFTA. None of us were yet in office, nor had we even been formally nominated, so it was really just a few private citizens talking.

Still, these conversations gave both sides a critical head start on what we knew would be one of the President's most important initiatives. We discussed the need for a protective mechanism to make sure the United States received substantial benefit from the new business activity a trade deal would bring to Mexico, and gave some thought as to how to prevent China and others from entering the back door to the United States from our southern neighbor. We also discussed the need for higher minimum wages in Mexico and for us to help to stabilize its currency. All of these concepts were ultimately reflected in the agreed-upon U.S.-Mexico-Canada Agreement (USMCA) that came into effect on July 1, 2020. For his efforts, Mexico appropriately bestowed on Jared the Order of the Aztec Eagle, the highest honor the country affords to foreigners. Jared should have also gotten many more international accolades than he did for his brokering of the Abraham Accords.

My working relationship with Ivanka centered on workforce development, one of her major initiatives. I thought her focus on this was very wise. When I was young, public schools all had what they called "manual training" programs, which prepared people who were not bound for college to have solid careers. Foolishly, a theory that everyone should go to college—an idea that is as wrong as it is unachievable—helped shut down these programs. Partly as a result, by 2017 the United States had one of the least developed vocational training systems of any Organization for Economic Cooperation and Development (OECD) country. In 2017, there were 6.6 million more job openings than unemployed people, partly because many unemployed people lacked the skills good-paying employers needed.[23] It is greatly to America's advantage to keep training our workers in jobs that are essential to the functioning of everyday life—and can never be exported overseas!

Ivanka and I knew it was time to reinvigorate pathways to prosperity for students for whom college is not the best choice. Ivanka invited me to cochair a major workforce development program, the main objective of which was to have each employer commit to specific numbers of apprenticeships in particular activities. Another objective was to increase workforce participation to something well above its relatively static historical level of 62–64 percent. Boosting these numbers will cause our economy to grow faster, and people will be better off.

She and I went all over the country to promote the initiative to employers. One of the events we did was a major dinner at the Indianapolis Motor Speedway. Neither of us had ever been there before, but the owner, Roger Penske, was a great host. He had a professional driver take each of us separately on a spin around the track. I have never been as terrified, whipping around a curve at more than two hundred miles per hour. It took a couple of stiff drinks to recover from the wild ride.

Ultimately, I would label our work a success. We convinced community colleges around the country to partner with local businesses to develop curricula that would produce qualified graduates. We also negotiated a treaty with Switzerland—a leader in this area—to share best apprenticeship practices. As for getting employers on board, Ivanka has her father's charisma and gift for making a sale. Employers were so charmed by her that they couldn't turn her down. She secured pledges from employers to create more than 6 million jobs over five years at a $60,000 average salary, which translates to almost $400 billion of income created for working-class people. One of the best parts about it was that we didn't spend any federal money, except a few plane rides and hotel rooms. It was an amazing return on investment!

Great Adaptations

Dinners and parties were only a small slice of my work commitments as Secretary of Commerce. Most often, they topped off a long workday. Unlike New York, Washington is an early-to-bed, early-to-rise community. Most parties start at 6:00 or 7:00 p.m. and rarely run much later than 9:00.

This was just one of the adaptations I had to make as Secretary of Commerce. Beginning with my arrival at Rothschild in 1976, and continuing with my namesake private equity fund, I had basically been my own boss for four decades. Having a boss—especially one as demanding as President Trump—was something I had not contended with for many years. Still, you are never too experienced to adapt your time and priorities to reflect your boss's. Additionally, working directly for the President of the United States presented the kind of fascinating new opportunity I'd chased my whole life.

My first day at Commerce was on March 1, 2017. The headquarters building sits right on top of a Metro station, and I went down to its entrance to greet employees arriving at work. I also held an assembly of key managers in the auditorium, where I explained my philosophy of management. "There will always be bad news, and screwups, especially with an organization of more than forty thousand people," I said. "But I want to hear about problems from you, and in a timely way, not days or weeks later in the *Washington Post* or CNN."

I knew—and still believe—that the vast majority of the people who work at the Commerce Department do their level best every day. But government workers are often captive to a mentality that would get them fired in the private sector. In that same initial talk with senior-level managers, I told them, "I want you to give me a one-page report each week of what you accomplished, what will you do next week, and what public promotion you have scheduled to highlight your work." One put his hand up and said, "It hasn't been our practice to do weekly reports."

"It is now," I said. "You can't manage things you can't measure."

In truth, accountability through measurable outcomes is a concept that is totally foreign to bureaucrats. Later, I said to one guy who made grants, "I've never seen any progress reports from you. Does your program really do what it says?"

He responded, quite nonchalantly, "We aren't equipped to monitor that."

I never quite got over the shock that employees were laying out large quantities of taxpayer money and never finding out whether it really made a difference, or if partners were upholding their end of the deal. In business, ineffective programs are swiftly eliminated. In government, outcomes are rarely measured because there is no intention to ever cancel the program, regardless of its effectiveness or the lack thereof. Once initiated, a program immediately develops a constituency of those whom it benefits. They lobby not just for its continuation, but also for its expansion. Temporary programs often morph into permanency, with no regard for the returns generated. It was the opposite of everything the business world valued.

Government bureaucrats also have a defensive attitude toward risk-taking. There is very little incentive or motivation for government workers to put forth good ideas that may be disruptive. Why is this? First, new ideas often ruffle feathers. Few people within the bureaucracy are willing to cash in their accumulated goodwill for the sake of an idea that may lead to turf wars or an upheaval of the status quo. Second, there is rarely a direct financial incentive to propose something new—a federal worker gets a paycheck regardless of how well he or she does the job. In the private sector, if someone takes a risk and succeeds, he or she is paid a bonus. In government, if the initiative fails, no problem, the checks keep coming. Additionally, there is always an inspector general and a congressional committee ready to disrupt your career if you sidestep established protocols or try to change something. This is a tragic risk-reward matrix, because many mid-level staff are quite capable of useful innovation but are locked into a dysfunctional organizational and incentive structure.

Federal agencies are also shackled by the invisible bonds of inertia. As Commerce Secretary, I often asked why the process for deciding a particular question or producing a certain result was so cumbersome. The answer typically was, "Well sir, that is the regulation." When pressed to show the regulation, staff could not point to one formally on the books. They were just doing things according to how they had always done them. I can even recall one instance where a bureau was so beholden to established processes that it took six months to produce a single letter to Congress on a matter. I don't mean to paint with too broad a brush. In fairness, we had many excellent folks at Commerce. We held multiple awards ceremonies at which top performers were honored. And I personally benefited from the great work of professionals such as James Uthmeier and Mike Walsh.

Weirdly, because pay in government is relatively low compared to the private sector, the thing that motivates many federal officials is titles. Heaven help you if you mistake someone's title, however meaningless it may be. You are challenging his or her very being. Titles determine where you are seated at dinner and where you stand at ceremonies. There is also a peculiarity to titles: Their power varies inversely with their length. "President" is very short and very powerful. "Special Assistant to the Deputy Under Secretary of State" is very long, but without much power implied. Nonetheless, people cling to such honorifics. Where certain Senate-confirmable positions are unfilled, career staff often have at the beginning of their title "Acting" or "Performing the Duties of . . ." Despite the temporary nature of the job, you can be sure that an acting appointee will have business cards printed on the first day they have the title. A king (or Assistant Secretary) for a day!

In the Spotlight

With a Cabinet post comes enormous scrutiny. Congress is at the top of the list of entities interested in your every move as a Cabinet Secretary. The House and the Senate are always eager for investigative hearings into federal agencies, and not necessarily because they are terribly concerned with improving them. As I first experienced when I was defending the work of investment bankers during the Federated Department Store hearings, members of Congress love hearings as a chance to preen before the cameras and make their constituents think they are working hard. The person testifying sits at a small table below encircled by the members, very much a star-chamber arrangement worthy of Kafka. Far from asking questions designed to elicit facts, it is not unusual for most of each member's five minutes allotted speaking time to be taken up by what amounts to a speech, often culminating in an attempt at a "gotcha" question. Very few hearings come to a controversial vote at the end, so there is little worry about making a public commitment that could become an issue in the next election.

To put it mildly, accuracy was not the priority at these hearings. At one hearing on tariffs, one Republican senator, a confirmed free trader, read a partial quote from some earlier testimony I had given, and tried to use that against me. I responded, "Senator, if you read all of the testimony, you would see that your quote was totally out of context." I then read the omitted section. He lost at the hearing, and because it had embarrassed him, he made himself a real enemy of mine going forward. I should have been less direct in my attack on him. It's always a struggle to get the votes you need, so antagonizing even a few relatively friendly individuals is counterproductive to getting things done. Senators are very sensitive to their own importance and hate the slightest bit of embarrassment. His strong reaction reminded me of the quip, "What a senator sees in his shaving mirror every morning is a future president."

While President Trump was a polarizing figure whose presence ratcheted up the animosity between Republicans and Democrats, he is by no means the only source of our country's division. While no one factor accounts for increased partisanship, I think decreased interparty socialization has contributed to it. In decades past, members of Congress typically brought their families to D.C. and lived there. Their children were at school together and they socialized with each other. Now, families stay back in their home state and the legislators commute on weekends. The House is only in session for an average of 147 legislative days per year and the Senate a few more.[24] Almost none of those in-session days fall on a Monday or Friday, which members use to travel. With members back in their home areas on weekends, there is usually very little time for fraternizing with the other side.

Polarization has also increased because House of Representatives districts have been so gerrymandered that there are very few swing seats. The vast majority are either solidly Democratic or solidly Republican. Thus, the primary is the real election, not the general election. Clearing the primary hurdle makes it very hard for a moderate to be nominated by either party. In the old days, when districts were more heterogeneous, candidates had to account for moderate and independent voters in their campaign promises and legislative votes. Alas, those politicians are a rare breed today!

I have two major recommendations for how to improve the political system. One is higher compensation for senior executive branch officials and for members of the House of Representatives and Senate. If those jobs paid better, they would attract a bigger talent pool. Most people in business or elsewhere in their forties don't want to interrupt their career progression and simultaneously take a big pay cut to go into government temporarily. The easy recruits are people in their twenties or early thirties and people near retirement. But that does not always mean they are the best.

My second recommendation is that instead of two four-year terms, presidents should be elected for one six-year term, the same as senators. The problem with four years is that it takes close to a year for a president to get a team in place because of the Senate confirmation process and the prevalent fierce partisanship. Once a Cabinet member is in place, it takes a bit of time to understand how the system works, especially for those who are not Beltway regulars. Similarly, it takes time to understand how to get legislation enacted. I believe that, if given a six-year term, Trump would have gotten even more done in two additional years than he did in the first four. Depending on your political views, that may or may not have been something you would like.

Even more hyper-focused on my every move than Congress was the media. I had an inkling of their obsessiveness one day when Hilary and I dined at the Four Seasons in Georgetown on our first Valentine's Day in Washington. The next morning *Politico* breathlessly reported that we were seen sitting side by side in a booth. If I had been with another woman, I could understand why it would be newsworthy, but not a story that a married couple was sitting together. The media may be so inured to infidelity that togetherness seemed unusual.

The media's favorite topic was seeking potential conflicts of interest discernible from my financial disclosures. I complied scrupulously with the ethics officials' insistence that I divest myself of most of my holdings prior to confirmation, but they did allow me to keep oceangoing vessels. One reporter complained that ships in which I had financial interests sometimes carried cargos to or from China. They overlooked that we did not own the cargos, just hauled them for the owner, and the owner designated where the goods should be picked up and to where they should be delivered. Another reporter was upset that Navigator Holdings, a company I part-owned, had chartered a tanker to a large Russian gas company, two of whose shareholders were oligarchs. The *New York Times* reran the story, though they knew the two oligarchs only owned 15 percent of the public company.[25] The *Times* also ignored that I had never met the gas company officials nor the two shareholders, nor had I even been on Navigator's board when the deal was signed, nor had the gas company been sanctioned. They omitted that my ownership had been disclosed publicly before I entered government, and that the freight carried by this ship was small relative to Navigator's overall business. Perhaps the media's zeal was tied to their inquisition related to all things Russian in our Administration. The facts they did cite were accurate enough, but the article was far more accusatory than the facts warranted, and seemed to insinuate that I actually did a favor for Russia. By contrast, another article by a different reporter from the same newspaper ran the correct story that, while vice chairman of the Bank of Cyprus, I pushed Russian representatives off the board. Guess which story was repeated the most?

In the months and years that followed, I was subject to endless attacks. In January 2019, I had gone on Maria Bartiromo's Fox TV show offering friendly advice to workers who had been furloughed by a government shutdown by pointing out that eventually they would recoup their lost pay and that if they were meanwhile short of cash the credit unions at Commerce and other departments would make bridge loans to them. The media, which sought to blame Republicans for the shutdown and the hardships it created for federal employees, were all too happy to distort my remarks into a Trump Administration disregard for government workers.

The following Saturday, a cartoon in the *Washington Post* depicted me on the balcony of the Department of Commerce building with the made-up quote, "Explain to me again why these folks not getting paychecks can't just live off the dividends in their portfolios!"[26] It was meant to show I was out of touch with the plight of government workers during the shutdown. It wasn't fair, but I had to live with it. I was also parodied on *Saturday Night Live* three times, and I must give credit to Kate McKinnon for a pretty amusing representation. In fact, being lampooned was a rare honor. As a friend said, "You know you have arrived when *SNL* caricatures you."

Forbes also criticized me for not correcting exaggerated estimates of my net worth. They were correct in calling me out for this foolish lapse of judgment. I am less charitably disposed toward a hit piece written in September 2019 by a Style section reporter at the *Washington Post*. He had covered a civil service award gala at the Washington National Cathedral. As I was leaving the event, he accosted me for giving a speech presenting an award to former Commerce Secretary Norman Minetta. He admonished, "It is really inappropriate for someone like you to be praising Norman Minetta." He then ran a similar column dripping with venom, saying, among other falsehoods, that I was "too rich to remember how the real world works."[27] That was ridiculous. Only in Washington would a style reporter be so political. America is in a sad situation when a media class that boasts about objectivity in coverage demonstrates so little of it in their reporting.

Bloomberg Businessweek's cover story "Wilbur 'Killer' Ross Isn't Worried About the Trade Wars" reported an apparent contradiction: My funds' businesses in many countries had benefited from the regnant international frameworks of free trade, but now that I was in office I was advocating for protectionism.[28] The magazine's chronology was correct. As a private businessman, my task was to deal with the world as it exists, but my government role was to try to correct what was wrong. And besides, the notion that world trade is over-whelmingly free is fiction. No major country is less protec-tionist than the United States. In fact, other than Singapore, there probably is no country anywhere that was less protec-tionist. Every country acts in its own self-interest and most have trade deficits with other countries that they partially off-set by their surpluses with us.

Telling my side of the story when attacked wasn't so easy. Other than the *Wall Street Journal*, mainstream media out-lets were reluctant to take editorials from Trump Cabinet members. The great exception was when the *New York Times* published one of mine touting the importance of the Administration's work creating commercial opportunities in outer space.[29] Most often, I made my arguments through preset speeches and fireside chats, which I gave two or three times per week at places such as the National Press Club, the Economic Club of Washington, the Business Roundtable, and think tanks and various trade association headquarters. Most were friendly audiences eager to learn about our policies. The think tanks, however, generally favored free trade, so we had some lively discussions there. Occasionally a staffer would pose a zinger I was able to parry. A glaring exception was one event at the Woodrow Wilson Center. Its chairman, my friend Fred Malek, had me speak at a luncheon. One of their staffers who interviewed me afterward became so belligerent during the Q and A period that Fred called him out for his rudeness right in the middle of the event.

The most active host for my remarks was, understand-ably, the U.S. Chamber of Commerce. At least once a week a foreign dignitary was its luncheon speaker, and quite often I gave introductory remarks. These were friendly sessions because the American participants were already in that country or wanted to be there. Tom Donohue, the longtime chamber CEO, was an ardent free trader, but we had a good personal relationship and just one big public disagreement. We both spoke at the U.S.-Mexico Chamber of Commerce during the USMCA negotiations. Tom stated his very pro-Mexican policies. I responded, "Tom, I love you dearly but that is not Administration policy, so no one should base their business plans on it."

Most annoying were the baseless leaks from someone in the Administration who wanted my job.

Shortly after confirmation, Bob Woodward, the famous author and *Washington Post* reporter, said to me very bluntly, "There are only two types of high officials, leakers and targets. You need to decide which you will be." I, perhaps stupidly, decided not to leak. Given the media's general animosity toward the Trump Administration, it might not have made much difference, but I felt good about not violating secrecy laws or protocol and not propagandizing.

Nonetheless, I dealt often with the false stories planted by some backstabber who repeatedly convinced the same CNBC reporter that my firing was imminent. Another reporter named a person who allegedly was being considered for the job. Denials by both the White House and me did not stop the incorrect coverage. My guess is that the source was a habitual leaker who wanted my job. Tough luck for him. There was indeed a lot of Cabinet turnover, but I was among the first and most loyal appointees and stayed until the last day of the Administration.

One unexpected effect of media coverage was how it often spurred the President to action. I would occasionally receive phone calls from the President at 6:30 a.m., with him complaining about something he had just seen on TV and which

I had to fix. The one I remember best was one that happened after some economist with the Federal Reserve Bank went on TV to defend the Federal Reserve's decision to raise rates. It wasn't long after his appearance that the phone rang, with Trump ordering me, "You need to go on TV with the opposite point of view." Unlike many members of our Administration, I followed his orders.

Protesters had me in their sights, too. The only prior time I was picketed was when the Communist Party of America besieged my apartment in New York because of my steel company acquisitions. Occasionally, someone would accost us at a D.C. restaurant, but it never became violent. The worst we received was at the Hirschorn's Kusama opening dinner, when left-wing activists noticed us and organized impromptu pickets to protest my presence. Sometimes social media vitriol bubbled to the surface, as well: One site sold T-shirts saying in large red letters on a black background, "Wilbur Ross must resign." They did not sell too well, but I did buy one of my own to wear on some appropriate occasion, perhaps Halloween or April Fools' Day.

Absorbing slings and arrows from the media and various haters was unpleasant, but it came with the territory. Eventually, I realized something: After the first hundred poisoned darts, they don't hurt anymore. I didn't respond to many of the hit jobs, because doing so would simply beget another one. As my dad used to say, "There is little point fighting with someone who has more ink than you do." It made sense. The better tactic when unjustly criticized is to tune out the static, put your head down, and keep going. Good leaders are not preoccupied with making difficult choices that will make everyone perfectly happy, thus minimizing criticism to yourself. Good leaders make the decision they believe to be right, and remain willing to accept the criticism that follows. The media howled day and night that I was unfit to be Secretary of Commerce, trying to claim a trophy for their wall in the form of my resignation or firing. I never capitulated to them, nor ever thought of doing so. Retaining the President's confidence in my ability to serve was what really mattered.

CHAPTER 11

Swimming Against the Tide

My first-ever interactions with Federal Reserve Chairman Jerome ("Jay") Powell came at President Trump's suggestion. Following a recommendation from Treasury Secretary Steve Mnuchin, Trump had appointed Powell as chairman in February 2018. By late March, the Fed had raised rates twice, even though inflation was well-controlled, jobs were growing, and corporate earnings were booming. President Trump was concerned that rate increases with questionable rationale might wreck the economic recovery, so he asked me to talk with Powell and get him to reverse course, or at least stop pushing rates up. He wasn't kidding. As I recall him saying, "Please call this idiot and explain to him that I will repudiate his nomination, even though he has been confirmed."

I said "Mr. President, I agree that Jay is pursuing a wrong policy. But it's not clear to me that it would be in your interests to threaten to replace him or take some other big action against such an important independent agency."

"OK," said the President. "But you have to call him and talk some sense into him."

"Yes, sir, I will report back to you once I have spoken with him."

As soon as I reached Jay by phone we had a brief conversation. "Jay, I am calling to request a meeting with you to try to convince you that your two rate increases were unnecessary, and that any further ones could be very bad for the economy."

Powell was defiant: "No—anything I say to you will just go back to Trump!"

"Well, it shouldn't surprise you that a Cabinet member would discuss this topic with the President, but that should not prevent us from having a discussion. As you know, I have made my living by anticipating cyclical events. I cannot understand why you don't wait until the data shows some evidence of inflation."

He wasn't convinced. "The Fed models show that when unemployment is down around 4 percent and heading lower, inflation will pick up strongly."

"Jay, if you are right, the worst case is that there will be a month or two of inflation before you squash it. Also, the Fed models have not materially changed since the 1970s. The economy is very different now. Plus, there is no Arab oil crisis today. The one in the 1970s hugely distorts things. In any case, no model is 100 percent accurate."

"I have no obligation to debate with you and I am not going to do so." The call ended shortly after that. A few weeks later, Powell reversed his policy. I have no idea whether my call helped change his position.

Later, Powell began an aggressive program of quantitative easing—increasing the money supply in order to keep interest rates low and business humming. By most professionals' reckoning and mine as well, he continued it for far too long, with high rates of inflation the product of his decision. I have no proof for this, but I believe strongly that one motivation for Powell's decision to continue printing money under Biden was that his six-year term was ending, and tightening the money supply might have jeopardized his chances for reappointment. Perhaps it was just coincidental, but very shortly after he gained a new six-year term he did begin gingerly tightening. Now, as the next presidential election looms, he has stopped tightening and talks about loosening, even though unemployment is below 4 percent. Perhaps the Fed has changed its models, though I have not seen an announcement to that effect.

I share this vignette as a window into one of my main responsibilities as Secretary of Commerce: battling a regulatory and bureaucratic superstructure that did not always serve American prosperity well.

Cutting Red Tape

To describe the regulatory environment of the American economy as complex is an understatement. Millions of businesses must make decisions in the context of state, federal, and local regulations. Some regulations are good and necessary for protecting consumers. But the cumulative effect of too much regulation is depressed economic activity. Not only do regulations drive inflation and scarcity, but if leaders know that their industry or business is under regulatory attack it discourages business investment and decisions. Even if new regulations are only announced as being planned, there's no real statutory period by when they must be killed or approved.

Executives can cope with even bad news, but uncertainty paralyzes decision-making. The uncertainty and distraction associated with long timelines is enough to make companies decide, "let's not bother." Additionally, regulation makes decisions open to costly and protracted litigation. People who want to kill a project can just tie it up in the courts.

I saw the ill effects of overregulation in my business career over and over again. I remember one time when my private equity fund had oil investments. One day one of our local managers called to say that the regional Environmental Protection Agency (EPA) person was now requiring him to seek a permit to install a Porta Potty at a well site.

I said, "There is no such rule. Tell them to go to hell!"

He very sensibly responded, "If I do that, imagine how they will torture me on the next permit I really do need." Such tyrannical behavior is an obvious outgrowth of an environment of overregulation.

Recognizing the counterproductive nature of regulations, President Trump wisely mandated that for every new regulation a federal agency introduced, it had to cancel at least two of similar scope. I was proud that by the end of 2017, we at the Commerce Department had exceeded that ratio, cutting seven regulations while adding none.[30] Not only did this effort remove harmful regulations, but businesses quickly got the message that we would not stand in their way. This signal helped create the Trump economic boom for which many Americans remember his presidency. In fact, when I was Secretary of Commerce, most of the businessmen who thanked me for what the Administration was doing were more grateful for regulatory relief than for tax relief. Given my passion for commercial space activity, I am also proud of effectively having taken charge of the Office of Space Commerce and the Commercial Remote Sensing Regulatory

Affairs office from the National Oceanic and Atmospheric Administration (NOAA). It let me personally make smarter—and faster—decisions on space commerce issues than NOAA could do.

The most aggressive and litigious advocates for regulations are environmentalists and wildlife conservationists, with whom I dealt frequently. The Department of Commerce oversees all the fishing in U.S. ocean waters and the Gulf of Mexico, mainly setting quotas for catches. The politics surrounding any fish are unbelievable—especially for red snappers. Many states have them, and each had different nuances to the problem. I wouldn't eat a red snapper for a year because everyone had an interest in it. The general issues were the total annual quota and the allocation of the quota between commercial and sport fishermen, but the actual facts varied from region to region, and so did the politics. Given their role of assuring that the catch did not exceed maximum sustainable levels, the NOAA staff tended to be somewhat conservative in their actions. A desire to hit the right target occasionally led to discussions with local independent consultants who generally supported higher quotas. Usually, we were able to come to a reasonable conclusion, but there was also some litigation.

By far the most memorable fight surrounding environmental issues was in California. The Delta Smelt—a three-inch fish—is native to the Sacramento-San Joaquin River estuary, and has been labeled an endangered species since 1993. Part of its importance lies in the fact that salmon feed on it. Never missing an opportunity to create a huge fight over an issue of relatively limited significance, wildlife activists have successfully lobbied to protect the Delta Smelt by convincing the state to divert a high level of water flowing from the Sacramento-San Joaquin River into the estuary. Meanwhile, farmers across the state of California have suffered from inadequate water supplies for years. The billions of gallons devoted to protecting the smelt could have been used to irrigate their lands, but there was a huge fuss over it. The insistence on protecting the smelt was a microcosm for how many environmentalists have their priorities out of whack. The local fisheries supervisor ultimately agreed to hire an outside consultant and abide by his recommendation, which was to allocate more water to farmers. It was a victory for America's food supply and common sense.

Sadly, people who propose and write regulations often complicate matters with mutually inconsistent objectives. For example, tax credits given to unionized electric vehicle manufacturers are not available to Tesla, the EV industry pioneer and leader, because it is nonunion. But is there more environmental benefit from an electric vehicle built with union labor than one built without it?

Such incoherence exposes a constant feature of left-wing programs: They often try to solve too many problems in one piece of legislation or one executive order. In the case of electric vehicles, the Biden Administration is trying to force companies to unionize even in right-to-work states. That objective conflicts with the Administration's desire to make EVs cheaper, which is necessary for their mass adoption. Instead of such mutually inconsistent policies, a better idea would have been to condition federal tax credits on the adoption of a uniform charging mechanism which all makes and models of electric vehicles could use. That would solve a lack of uniformity in charger design, one of the problems hindering EV adoption. It mystifies me that this has not been accomplished already. At Commerce, I asked the car companies, "Can't you all agree on the interface between the car and the charging system? It would make recharging much more feasible." No dice. However, Tesla has begun the process of making its charging station available for anyone whose systems can connect with Tesla's. I hope this is a positive step toward a consistent standard across the industry.

Being Secretary of Commerce also gave me a close-up look into the thicket of regulations swamping the U.S. health-care system. Though not under my remit, the Food and Drug Administration (FDA) had a bedeviling level of red tape. Obviously, assuring the safety and efficacy of medical and pharmaceutical innovations is of paramount importance, but the FDA seems painfully slow and bureaucratic. The process for conducting trials of drugs is especially cumbersome. It starts with companies testing products on rats or mice to establish a basic level of safety and efficacy. If the drug passes that point, it typically takes the FDA ninety days to decide to permit the Phase I test on humans. Surely this could be shortened to thirty days. Similar lags characterize each of the four subsequent phases. When a test in any phase is underway, no interim results are reported to the pharmaceutical company. Early warnings that the results do not look successful would let the companies cancel the tests early, thereby saving them time and money. Standardizing the number of patients participating in the trial at the lowest number that could produce statistically significant results would also be beneficial. But currently, each step entails its own negotiation on the number of trial patients specific to each product. Again, this burns time and money. The final approvals can also take six months, even if several intermediate tests are successful. (At one point in the clinical testing of an Alzheimer's drug, the FDA delayed approval until autopsies could be performed on test subjects, a huge delay.) Then a separate investigation by a different federal agency, the Center for Medicare and Medicaid Services, determines whether or how much the federal government will reimburse payers for the drug under Medicare or other programs. In total, the process can take as long as four years and cost hundreds of millions of dollars. This, plus R&D money spent on fundamental research that never gets to Phase I, are among the real reasons pharmaceuticals are so expensive. The actual manufacturing is not very costly.

The 2020 Census

No area of my tenure as Secretary of Commerce indicated the intricacies of government more than the Census, the nationwide counting of people that has taken place every ten years since 1790. At the time I was confirmed in 2017, I had three years to prepare for the 2020 Census, which falls under the jurisdiction of the Commerce Department. Sometimes I felt like I needed thirty.

I was already familiar with many of the difficulties of conducting the Census because of my own experience as a census taker—one of the several jobs I held as I worked my way through Harvard Business School. Each day I set out wearing a white canvas duck belt around the waist, with my Census badge attached to a strap on one shoulder. My territory was a tough neighborhood in Boston where residents did not react well to anyone claiming they were there from the government. Some residents threatened to unleash their pit bulls. Others simply refused to open the door when I knocked. In some cases, a voice would cry out, "There ain't no one here!" I would respond, "Well, then, I will just talk with you!" This was no easy job, and I appreciated the difficulties the 2020 census takers would be facing. I wanted to make it as smooth as possible for them.

Unfortunately, things did not get off to a good start. Shortly after my confirmation, the House Committee on

Oversight and Government Reform held budget hearings on the Census. I testified that the $12.3 billion budget proposal which predated my arrival seemed too low, and that I would return with one that was definitive and thoroughly researched. Within two months there emerged a 40 percent cost overrun in a critical early phase of introducing new technology. Meanwhile, on June 29, the NAACP filed a Freedom of Information Act (FOIA) request for documents relating to a planned minority outreach program that we had not even finalized. That should have been a clue to the torrent of FOIAs and litigation that was soon to come. After studying up on the budget, I concluded that it had to be revised upward to $15.6 billion, including a $1.2 billion contingency reserve. The level of scrutiny performed prior to my arrival was totally inadequate. Census officials had not even included all the rents on the two-hundred-plus offices we would temporarily open for 400,000 contract workers. Instead of gunning for the whole thing at once, we initiated an increase of $187 million just for Fiscal Year 2018. Even before I went back for the next hearing, Representative Carolyn Maloney introduced a bill seeking a $441 million increase in 2018 funding, more than twice the increase I was about to propose. The congressional feeding frenzy had now begun!

There were many other problems as well. Many of the contracts with vendors were dangerously based on the vendor's self-reporting of time and materials, with no actual price quoted for the job. This meant, for all practical purposes, the vendors had blank checks. The budget's estimates also seemed to vastly underestimate how much they would have to pay the census takers. Finally, the budget had been prepared by subject matter experts, not by professional estimators, contributing to its questionable accuracy.

Day by day, the litany of glaring problems grew. Eventually, I had enough. One Friday, I called the then–Director of Census Bureau, John Thompson, and bawled him out: "John, a few weeks ago, you testified to Congress that your budget numbers were valid. Now you have agreed with me that those numbers were way too low in many categories. This is unacceptable!" A few days later he resigned. We quickly approached several possible replacements, but they did not want the job. Meanwhile, I had gotten to know the Acting Director, Ron Jarmin, and convinced him to remain through 2020. He diligently stayed on until Steven Dillingham became his White House–proposed replacement in December 2019.

Soon, we encountered another problem: Cenveo, the vendor the U.S. Government Printing Office had chosen in October 2017 to print up the Census's millions of forms, envelopes, and other materials, went bust at the beginning of 2018. Financial problems aside, although Cenveo had bid the lowest, the company wasn't equipped to handle the size of the job. I was mad as a hornet at the Government Printing Office's failure of due diligence. I demanded of them, "How the hell did you let a company that was practically insolvent take this contract?"

They gave me a classic government response: "We were required to take the low bid."

This was one bankruptcy I couldn't salvage. That oversight caused us to pay millions of dollars to get the bankruptcy court to release us from the contract and give it to the only other bidder, R.R. Donnelly, whose price was much higher.

The personnel aspect of the Census was a monumental challenge, as well. Being a census taker is an unglamorous, short-term job. As I knew from my own experience, like all door-to-door solicitors, census takers have lots of doors slammed on them. It also is physically tiring for people in our couch potato society to walk from door to door for many hours each day. Thus, in the 2010 Census, 25 percent of the staff quit after the first couple of weeks and were not replaced. The hiring and training itself was also complicated. Everyone had to be fingerprinted and checked for a criminal record, and be trained to intake data via cell phone rather than pen and paper. Even more complex was the fact that Census had earlier lost a court case that prevented it from turning down people who had been convicted of certain crimes. We actually had to prove that we were hiring some convicts!

I implemented a few directives that helped improve motivation and reduce attrition rates. First, we started a bonus system to encourage people to stay on the job and work certain levels of hours. I also went around to visit some of the offices with the lowest retention rates to see how we could improve them. I also ordered that once a state reported 99 percent of its expected population total, Census workers would be redirected to lagging states, rather than just simply let go. Later, when COVID-19 hit, we faced a logistical nightmare in setting up a COVID-19 testing program for more than 400,000 workers scattered across the country and acquiring and distributing personal protective equipment to them. But we muddled through.

Fights with Congress also consumed the process. One of the main ones was over contingency reserves in the budget. In the private sector, you always book a contingency reserve to cover cost overruns, typically 10 percent on large multi-year contracts. Some members of Congress balked at the concept, saying people should be accountable for their estimates. They had a point, but it was silly to ignore the inevitability of things going wrong in a complex, multiyear, multibillion-dollar project with more than eighty vendors. In addition, subject-matter experts are vulnerable to approving change

orders suggested by vendors or initiated by the experts themselves as they think further about the project. To bring cost
overruns under control, I put in a rule that any change orders
needed my personal approval. The Census budget eventually
included a contingency fund divided into one category of
Known Variables and one of Unknown Variables, the latter
of which could be released only with my written approval.
We needed these reserves when COVID-19 hit.

But by far the most frustrating aspect of the Census was
my decision to include a question of citizenship on the form.
In my mind, having this question should not have been so controversial, because previous censuses had included it, and it
has major relevance for understanding the composition of the
country and how resources and representation are allocated.
The left was loath to include this question to begin with. At
one early hearing, New York Congresswoman Alexandria
Ocasio-Cortez ranted against it. She asserted, among other
claims, that asking it was unconstitutional. I responded by
asking something to the effect of, "Was it also unconstitutional when it was asked during the Clinton Presidency?" She
fumbled a bit and then blurted out that it must have been
phrased differently.

As the controversy raged, the enormous amount of press
coverage opposing the inclusion of the citizenship question
hinted at the media's bias. Some alleged that the real reason for reinstituting the citizenship question was to suppress
minority participation and possibly to provide information
that would lead to deportations. Those repeated accusations,
despite being false, predictably did lead to some of the very
same suppression that was their stated concern. Our arguments that many countries, including Canada, Mexico, the
UK, Ireland, and Germany asked the same question and
that the United Nations recommended that all countries do

so were ignored. Some of the same states that claimed we wanted to undercount their residents rebuffed our requests for administrative records such as drivers' licenses and social benefit payments, which would help cross-check Census data. Their specious excuses centered on privacy concerns and the potential that these records might be inaccurate.

Eventually, the House of Representatives held hearings about the 2020 Census and issued a subpoena for privileged communications between me and the President on the matter. Both Bill Barr, the then Attorney General, and I refused to obey the House Oversight Committee's subpoena on several bases, including the time-honored principle that communications between the President and his Cabinet members were subject to executive privilege. The Committee recommended that the full House hold us in contempt of Congress and refer the matter to the Department of Justice (DOJ) for possible prosecution. It was unnerving to watch on TV as members voted on the motion to hold us in contempt, going up one by one to the platform to cast a ballot. I knew what the outcome would be. Yet I kept hoping that somehow, the Democrat-controlled House would vote no. This must be the way a defendant in a trial feels as the jury is about to announce its verdict. However, the vote is not a conviction, just a consensus to refer the matter to the DOJ. It was more than a little scary, but not scary enough for us to give in to them. The DOJ declined to prosecute us, so that ended the exercise. Even stranger was the allegation by some members of Congress that I lied when I testified about my reasons for wanting to include the citizenship question on the census because they believed I had some sinister ulterior motive and that my failure to confess that was tantamount to perjury. They must have been omniscient and therefore knew better than I did what my motives were.

Outside of Congress, there was an enormous amount of litigation on the question. I won't rehash all the complexities here, but in the end the U.S. Supreme Court ruled 5-4 in June 2019 that the citizenship question could not be included. I will not comment on the ruling except for one fact: The same Supreme Court that had voted that I not testify in the case ultimately based much of its decision on what they divined was in my mind. I am not a lawyer, but this seems like a bizarrely mismatched set of decisions.

Before the counting got underway in early 2020, to attempt to maximize participation in the Census, I authorized a record-breaking $675 million budget for communications in English and twelve other languages, double the amount spent in 2010. We monitored the census takers' progress with detailed daily reports by every census taker. I also wrote to the mayors of certain cities with populations of a hundred thousand or more to encourage them to foster participation. After a few weeks it became clear that some states were way behind in terms of response rates, so I called their governors personally to encourage them to supplement our own efforts. I also made personal calls to the mayors of the fifty cities lagging the worst. Most of them were Democrats who were quite surprised that a Republican Secretary of Commerce would reach out to them. I got more than a few strange responses. I began each call by asking how COVID-19 was affecting their city. One mayor who sounded like he might be high responded, "Oh it's great! Now I can stay home with my dog while I work." Another asked me to remind him how many people lived in his city. By and large though, the calls did stimulate some corrective actions. One mayor went around his city atop a fire engine with a loudspeaker urging people to participate. Another gave prizes to the ward leaders who scored the largest improvements in responses. Many repeated our messages on their political websites. No prior Secretary of Commerce personally worked as hard as I did to maximize the coverage and accuracy of the process.

More litigation ensued in July 2020 when President Trump announced that he wanted to exclude illegal immigrants from the final count so that he could avoid factoring them into the allocation of congressional seats. This further contributed to progressive animus against the question and initiated many legal challenges. The President also decided against our recommendation to extend the Census beyond December 31. This decision required that we complete the fieldwork of enumeration by October 5. Between the short time window, lawsuits, COVID-19, and Democrat opposition, it would have been easy to just give up. Instead, we initiated bonuses to encourage Census takers to work more hours and hired more enumerators so that we would match the originally planned enumerator hours, even though we were operating for fewer calendar days. But these steps did not end the opposition's claims that we were deliberately cutting the process short.

Thankfully, by October 2020, when the counting stopped, field reports indicated that except for Alabama, a traditional Census laggard, every state had achieved success rates of more than 99 percent, and more than 99 percent of addresses had been accounted for. However, after the presidential election, Census staff indicated that there had been computer problems which would delay the final count until after President Biden was inaugurated. This outcome prevented Trump from allocating House seats and made him furious. Still, I can say with pride that the Census count was overwhelmingly thorough and accurate.

The final tally caused Texas to gain two seats, while five other states gained one seat each, with seven states losing one seat apiece.[31] The Pew Research Center, which I regard as left-leaning, published an analysis suggesting that the Caucasian and Asian American populations appeared to have been overstated and the Black and Hispanic groups under-counted. They said the same had been true directionally in 2010, but to a lesser degree. [32] It is odd that anyone thought they could estimate with precision the degree of undercount-ing, since neither they nor anyone else could be certain of what the actual numbers were.

I have several ideas for how to improve the Census and its usefulness. First, children are one of the most under-counted Census groups. Schools obviously have the names and addresses of the children attending them. Using school data for Census purposes in a way that protects privacy rights would reduce the problem of undercounting, espe-cially of minority groups. Second, I recently learned that there are more than 6 million accounts totaling many billions of dollars of payments held in suspense by Social Security, because no such person is known to exist. Many illegal immi-grants create fake Social Security accounts which are submit-ted to employers, who then make the requisite withholding payments. In effect, these people are stealing the employer contributions. With the advent of artificial intelligence, we could use Census data to readily identify such anomalies, stop fraud, and use the resulting information to improve the completeness and accuracy of the next Census. Third, it would help participation to have federal legislation requiring that all administrative records related to government trans-fer payments to individuals be available to the Census. This would help as a cross check on field data. It is ludicrous that people receiving support from federal, state, or local govern-ments are not held accountable for their participation in the Census. It is technically a crime to refuse to participate in it, but I am not aware of any prosecutions for such refusal.

Doing so probably wouldn't help boost participation and would inflame political tensions. Perhaps we could pass legislation that terminated federal payments for people who don't participate in the census.

CHAPTER 12

Looking Abroad

Being Secretary of Commerce presented a remarkable opportunity to re-analyze commercial ties between the United States and countries around the world. The United States is the world's largest goods importer, world's second-largest exporter, and the top recipient of foreign direct investment, translating into millions of American jobs. I made approximately forty trips overseas in the course of my duties, each one designed to win business and create new opportunities for American companies and workers, or to redress unfair trade practices.

None was as memorable as my visit to Saudi Arabia in 2017.

I had been several times to the Kingdom of Saudi Arabia to raise capital for my private equity funds, so the country was familiar to me. Additionally, years before, Princess Muna had been a neighbor in the Dakota. One day her father-in-law, the late King Faisal, was scheduled to visit her there. But as his limo pulled up to the gate, he sent her a note saying,

"Muna, you really must have the exterior cleaned if you want me to visit." He assumed that Princess Muna and his son, Mohammed bin Faisal, owned the whole building, not just a spacious apartment.

Saudi Arabia remains a monarchy today, but the Kingdom has made great strides toward modernizing both its economy and its society, and has grown as a global player. On security, it is a helpful bulwark against Iranian aggression. Economically, its sovereign wealth fund has hundreds of billions to invest around the world. And its status as one of the world's leading oil-producing nations gives Saudi Arabia significant power over global energy supplies and inflation. Recognizing the increasing importance of Saudi Arabia in world affairs and its value as a partner for the United States, President Trump launched a combined trade, diplomatic, and security cooperation mission to the Kingdom in May 2017.

The Saudis were eager to welcome a large delegation of senior Trump Administration officials, headed by the President himself. The Kingdom is historically pro-America, but they felt disrespected by President Obama's foolish decision to effectively strengthen Iran through the 2015 nuclear deal. Trump was an avowed enemy of the agreement, so the first day of our engagements was totally positive. We had many pre-negotiated trade deals to announce, including $110 billion worth of defense equipment sales to the Kingdom, including tanks, ships, planes, and air defense systems. The Saudis sorely needed these items for defense against Iran and its proxies. We also announced transactions in the health sector and several others.

Following the trade announcements, there was a lavish ceremonial luncheon, naturally dominated by President Trump, King Salman bin Abdulaziz, Saudi's de facto ruler Crown Prince and Prime Minister Mohammed bin Salman

(MBS), and other members of the royal family. It went on for hours, a wonderful opportunity for public officials and private sector executives to get to know each other in a relaxed social setting. That evening, just a few of us met with the King at a museum on the outskirts of Riyadh, a former royal residence. Rex Tillerson, our Secretary of State, and I were the first to arrive at the nonalcoholic cocktail party. International TV cameras were all over the place, filming twenty men in Saudi tribal garb performing a traditional Saudi sword dance. After we had a quick fruit drink, Rex and I were invited to join the sword dance. Dancing is not really my forte, especially not while waving a thirty-pound sword to music, but, in the interest of being a respectful guest, how could I say no? The sight of me clumsily lurching with this wide-bladed, pearl-handled ceremonial sword quickly went viral around the world. Even today, if a discussion with friends turns to Saudi Arabia, someone is likely to bring it up. Fortunately, the President soon arrived, and the attention all focused on him and the Saudi royal family.

We then went inside to a large, open-air room. There, more local dancers, acrobats, and singers performed as we indulged in course after course of delicious Arab food. When we finished the main course, in came the royal falconer with an enormous bird sitting on his heavily gloved forearm. He explained how the Saudis used falcons to hunt small game, especially rabbits. It was news to us that rabbits were indigenous to the region, but apparently they are.

After a few minutes, the royal falconer asked the President if he would like to hold the bird and teach it something. Trump declined. Instead, he pointed at me, and exclaimed, "Wilbur will do it!" I stood up and watched the falconer put the bird on my gloveless left arm. At least he didn't burden the right arm, which was worn out from the sword! The falconer then had me move to the center of the room and said, "Now, the test is whether you can get him to open his wings to their full width."

"OK, how do I do that?"

He responded, "By gently jiggling your wrist. But don't do it too vigorously or you may upset him."

As I stood there with his huge claws all the way around my forearm, I worried what would happen to me if he did get upset. The first few little jiggles did nothing, nor did a slightly more vigorous one. Finally, after still more vibration, suddenly his six-foot wingspan opened up with no sign that he was upset. Everyone applauded. The falconer left. My arm remained intact.

The delegation's hotel was the Four Seasons Riyadh. My room was the largest suite you can imagine, boasting not just a foyer but a waiting room with chairs and couches, a fully equipped private office, a private dining room that could seat eighteen people, a library with hundreds of books, and a bathroom that had tons of marble and solid gold fixtures. The bedroom had a 120-inch TV and a four-poster bed that was twice the size of an American double bed. Wow! This was high living. I could only imagine what the President's accommodations looked like.

The next day mostly consisted of one long meeting in a vast hall with a circular crystal chandelier about twenty-five feet in diameter. Several hundred comfortable, well-spaced seats accommodated not just the Saudi delegation and ours, but also the leaders of leading Muslim nations and their entourages. Each leader had a large desk that could seat three people, in front of which was a big couch on which more staff sat. This was the largest gathering there that anyone could recall. Not that there were many of them: One of the Saudi staff volunteered, "I have been here for two years, and this is the only time this room has been used." Ivanka Trump, Jared Kushner, Reince Priebus, and I sat together in the audience facing the leaders. We were delighted at the extraordinary warmth and friendship everyone exhibited toward the President. They clearly knew that he was on their side in the fight against radical Islamic terrorism and Iranian mayhem.

Additionally, President Trump's trip early in the Administration paved the way for the Abraham Accords, which continue to offer the best prospects for lasting peace in the region. Jared Kushner was so influential in this work of diplomacy that Rex Tillerson, Secretary of State from 2017 to 2018, once complained to me that President Trump had "too many Secretaries of State." He was referring to himself, Jared, and Nikki Haley, who had convinced Trump to make UN Ambassador a Cabinet position. Trump ultimately ended that confusion by empowering Mike Pompeo as Secretary of State, who was able to work cooperatively with Jared. Jared's work on the Abraham Accords occurred through very quiet diplomacy. The announcement in August 2020 that the United Arab Emirates and Bahrain had normalized relations with Israel stunned the world, both because of its significance and because few knew such discussions were afoot. While the barbaric Hamas assault on Israel and subsequent Israeli invasion of Gaza have dealt a setback to normalization of relations between Israel and Saudi Arabia, there is no reason to stop trying. It may well be that the ethnic warfare in the region is so long-standing and deeply rooted that sustainable peace between Israel and the entire Muslim world is simply not possible. But the Abraham Accords give more hope for that outcome than ever before.

Sometime after this trip, MBS came to Washington to meet with U.S. business leaders. He generously seated me on his right and my wife Hilary to the right of Masayoshi

Son, the founder of the Japanese investment firm SoftBank, in which the Saudis had invested billions. MBS then went on to New York and elsewhere building goodwill. MBS will be a force to be reckoned with for years to come, having developed the most detailed long-term plan for modernizing his society and diversifying the economy of his developing country I have seen. He even has specific targets for how many peer-reviewed papers their scholars will publish each year in leading Western journals. That session, plus others with the Saudi Ambassador to the United States and various government officials who came to Washington, continued to impress me. The Saudis were well-educated (mostly in the United States or the UK), well-prepared, and fully committed to favorable relations with the United States, while anxious to reform their own society. They know their oil reserves cannot last forever and have taken important steps to diversify their economy. Additionally, the Saudis have backed off from their financial support for hardline Islamic ideology that contributes to full-on radicalization and terrorism. The human rights picture inside Saudi Arabia is also improving, albeit slowly.

It thus made me very sad to see President Biden begin his presidency by damaging U.S.-Saudi relations. On the campaign trail, Biden said he would make Saudi Arabia a "pariah."[33] This kind of language is so counterproductive to a good relationship. During his first week in office, he froze billions of dollars' worth of arms sales. This signaled to Iran that Biden was not remotely as supportive of the Saudis as Trump had been, and within a few weeks the Iranian-backed Houthis started firing at the Saudi oil fields. Moreover, the Biden administration ignored MBS's efforts to liberalize his society and economy, especially by improving the status of women and lessening the country's dependence on hydrocarbons.

The Saudis' slaying of the journalist Jamal Khashoggi—the source of so much animus—was inexcusable, but the price for that horrendous act cannot be a total severance of ties. Later, Biden went begging for Saudi Arabia's help with oil prices, but they were slow to respond. In fact, on one recent visit to the Kingdom, a Minister told me that MBS ignored the first three calls made by President Biden. No sword dance and no falcon for him!

Moreover, in a subject that goes hand in hand with relations with Saudi Arabia, Biden needs an overhaul of his Iran policy. His reversion to Obama-era appeasement has clearly failed, as Iran's nuclear effort has gone well beyond where it was in the Obama or Trump presidencies. His ill-considered decision to pay $6 billion to obtain freedom for some innocent Americans held as hostages by Iran, in my opinion, might have encouraged the Hamas attack by creating a perception of weakness. Later, the Administration reversed this $6 billion decision. Decisions like these must be thought through in advance, not retracted when their erroneous nature becomes obvious.

A timid posture toward Iran borders on imbecility and increases exponentially the danger of war. The United States has only launched token responses to hundreds of Iran-supported strikes at U.S. bases in the Mideast in the wake of Hamas' October 7 attacks, as of this writing. Similarly, when the Houthis started attacking merchant vessels in the Red Sea, I would have suggested launching significant airplane, missile, and drone attacks against them. Instead, our initial response was so feeble that the Houthis have become bolder and bolder. Nor have we appropriately punished the Iranians for helping Russia against Ukraine. I greatly fear that our cowardice everywhere will blunder us into a global conflict.

Finally, the Biden Administration's mishandling of the Middle East has given China greater opportunity to gain influence in the Middle East. In 2023, when Saudi Arabia and Iran announced new steps to improve diplomatic ties, they did so from Beijing, and China depicted itself to the world as the intermediary responsible. The United States has tragically lost ground in the Middle East. The formerly strong relationship with Saudi Arabia and the other Gulf states may be retrievable, but only if we are consistent in our dealings with them. Any relationship features ups and downs, but when either side makes a mistake, the other needs to provide a bit of slack. Too much is at stake to do otherwise.

Tangling with Turkey

Like Saudi Arabia, Turkey was also another strategically important country where the relationship required a lot of give-and-take. I had first met President Erdoğan several years ago when Mike Bloomberg invited a dozen professional investors to meet him in his hotel room in New York City. There was very strict security both in the lobby and on his floor, indicating his preoccupation with possible assassination attempts. Additionally, the day we met was a swelteringly hot summer afternoon, but the air-conditioning in his room was turned off. When asked why, Erdoğan's security head said, "We are afraid that someone might put poison gas in the air conditioner."

Prior to Trump becoming President, President Erdoğan had made a deal to buy F-35 fighter planes from the United States. But President Obama canceled the sale because of human rights issues. The Turks then contracted to buy the S-400 air defense system from Russia. President Trump and

Jared were concerned about a NATO member country bringing in a Russian defense system, something that would pose a
risk to NATO planes and also further deepen Russo-Turkish
ties. Turkey's economy was already heavily dependent on
Russia for natural gas.

To try to solve the problem, the President was prepared
to reinstate the fighter contract. But the Russian air defense
system had to go. As a sweetener to induce Erdoğan to drop
the Russian deal, Trump was willing to promise a massive
trade program. Jared asked me to develop in great detail one
that would build up to $50 billion of annual trade in each
direction after five years. At the time, Turkey imported about
$11 billion from us, and we imported about the same amount
from them, so the solutions for boosting those numbers took
a great deal of creative thinking, to say the least. I was then to
go to Ankara and Istanbul and sell the proposal to Erdoğan
and the Turkish business community.

The plan we developed to reach the targets had an abun-
dance of ideas. For one, most individual Turkish companies
were too small to be able to service the U.S. market, so there
would have to be a government-led consolidation effort in
certain industries. Second, while the average Turkish wage
rates were relatively low, the economy needed an injection of
automation to bring labor costs in line with Asia and Mexico
and make Turkish production of textiles, shoes, apparel,
and fashion accessories even more competitive. Turkey also
would need to create trade missions to the United States and
permanent marketing presences here, in large part to sell their
fabulous resorts, beaches, and historical sites. To help the
nascent Turkish aerospace industry, we would agree to have
a substantial percentage of the F-35 fighter parts made there.
Turkey's strong food processing industry would receive our
help in getting clearances for the U.S. market. Turkey would

also need to change its patent and trademark laws and commit to strict enforcement. The list went on and on.

The Turkish finance minister—Erdoğan's son-in-law—liked the specificity of our proposals and recognized the impact they would have on their struggling economy. He agreed to take me to the President and strongly support the deal. He did ask for one favor in return. He was trying to convince his father-in-law that it would take massive interest rate increases and devaluation of the currency to curb the inflation that was ravaging the country. He asked me if I would help him convince the President to adopt those policies. I did not want to detract from my own agenda, so I simply agreed that if Erdoğan raised the question I would respond that such programs had worked in other countries, but I did not know enough about Turkey to be sure it would work there. I also volunteered to recommend some international economists who can provide technical assistance if they felt that would be useful. The meeting went well, although Erdoğan was a bit skeptical about the scale of the proposal. He agreed to have his commerce minister set up meetings for me to meet with the major business groups and said that if I could convince them he would give the proposal serious thought.

With this level of cooperation secured, I met during the next several days in Turkey with every industry association and the heads of several major individual companies, with lavish entertainment and dinners every night. By the end of the week, there had been enough media coverage and enough words of support going directly to Erdoğan that he invited me for a debriefing. He said he was going to New York in a couple of weeks, where he would put on a dinner for the leaders of the 350,000–500,000 Turkish Americans. He wanted me to be the featured speaker and describe the program.

True to his word, a few weeks later, he took over the party space at Cipriani in New York City, which had formerly been the vast ground floor of the Drydock Savings Bank. His commerce secretary gave me a glowing introduction and there was lots of applause after my talk. Erdoğan then stood up and said, "Ross gets it." But he also went on to propose that Turkey would both keep the Russian defense system and buy American F-35s while executing the trade proposals. Clearly his strategy was to have the dinner guests pressure our Administration to accept this "compromise." His strategy of having his cake and eating it too did not work. Our military could not accept the package. Despite all sorts of assurances by the Turks, there was a great danger that the Russians would learn too much about our stealth fighters as the Turks programmed the S-400 to avoid shooting at them. The big trade deal did not go forward, but its negotiation did a lot to ease tensions between the two nations. It also once again demonstrated the President's and Jared's ability to think outside the box.

On a personal note, I was very impressed with Istanbul. The days I spent there selling the trade deal was my first visit to one of the world's most historic and exotic cities. The people seemed to be very pro-American, notwithstanding their country's involvement with Russia. Erdoğan himself is a very tough and sophisticated negotiator. After the outbreak of the war in Ukraine, he extracted meaningful concessions in connection with the admission of Sweden to NATO and has positioned himself cleverly relative to the EU. Turkey is exempt from tariffs on its exports to the EU but is not subject to EU governance. Thus, Turkey has been able to borrow a bit from the Trump Administration's trade plan and become a major supplier to the enormous Spanish merchandiser Zara.

Free and Fair Trade?

You don't normally think of someone who founded a non-profit organization as an entrepreneur, but Klaus Schwab is an exception. In 1971, Klaus held the first-ever World Economic Forum (WEF) conference in Davos, Switzerland. The WEF has since grown into a hundred-million-dollar conference business, and its centerpiece event remains the five-day conference in Davos, Switzerland, a small ski resort with a surprisingly large building that can accommodate thousands of attendees. The guest list includes political leaders from most major and many minor countries as well as CEOs of multinational companies, private equity funds, hedge funds, and sovereign wealth funds. The mainstream media camps out there, too, and constantly interviews participants, usually outdoors in the freezing cold. Some liberal pundits have accused Klaus of selling out to big business, but I think that if anything Davos remains to the left, or at least to my left.

President Trump had an opportunity to speak at the 2018 gathering, but he was on the fence about it. For one thing, Davos represents a collection of global finance and business leaders who mostly were opposed to President Trump's attempts to correct trade imbalances through tools such as tariffs. Klaus asked me to help convince President Trump to lead a U.S. delegation and be the keynote speaker. My pitch to the President was, "President Xi stole the show last year and this would be an easy maiden appearance for you before a very influential audience with no worry about a hostile Q and A."

The President ultimately overcame his visceral aversion to multinational conferences and attended. Once on the ground, the biggest problem our delegation faced was that in the two days before we arrived thirty-six inches of snow had fallen, so we had to attach cleats to our rubber boots. In general, the President's speech focused on the unparalleled opportunities the United States affords foreign investors, and how his Administration's efforts at tax reform and deregulation were making the business environment even more hospitable. The speech received an excellent response, benefiting from being carefully worded to avoid the stridency that sometimes is part of Trump's stump speeches.

For my part, I had about thirty small "pull-asides" with other attendees, usually friendly get-togethers with counterparts from other governments. My best engagement, however, was a small dinner hosted by Klaus and his wife. The only other attendees were the kings and queens of Netherlands and Belgium, a few lesser European royals, and me. I guess that was my reward for encouraging Trump's participation.

The most amusing meal was a luncheon hosted by my friend Lally Weymouth of the *Washington Post*. It was largely a humorous event with the amusement led by David Rubenstein, a cofounder of the Carlyle Group. David began his remarks by saying he hoped Trump would make his mark on the economy faster than Jimmy Carter, in whose White House David had served. He added, "After all, it took our administration several years to create rampant inflation!" David brought the house down with laughter at this self-deprecatory remark. He then went on to say, "I hope the new administration's policies will be supportive of the most important underpinning of our economy—the private equity industry." More laughter, and so it went.

But Davos was not all laughs. The panels I participated in— mainly on issues related to trade, export controls, or maritime matters—were mostly hostile. They featured self-avowed free traders challenging our Administration's policies. Thus, President Trump's speech, for all its appeal, also made an important point to the Davos audience about his efforts to reform free trade:

> We are also working to reform the international trading system so that it promotes broadly shared prosperity and rewards to those who play by the rules. We cannot have free and open trade if some countries exploit the system at the expense of others. We support free trade, but it needs to be fair and it needs to be reciprocal.[34]

This was a courageous message to deliver to the Davos crowd, which needed reeducation on the concepts of free trade. Primarily, the use of tariffs as a tool of economic policy is not an historical aberration. For more than a century after the American Revolution, tariffs were the U.S. government's main source of revenue, before the federal income tax was introduced in 1913. The United States even continued tariffs throughout the Depression. After World War II, U.S. policy was to rebuild Europe and Asia through both direct aid programs like the Marshall Plan and low tariffs. The United States was then the dominant economic power, exporting our goods all over the world, so these unfavorable arrangements were a smart temporary policy to help war-torn nations resist communism. But asymmetrical trade relationships were not time-limited, as they should have been. Instead, they were formalized, first by the General Agreement on Tariffs and Trade and later by the World Trade Organization (WTO), an entity that outright encourages countries to export to the United States. As a result, by the 1970s, the United States had major trade deficits instead of its traditional surpluses. The problem was compounded when we accepted China and others into the WTO on the theory they would play by the rules. With no effective and prompt enforcement mechanism to hold them accountable, they didn't.

To compound the difficulty of reversing the tide, international trade negotiations are far more complex than commercial negotiations, potentially covering thousands of categories of economic activity. Therefore, the parameters for a mutually acceptable deal are similarly more complicated. Additionally, true reciprocity, as measured by a bilateral trade balance, is difficult to obtain for the U.S. Because our internal market is so much bigger than any other nation's, any truly fair trade deal we strike would entail a vastly asymmetrical outcome for them. Even China, in a true reciprocal scenario, would have to increase access to its economy by as much as 50 percent of its current GDP just to maintain the present U.S.-China trade deficit. Insisting on strict reciprocity has not been our historical pattern. Nor have we in many cases insisted that agreed-upon provisions be implemented simultaneously. U.S. concessions often have come into effect years before our counterparties' do. They have usually materialized belatedly, if at all, because our trade deals too often have had no effective enforcement mechanisms.

Today, free trade has become a delusionary dream. China's threat to American global leadership is substantially due to the benefits it derives from WTO membership and from American direct investment. Our corporate investments in China during the last ten years alone have been about $1 trillion, while our trade deficit in goods from 2017 through 2022 was approximately another $2.1 trillion. Many of our investments have happened though of joint ventures which open opportunities for intellectual property theft. China has also deployed a strategy wherein it creates excess capacity in a certain product category to drive global prices down and attempt to put competitors out of business. This has already happened with solar panels and LED screen televisions, and the playbook is now being run with semiconductors and electric vehicles.

The Trump Administration saw this happening with steel, as well. Global steel demand is about 1.5 billion tons per year. But global supplies amount to about 2 billion tons per year, with China responsible for about half of that. That kind of excess production, which drives prices downward, has contributed to the hollowing out of the American steel industry. To restore the equilibrium lost long ago, the Administration slapped tariffs on Chinese steel using national security authorities. But doing so was not without controversy. Many American interests—factories, assembly plants, etc.—are tied up with China, and U.S. businesses didn't want to absorb new costs for raw materials. Still, these tariffs were necessary, and we imposed steel tariffs on thirty-five countries over offenses such as countervailing duties, anti-dumping, and illegal subsidies. Even with tariffs in place, China got sneaky in trying to dodge them. Under WTO rules, countries don't just tariff "steel" as an amorphous entity. Tariffs must be applied via specific product codes tracked by customs authorities. The Chinese would make a little adjustment to each steel product in such a way that the codes didn't apply.

Another product that deserved and received tariffs were Chinese electric vehicles. The Chinese car industry has grown significantly in the past two decades, and the Chinese were (and are still) positioning their electric vehicle industry to dominate the world. I had a feel for what was going to happen because I had seen the Chinese run this strategy with success in the auto parts industry. At the time, the Chinese were barely exporting any EVs here, so they didn't put up a big

fight. But now that the Biden Administration has incentiv-
ized EV adoption and Chinese companies such as BYD have
gone global, I say with humility that it was a prescient move.
Much of the credit for implementing these tariffs goes to Bob
Lighthizer, the U.S. Trade Representative, who was an outstanding advocate for sensible trade policies. The title of his
book alone—*No Trade Is Free*—is enough to give you a fla-
vor of his views.

Bringing reciprocity to trade deals with the United States' North
American neighbors was also a priority for the President. As
just one example, Canada's heavily subsidized timber exports
crossed the border freely, depressing the American logging
industry. Commerce levied a 20 percent tariff on Canadian
lumber. We also fought against Canada's exclusionary measures
against American dairy farmers. But the main trade instrument
that needed to be fixed was the North American Free Trade
Agreement (NAFTA). Among other flaws, NAFTA was obso-
lete because it took effect in 1994, before the modern digital
economy emerged. Second, the rules regarding the origin of certain products were outdated. NAFTA specified exactly which
parts had to be made in the United States. Half the parts used
in cars back then aren't used anymore, and many electronic
components are now found in automobiles which didn't exist
when NAFTA entered into force. Over time, it became easier
and cheaper for Mexican companies to export parts into the
United States that were not covered under NAFTA.

To that end, talks on the U.S.-Mexico-Canada Agreement
began in the spring of 2017. A great deal of our strategy centered on how Mexico would benefit under a new deal. As
we reduced trade with China, Mexico would be the prime

beneficiary if it could develop a workforce that was less transitory (Mexican workers would often migrate from job to job and send remittances home). Additionally, opening hydrocarbon development in Mexico to American companies would reduce fuel prices and increase exports because Pemex, the Mexican state-owned oil company, was not well run. Finally, the renegotiation presented a long-desired opportunity to resolve long-standing agricultural issues, as I recently had done for Mexican sugar and tomatoes in separate negotiations with Mexican representatives. We also had a positive predicate for the USMCA in an agreement I had negotiated with my Mexican counterpart providing for a reciprocal enforcement of patents and trademarks. Mexican companies loved this, because they had developed some important brands that wanted American legal protections as they tried to capture the ever-growing Hispanic population here. In the end, the USMCA was clinched at the end of 2018. I can't take credit for negotiating it—that overwhelmingly belongs to Jared Kushner and Bob Lighthizer. But I was proud to help contribute to this landmark trade agreement that restored a sense of fairness to the trade ties with our closest neighbors.

President Trump also aggressively defended American businesses against other unfair foreign actions, such as his campaign against India's confiscatory import tariffs on Harley-Davidson motorcycles and medical imports. I had a huge debate with the Indian Health Minister over stents. There are many sources of commoditized stents sold in India at low prices, but when Johnson & Johnson introduced a new and greatly improved version, India ordered that it be sold at the same price as the inferior ones. In response, J&J tried to withdraw the product from the market, but the Indian authorities said they must then withdraw all their products, an obvious incident of blackmail. I argued that this was manifestly unfair. Ultimately, India relented a bit.

The OECD

The Trump Administration also tangled with European nations quite a bit on trade. I led talks with the EU before Lighthizer was appointed U.S. Trade Representative. One of our major complaints was that EU rules were too prohibitive of American food exports. At one point in the negotiations, I told my EU counterpart, "You refuse to allow importation of U.S. livestock and agricultural products claiming they are unsafe. Well, the President and I eat lots of the dangerous foods every day and there is no sign that we are more prone to illness than our European counterparts. In fact, there is no empirical evidence that Europeans live materially longer than Americans, so your food claims are obviously make-believe."

His response was, "Europeans won't buy the American products."

"Then why won't you permit them to be on grocery shelves? If Europeans really don't buy them, we will stop shipping them over."

They had no reply. Ultimately, there is still much work to be done to let American food products obtain access to markets in Europe and the United Kingdom.

Just as seriously, I had recommended steel and aluminum tariffs to the President, which he applied to the EU early in his presidency. Not only were these tariffs useful to protecting the American steel industry, but they signaled to the rest of the world—the Koreans, Japanese, Chinese, and others—that the United States was ready to play hardball on trade everywhere if we would tariff our closest allies. The Europeans were predictably furious.

Against the backdrop of these developments, President Trump appointed me to lead the U.S. Delegation to a 2018 meeting of the Organization for Economic Cooperation and Development (OECD) in Paris. The OECD was founded in 1961 to foster economic development and cooperation among its thirty-eight members, mostly European nations. It lacks enforcement power, but on the rare occasions when it takes a unanimous position, it does exert a considerable force of moral persuasion over its member states. Those countries, of course, hated our trade and tariff policies.

This milieu set the table for two controversial meetings at the OECD conference. The first was to inform the OECD Secretary General, Angel Gurría, that the United States would not support his reelection campaign. We couched it more politely, but he got the message. Gurría was a well-polished international diplomat, and he impressed me because he did not get heated over this bad news. He instead blithely described the election process: The search committee would screen internal and external candidates and would make their recommendations to the full board. In effect, he was saying, "I will try to talk my way to reappointment despite your opposition." But he never used those words, never raised his voice, and never showed any emotion. He didn't even so much as wince. And he did ultimately win reelection.

My other tense meeting was with the French Finance Minister, Bruno Le Maire, to explain that neither the EU overall nor France individually would be exempted from U.S. steel and aluminum tariffs, and that we intended to impose the maximum penalties on French exports for violations of WTO subsidy rules committed by the French aviation giant Airbus. Le Maire became furious, saying, "You should not treat your allies like that! Boeing committed just as many violations as Airbus did!" I simply responded, "I am sorry, Mr. Minister, but the decision has been made, and we believe the Boeing subsidies are a small fraction of those received by Airbus."

Indeed, French companies are among the most highly subsidized in Europe. But all of Europe, especially Germany, benefits from a sly subsidies scheme. Every European export obtains a rebate of the EU's 20 percent Value Added Tax (VAT). Since the VAT applies on all imports, but is rebutted on exports, a European export is cheaper in the United States than in its home country. Meanwhile, every American export costs 20 percent more in Europe than in the United States. This effectively is a huge distortion of costs for a direct subsidy for individual activities.

Those were a couple of difficult days at the OECD meetings, but Paris is still Paris, so I had a good dinner with our Ambassador to France, Jamie McCourt, and went back to D.C. in the morning. This OECD meeting and others with similar multinational organizations are mostly useful to the talking heads who populate them. At the end of the day, countries generally look after their own interests, as they should. Multilateral bodies tend to be biased against the United States because their member states all want something from us, so we are the odd man out.

This leads to my final comment on the postwar trade system: It does not create harmony between nations in the way free traders think it will. Our trade deficits with China prove this point. To a lesser extent, our trade deficits with Europe have not convinced NATO member states to pay their fair share for defense, and some parts of the EU have been very slow to help with Ukraine or Gaza. Germany has long depended on Russian natural gas, but that relationship did not deter Russia from invading Ukraine. Nor is free trade helpful in terms of climate cooperation. Germany has been reviving coal-fired utility plants and China's carbon dioxide emissions increase every year. Theories that free trade creates momentum in other policy areas are weak at best.

In the end, being Secretary of Commerce was often an international sales job. I sold the tariffs as necessary to reform trade relationships in ways that served the United States. And I also sold the United States as a foreign investment destination. At one point I spent ten days in southeast Asia, including becoming the first-ever Secretary of Commerce to travel to Laos. It may not sound like much, but that trip was of great strategic importance to our competition with China. Building up the Foreign Commercial Service—officers on the hunt for deals for American companies abroad—and bringing foreign companies to the United States every year for the Select USA summit were also part of the sales job. Many parts of the American economy must be fixed to stem the outsourcing of jobs and wealth abroad. But American prosperity in the twenty-first century will continue to depend greatly on our relationships with international trade partners. American leadership in both sustaining and reforming the global trading order will remain indispensable.

CHAPTER 13

Confronting China

As the Trump Administration was departing Washington, the President's economic advisor, Larry Kudlow, called and said, "Wilbur, I am jealous of you. I never made the cut!"

"What cut, Larry?"

"The Chinese government just announced that they have sanctioned you and Pompeo, but not me!"

It was true—the Chinese government slapped sanctions on twenty-eight former Trump Administration officials within minutes of President Biden taking office. To this day I have never been officially notified of the sanction or what it really means, but I am certainly not going to China anytime soon. This chapter explains why China levied sanctions on me and the other Trump Administration officials.

In 1985, Donald J. Trump bought the former estate of businesswoman Majorie Merriweather Post, a seventeen-acre parcel across the road from the exclusive Bath & Tennis Club in Palm Beach, Florida. Mrs. Post had bequeathed it to the U.S. government for diplomatic use, but the upkeep was too expensive, so the government returned it to the Post Foundation, which put it back on the market. With his usual cleverness, Trump bought it and recouped much of the purchase price by auctioning off the antique furniture and silverware, replacing them with good reproductions. Trump's original plan was to subdivide and develop the estate, but the town council turned him down, so he made it into a private club and lived there himself. Once he was President, it became a "Winter White House," just as President John F. Kennedy had created with a home several miles north of Mar-a-Lago in Palm Beach.

In 2017, President Trump hosted President Xi and a full delegation from China at his resort. The kickoff to the visit— billed as a summit—was to be a 6:00 p.m. formal dinner in Mar-a-Lago's Great Hall, with both parties seated on either side of one long table.

Shortly before the dinner, something big came up.

In the hours prior to the meeting, a White House aide called with a request for me to come to the Sensitive Compartmented Information Facility (SCIF) on the estate at 4:00 p.m. for an urgent meeting of the National Security Council. Naturally, she didn't give any details on an unsecured line. The SCIF was a small windowless room specially equipped with heavy metallic curtains to prevent eavesdropping, with a secure TV at one end. Once we were all assembled, the President announced that he might launch missiles into Syria in retaliation for a heinous chemical weapons attack on Syrian civilians. After about a thirty-minute discussion about what to do, including a recommendation from "Mad Dog" Jim Mattis, the Secretary of Defense, we decided to launch a strike at 7:50 p.m. that evening local time, with the admonition of secrecy until the strike occurred. I went back home, deflected all inquiries from my wife, got changed, and went back for the reception and dinner.

During the meal itself, President Xi dominated the conversation with his tediously detailed version of Chinese history. He explained how China had been the most powerful nation in the world, and a highly cultured one, when our European forebears were still running around in loincloths. He went through the maltreatment of China by the British and other Western nations, and was just getting to World War II and the Japanese occupation when a White House aide brought President Trump a note, which he read quickly and put into his pocket. He then said, "Please excuse me for interrupting you, President Xi, but there is an urgent message I must reveal to you. The United States has just launched fifty-nine missiles into Syria. I know your intelligence will soon pick it up, but I wanted you to hear it directly from me."

President Xi, who had been speaking in Chinese with simultaneous translation, said in perfect English, "Repeat please." His translator repeated the message in Chinese. In my mind, the whole scene showed that Trump is not afraid of Xi. Shooting missiles in the middle of dinner, it seemed, sent a very deliberate message to the Chinese leader.

Xi seemed equally steely. Without batting an eye, he said through the translator, "Mr. President, you certainly have been having a busy evening," and reverted to his history lesson exactly where he had left off, as though little had happened. Xi was determined not to let anything interfere with his lecture. It was characteristic of how Chinese representatives would always stay on message. Not even a missile strike can distract them. This is the kind of focused potential adversary that America is up against in the twenty-first century. As Secretary of Commerce, I was proud to have done my part to protect the American national and economic security from the Chinese Communist Party.

How the West Was Won Over

My experience with China and the Chinese people did not begin in government. Over the course of my business career, I had some investment in seventeen different plants in the country, manufacturing everything from auto parts, to electronics, to textiles, and more. As a result, I traveled all over China and made many friends there. If you are fortunate enough to make friends with a Chinese person, you have a friend for life. The Chinese also have an incredible work ethic. But China is not an easy country in which to do business. It's a highly corrupt society, where bribery and dishonoring of contracts are routine practices. When you try to collect on accounts receivable, the Chinese are slow to pay and often ask for a discount. Nor are Western concepts of intellectual property respected there, thus enabling lots of counterfeiting and other illegal transfers of proprietary knowledge. Years earlier when we owned Burlington, I was on a Commerce Department trade mission to Beijing. As we neared the U.S. Consulate, I saw that immediately next door was a block-long double row of outdoor stalls called Silk Alley. Each vendor had racks of knockoffs of famous U.S. brands at low prices. When we met with the Embassy staff, I asked, "What do you think about Silk Alley?" They answered in unison, "It's great! We buy all our clothes there!" That was my first real-world contact with how our government's trade policy teams worked, or more accurately, did not work, to protect U.S. interests.

The story of how the Chinese Communist Party (CCP) lifted millions of Chinese out of poverty is mostly a myth. Contrary to the government's official narrative, the CCP had little to do with it besides, ironically, opening the country to Western capitalists. Growth was extremely spotty until the first wave of economic liberalization led by Deng Xiaoping in the early 1980s, when a few select Western companies were allowed in. Growth did not occur in a smooth and rapid upward trajectory until China joined the WTO in 2001, further opening the floodgates for American companies. Between trade deficits and American foreign direct investment, the United States has put more than 10 trillion dollars into their country, to say nothing of the rest of the world. China's export surplus is 1.5–2 percent of world GDP, so that amount of all economic activity ends up to their benefit.[35] When factoring in China's mass intellectual property theft of Western knowledge, really it is the West that has created China's prosperity—largely inadvertently.

Why did the West decide to trade so robustly with a communist power? The answer is partly humanitarian: President Clinton liked lifting people out of poverty and made concessionary deals with many developing countries. All were at our expense, but the others were small compared to China. Clinton also hoped that more Chinese interaction with the West and higher standards of living would draw China away from communism and cause the country to play by the rules in the international arena. The mistake in allowing China into the WTO was failing to impose a rapid and effective enforcement mechanism in the accession agreement. Instead, the United States insisted upon a WTO appellate court, which arrogated policymaking to itself more than it impartially adjudicated disputes. The vast majority of cases that the court agreed to hear were actually brought against the United States, with the vast majority of those rulings adverse to us, as well. During the Trump Administration, the court specifically violated the WTO rule that each nation had the right to make its own national security determination by ruling against our decision to impose steel and aluminum tariffs, which we issued on national security grounds. We ignored that decision. The Trump Administration also vetoed all appointments of new court members so that they had no quorum. Bizarrely, the last remaining member was Chinese.

Chinese influence at the WTO reminds me of how China has pushed hard for leadership positions in multilateral commercial bodies. When the election of a new Director General for the World Intellectual Property Organization came up in 2020, the leading contenders were from China and Singapore. Nothing could be more absurd than to have China setting and enforcing international laws protecting intellectual property, so I lobbied hard for the candidate from Singapore, who ultimately won. At the International Telecom Union, I was able to lobby Americans into high positions, but not the highest.

Much of our ability to compete against China and other nations is hamstrung by leftists at home. They fight to sign treaties that implement feel-good policies, but whose substance is averse to American economic interests. Under the Paris Climate Accords, for example, the United States could incur billions of dollars of near-term costs associated with mitigation of climate change. But China is free to increase emissions with no constraints until 2030, with their only obligation in the meantime to make their best effort to control pollution. Once again, John Kerry traded feel-good headlines for a deal that neither achieved its stated objective nor made economic sense. Another case in point of a bad deal with China is the so-called de minimis provision governing international shipments from China. In 2016, President Obama signed legislation stipulating that any small package coming from China whose contents are worth less than $800 is not subject to import duties. Chinese retailers such as Temu and Shein have exploited this provision to build their business of shipping cheap apparel to the United States, while U.S.

companies pay millions in comparable duties. Even worse, only a tiny fraction of the packages shipped annually are subject to inspections, which occur randomly. God only knows how many of the roughly 460 million small packages that came from China in 2021 contained fentanyl components or other narcotics.[36]

Early in the Administration, prior to the confirmation of Bob Lighthizer as U.S. Trade Representative, the statutory authority responsible for negotiating trade treaties, President Trump sent me to China to try to negotiate some quick concessions so that he could have some early wins. I ultimately negotiated about $70 billion in immediate concessions, including some opportunities for U.S. beef. To celebrate the agreement, the President was scheduled to bring a small delegation to China, including the then-Secretary of State, Rex Tillerson. But by the time the trip was about to occur, my friend Bob had been confirmed. He advised the President that making too big a deal out of these concessions might make it more difficult to obtain major long-term concessions regarding intellectual property, industrial espionage, dumping, and other issues. Trump was therefore inclined to cancel the trip even though representatives from American companies were en route to the signings. Tillerson ultimately convinced him that cancellation would be viewed as a major faux pas, so President Trump made the trip but we low-keyed the concessions with the media.

Much later, Ambassador Lighthizer negotiated a more extensive Phase One agreement and plans were announced for Phase Two. But COVID intervened and our administration ended in January 2021. China has not followed through on many of its Phase One commitments and there has never been a Phase Two negotiation, although both Secretary of State Tony Blinken and the Secretary of Treasury Janet Yellen each have made several trips to China. Because China has not lived up to its initial Phase One commitments, the additional tariffs imposed as part of Lighthizer's strategy for restoring balance in the U.S.-China trade relationship have remained.

In retrospect, our trade policies should have been more precisely tailored, both in terms of what to keep out and what to let in. In my view, China's worst export to us is chemicals for the manufacture of fentanyl. When asked by President Trump in my presence if China had a drug problem, the answer from a Chinese official was "No! Selling narcotics to Chinese citizens is a crime punishable by death and we enforce it strictly." He could have added, but did not, "But we do not punish those who export the ingredients." Indeed, China sells the raw precursor chemicals to Mexico, where the cartels process it and send it to the United States. The renegotiation of the USMCA could have been an ideal opportunity for keeping these toxins out of the United States.

Equally as infectious as fentanyl are COVID-19 and TikTok. The debate about whether COVID-19 was developed in a Wuhan lab or not is almost immaterial, because we do know that early in the pandemic, the Chinese government banned flights from Wuhan to Beijing and other major Chinese cities but let them continue to the United States and Europe uninterrupted. This selectivity suggests an evil intent. Similarly, TikTok is not permitted to operate in China, but after the House of Representatives voted for ByteDance's divestment of TikTok in 2024 the Chinese government said they would not permit the sale of the company to American interests. My interpretation is that they like the anti-U.S. messages that go to our teenagers, and enjoy even more the fact that they know more about our young people than their parents might. When a friend of mine recently eliminated TikTok from her iPhone, the app notified her that it would no longer have access to her emails and photo library. The Senate has followed the House's lead in voting to force a divestment of TikTok from its Chinese parent company ByteDance, a praiseworthy instance of bipartisan cooperation.

But China is not without major problems of its own. A recent economic slowdown has exposed structural economic problems. Nearly all of China's vast economic improvement has been concentrated in urban areas, and there is at least a 3:1 income disparity in urban versus rural areas. When China was growing fast, ambitious young people would migrate to cities for good jobs and found a better quality of life. Now the jobs aren't there, and people are being forced back to villages, where they become disgruntled and make trouble by doing things like going on strike. Consequently, the number of incidents of violent unrest in rural China has grown. On a more macro level, besides foreign money coming in, China has always been driven by debt. As of 2023, debt was 287 percent of GDP.[37] This portends a heavy load for the government to manage in the future, one compounded by massive problems such as a real estate price collapse and a shadow banking sector.

Xi has decided to respond to economic woes by consolidating political control to an unbelievable extent. Many Chinese billionaires who have proven difficult to control mysteriously disappear. Chinese companies are forced to create political commissariats to ensure that business decisions accord with political ones. Within Chinese state-owned enterprises (SOEs), party secretaries are more powerful than CEOs. Most of them have little or no business expertise and instead are doctrinaire Communist ideologues. Their control is one reason why Chinese SOEs are so inefficient. China's exertion of total political control over its companies could be its biggest handicap in its technological race against us.

Xi's totalitarian behavior is economically counterproductive. But worse than that, it is truly frightening. Dictators love to start wars when things go bad, because they can blame it all on a common enemy, and the Chinese Communist Party regards no nation as an enemy more than it does the United States. Xi has said that he wants to "build a modern socialist country that is prosperous, strong, democratic, culturally advanced and harmonious" by 2049.[38] The centerpiece of his "great rejuvenation" of China is the conquest of Taiwan. Xi wants to go down in history as the equal or superior to Mao Zedong, who himself never accomplished the retaking of the island. If the Chinese military decides to launch an operation against Taiwan, it could trigger a military conflict with the United States.

China Tech Threats

During the Trump Administration, the United States underwent a growing realization of the potential national security threats associated with Chinese technologies. Telecom equipment and many other technologies made by Chinese companies can be used to surveil, propagandize, and steal data from Americans. ZTE Corporation—China's second-largest telecom equipment company—presented one such threat. The Department of Commerce's Bureau of Industry and Security (BIS) is responsible for stopping the export of American technologies of national security significance and enforcing bans on the sale of such technologies to sanctioned countries. BIS investigators determined that ZTE covertly sold products with American components to two sanctioned countries, Iran and North Korea. Our team sent the information to the Department of Justice, which brought a case against ZTE.

In March 2017, ZTE pled guilty. ZTE was so brazen that it continued the prohibited sales even while it knew the United States was preparing to bring charges against it. As a result, we prepared to ban ZTE from purchasing every high-tech American component and impose other penalties.

Unfortunately, the pending action prompted President Xi to call President Trump twice to ask that we not put ZTE out of business. The President thought that agreeing to Xi's request would help him negotiate on broader issues, specifically a trade deal, and asked me to work out a different solution. ZTE was privately owned, and I suspected that high officials in the Chinese government or their families may have been big shareholders. Unfortunately, it was not within our purview to work through ZTE's deliberately confusing mazes of ownership with the goal of targeting its owners for penalties. The Commerce Department negotiated with the company and imposed a fine of $1 billion, the largest fine we had ever levied for export control violations. We also designated a firm to monitor ZTE's compliance with U.S. export controls for ten years on our behalf at their expense. Our monitor would have the right to make unannounced inspections of any of their five hundred related companies at any time and would report its findings to the Department of Commerce every month.

Our work on ZTE led to our battle with Huawei, the world's largest telecom equipment company. Huawei made better technology than ZTE, making them even more dangerous. They too were illegally selling gear to Iran in violation of Americans sanctions. As a result, in 2019, at the president's direction, and on the Commerce Department's recommendation and evidence, the Department of Justice brought charges against them, even levying a charge of bank fraud against its CFO, Meng Wanzhou, the daughter of the CEO.

Canadian authorities apprehended Meng in Vancouver while changing planes and she was kept under house arrest in her home there, pending extradition to the United States. In the meantime, we started imposing export controls on the company. Targeted technologies included the Google Android operating system for its cell phones and every other high-tech item we could identify that the company used to manufacture its products. Without access to cutting-edge American components, Huawei's revenues declined by nearly 30 percent in 2021 from 2020.[39] Unfortunately, China unjustly took two Canadian diplomats hostage in retaliation for Meng's detention, and she eventually was allowed to return to China in 2021 after a prisoner swap and dropped charges.

But our work on Huawei was not finished, even as Meng's fraud case dragged on. Thanks to Chinese state subsidies, Huawei (and ZTE) had destroyed the price structure for 5G equipment worldwide, leaving a huge opening for them to dominate the world 5G market. Our concern was that Huawei phones, routers, and other technologies might be leveraged as devices for reporting sensitive data back to China. We referred to it as "calling home." Not even carefully screening the devices was a sufficient solution, because the Chinese designers would know them far better than we ever could. And even if a product was clean originally, there would be multiple opportunities to infiltrate something into it via the monthly maintenance and periodic updating processes. Multinational Huawei-led 5G networks were unacceptable from a national security perspective, so Secretary of State Mike Pompeo and I convinced many foreign governments not to buy from them. As noted, there was no American company to provide the whole system, so we effectively were lobbying for Samsung and Ericsson as the alternative—albeit a more expensive one. The Chinese continued to compete, as well.

After I had convinced Argentina not to buy Huawei phones, the company had the nerve to go back to the Argentines and ask if it could get, as a consolation prize, a commitment for equipment just for the Argentinian national security agency. There is still much work to be done to convince nations to keep Chinese tech out of their diplomatic and military networks.

In total, export controls are a very useful weapon for stopping China's tech dominance, but administering them entails difficult choices. Every dollar of exports curtailed is a dollar of sales lost by an American company, so the Commerce Department must balance two conflicting goals: maximizing national defense objectives and minimizing the collateral damage to our economy. It took some courage to impose export controls on a couple of hundred products in total. These were mostly to China, but every sanctioned country also was on the list. Almost equally complex were Committee on Foreign Investments in the United States (CFIUS) cases examining whether certain foreign acquisitions of U.S. companies presented national security risks. A key problem is that China routinely pays a much higher price to purchase American companies than any other suitor would, and the American sellers usually campaigned hard for the federal government to approve deals. The departments of Treasury, Commerce, Defense, and State are the decision-makers on CFIUS matters. I generally voted to ban transactions outright, because I knew from export controls that monitoring complex international deals is very difficult. The other agencies tended to prefer contractual limitations on behavior—something that was naive because of the CCP's proclivity to dishonor agreements and lie about what it is doing.

Our Administration's China efforts won mixed levels of support on Capitol Hill. Some Republican senators, most notably John Cornyn, Tom Cotton, Marco Rubio, and Dan Sullivan, were strongly supportive, but many others were ardent free traders. Interestingly, Senator Schumer was aggressively anti-China. Every time I would pass by him at a White House function, he would wag his right forefinger at me and say very loudly, "Wilbur—China! More effort against China!" As indicated at the beginning of this chapter, Larry Kudlow also supported our China policies even though he is an ardent free trader. He recognized that China's egregious behavior put it into a category of its own. That is why he made the call to me described at the beginning of this chapter. Unlike so many economists, Larry knows that economic theory must accommodate actual reality.

The CHIPS Act

American semiconductor needs are vast. The United States consumes 25 percent of the world's chips used in electronic goods,[40] but only produces about 12 percent of global supply inside our borders.[41] We import the rest, mainly from fabrication plants (fabs) in China, Taiwan, and elsewhere. Our economy cannot function, even in peacetime, without these imports, so we are terribly vulnerable in the event of war.

In the case of semiconductors, the Trump Administration was not too worried about the older, less efficient chip designs, but very concerned with the most advanced, smaller ones. The smaller the basic chip, the more room for adding power and capabilities. When I say small, I mean miniscule in the extreme. Chips are measured in terms of nanometers (nm), or, the size of each transistor that can fit on a chip. For reference, the width of a human hair is 80,000-100,000 nanometers. The most abundant chips are those with transistors fourteen nanometers or larger. The Chinese at the time were not capable of producing anything smaller than ten nanometers, while Samsung and Taiwan Semiconductor Manufacturing Company (TSMC) already had developed five-nanometer ones involving a technology called extreme ultraviolet lithography. Only TSMC and Samsung currently produce quality five-nanometer chips, and both are pushing toward three nanometers. The smaller sizes enable quantum computing, military, and high-end artificial intelligence capabilities. We targeted Chinese advanced chip design and fabrication capabilities with export controls. Much credit for cooperation goes to the Dutch, which has convinced ASML, the sole producer of extreme ultraviolet lithography technology, not to sell the highest-end equipment to China. China is still throwing untold tens of billions of dollars into catching up at the smallest node sizes, but they are probably five to ten years behind, and the world's nanometer targets continue to go smaller, so it will be hard for Chinese companies to be totally competitive with firms domiciled in free nations for many years.

Between the United States losing its status as a chip manufacturing nation and the dangers of depending on Chinese supply chains for technologies as fundamental as semiconductors, I initiated what eventually became the CHIPS Act—a subsidy program to incentivize companies to build chip fabs inside the United States. Republicans generally don't like subsidies, which today often go by the name of "industrial policy." But we reasoned that supporting the chip companies was a wise expenditure of government money. Trump was initially lukewarm on the idea, because, as he explained, "I don't want to have government money going to a piss-poor business like Intel." It was true—Intel had lost much ground to competitors like AMD and Qualcomm since its peak boom years of the late 1990s and early 2000s. Intel now has a new CEO, so hopefully they can turn it around.

While the CHIPS Act was not officially passed until 2022, our Administration did much of the early advocacy on Capitol Hill. We also illustrated a proof of concept for reshoring chip manufacturing by working with the state of Arizona and TSMC to convince the company to build its first-ever American factory there. I also wrote to every House Republican member of Congress urging that he or she approve the final bill, even though the Democrats had loaded in so many extraneous provisions. Semiconductors were and are so important to our national security and to our economy that some pork had to be tolerated.

Even though the final bill did pass, the Biden Administration added tens of billions in spending unrelated to producing semiconductors. The Democrats loaded CHIPS with so many expensive frills, such as mandatory childcare centers and union labor mandates that inflate construction costs, that the program became much less attractive than what we had introduced. It makes no sense to create a subsidy and then destroy the economic benefits from it. Once the legislation did pass, the Department of Commerce added provisions to the cost of constructing and operating new chipmaking facilities. The allocation of funds is now subject to so many factors that Commerce hired five young Wall Streeters to act as an in-house investment bank. How ridiculous is it that they made the programs so complex and unwieldly that they had to bring in young outsiders to sort it out for them?

There are two problems with bringing these young guns aboard. First, their presence does nothing to address all the regulatory impediments to new fab construction to which the industry objects. For example, TSMC, the acknowledged world technological leader in chip fabrication, has delayed construction of its fab in Arizona in part because of slow disbursement of CHIPS funding. I take this setback personally, since my staff and I spent two years working with TSMC to build this state-of-the-art facility there. The second problem with adding this new staff will mean more delay while the new group gets up to speed and then proposes and finally implements the process. We don't have the luxury of time. There is also a strong possibility that the worst performing chip company (Intel) will receive the most money.

Additionally, while some of the $39 billion in manufacturing incentives has begun to trickle out, the Commerce Department has established regional technology innovation centers to encourage new technology.[42] Such centers have been tried before and have proven ineffective. They waste appropriations by spending it on feel-good activities that accomplish little or nothing. In fact, my Commerce Department did an analysis by the National Institute of Science and Technology proving that university research was far more productive of commercially usable products than government-sponsored research. Naturally, no mainstream media picked it up. My guess is these centers will waste more money on start-up companies with dubious qualifications instead of committing it to proven industry leaders to make their U.S. plants more competitive with those in Asia.

The bungled implementation of the CHIPS Act is unfortunately proving that the Biden Administration is incapable of implementing an effective industrial policy. If we are to maintain technological leadership, we must win the semiconductor war. There is no room in the cost structure to pay for sociological experiments, however worthy they may seem. Jamming other policy objectives into industrial policy is a major reason why massive European industrial subsidies have been relatively ineffective. We should learn from their mistakes.

Similar inconsistency has arisen regarding the so-called rare earths minerals. Instead of extracting what we need, the Biden Administration is letting climate concerns and other social issues block the mining of the rare earths necessary for high-tech products. From a national security perspective, we cannot afford the risks of continuing to depend on China for these essential materials.

The risks of dependence on China for rare earths were even more clearly brought into focus by my negotiations with Russia, another adversary, over American supplies of uranium. Near the end of my stint as Secretary of Commerce, a prior trade dispute settlement with Russia over purified uranium came up for renewal. Russia is the largest source of enriched uranium used in U.S. nuclear power plants because the supply is so inexpensive. Relying on Russia for power generation is an obvious national security issue, but the utility companies said that scrapping the agreement would cause electricity rates to rise in many markets. My solution was to create a new long-term contract that preserved low rates but gradually reduced the import levels, thus limiting the amount Russia could export to the U.S. I worked the numbers with the few interested U.S. vendors so that they would expand their facilities to provide growing alternative supplies of uranium with no noticeable impact on utility rates, thereby providing the U.S. with an increasingly useful alternative.

Our country, however, remains dependent on imports, mainly from China, of rare earths: lithium, beryllium, and other minerals used in advanced technologies. These are actually not rare because the U.S., Canada, and Australia all have huge reserves. But the processing of these minerals is pollutive, and China has also driven down the price of processing to levels with which the U.S. cannot compete. As a result, the U.S. has had no mechanism prepared for solving this problem.

The environmentalists were totally opposed to the issuance of new permits necessary for extraction, and there was little interest elsewhere in the Administration to do more than commission a study on the matter. I tried to convince the mining authorities in Australia and Canada to jointly subsidize a common processing facility in the U.S., but got nowhere. Nor did the Department of Defense—which needs supplies of rare earths for items such as the F-35—have interest in paying higher prices, so the initiative went begging. The scenario of an America bereft of critical minerals is not a far-fetched hypothetical. In 2010, China restricted exports of certain rare earths to Japan in retaliation for Japan's detention of a Chinese fishing boat captain. More recently, in 2023, China decided to restrict exports of germanium and gallium, elements used in semiconductor production. Perhaps the wars around the world and the COVID-19 pandemic will help people understand the risks involved of depending on China or other adversarial nations for the foundational elements of high-tech products.

COVID-19 Complications

The ultimate Chinese challenge during the Trump Administration was the COVID-19 pandemic. Whether you believe the virus came from the Wuhan wet market or the Wuhan Institute of Virology, it was undoubtedly of Chinese origin and cost more than one million American lives and trillions in economic activity. The public health response mostly came from the National Institutes of Health (NIH). My main direct challenges, as noted elsewhere, were recruiting, training, and equipping more than 400,000 census takers with PPE and managing nearly 50,000 Commerce Department employees now functioning remotely.

The FDA was of practically no help in developing the COVID-19 vaccines. On February 4, 2020, my friend, Department of Health and Human Services Secretary Alex Azar, filed the statement of emergency necessary for the FDA to take emergency action regarding COVID-19 vaccines. Soon thereafter, Pfizer-BioNTech ran a clinical test of approximately 44,000 patients in the strictest format: double blind, placebo controlled.[43] As the seriousness of the pandemic revealed itself, President Trump took the unprecedented step of federally funding the creation of a facility to produce the vaccine once it was approved. Normally, large pharmaceutical companies wait until after approval to spend money on a production facility, but the President correctly decided that the usual cautious approach would delay delivery of the vaccine by six to eight months and result in huge numbers of likely avoidable deaths.

The FDA became furious at this end run around their bureaucratic authority. As we got to early fall, the crisis had intensified, so Trump pressured the FDA to grant an Emergency Use Authorization (EUA) that would permit the vaccine to be used on the highest-risk part of the population. He wanted it cleared before Thanksgiving to protect people attending large family events, but the FDA was unresponsive. It finally granted the EUA on December 11, 2020, but did not give full, final approval for broad use until August 23, 2021. I am not a pharmacological expert, but the FDA's decision-making seemed to me (and certainly to the President) to be inconsistent with the country's needs. While it is easy to second-guess things in hindsight, I have never heard a real explanation of what the FDA learned in the last few months before final approval that wasn't clear at the outset. The nation should be grateful that President Trump had the courage to gamble on prefunding the vaccine's production. My own direct participation was negligible, but I know from personal conversations the extreme annoyance the President had at what happened. This is a particularly pungent example of how overregulation can be problematic, and in this case, dangerous.

This dithering over the vaccine, plus Dr. Anthony Fauci's controversial congressional testimony in early 2024, made me skeptical about how our public health experts operate. My most vivid recollection of the Fauci testimony was that he was repeatedly vague or had no recollection of many events, but did state that the oft-repeated mandate to stand six feet apart had no scientific basis. Rather, Fauci said, "It just somehow appeared."[44] Since this edict caused the closing of schools and businesses, it is shocking that such a consequential policy had such questionable provenance. Moreover, Fauci's initial denial and subsequent admission that federal funding was provided to the now infamous Wuhan, China virology lab was even more unsettling. Fauci's subterfuge makes it hard for me, as a layman, to place much faith in the scientific establishment. Scientific autocrats are so used to being unchallenged by non-experts that they ignore practical realities.

Saving U.S. Steel

Not to be downplayed is the economic damage that China inflicted on the United States by failing to properly report the existence of a dangerous new coronavirus before it spread wildly out of hand. After recovering from problems in the early 2000s, U.S. Steel Corporation began to suffer from the economic slowdown caused by COVID-19. David Burritt, the CEO, called to tell me that the company had only two options. The first was to find $1.5 billion or so to finance building the largest and most energy-efficient mill in North America—a very difficult proposition in the company's current state. The other was to forgo that effort, file for Chapter 11, and clean up its balance sheet to fund the mill as part of its bankruptcy reorganization plan.

I immediately called President Trump and explained the situation. He said, "I don't want U.S. Steel to go bust while I'm President. Find a way to fix it!"

"Mr. President, are you authorizing me to push every part of government to solve this problem?"

He responded, "I am directing you to fix the problem and authorizing you to do whatever is appropriate to accomplish that."

"Yes, sir."

I called Burritt back and said, "This Administration has no intention of having U.S. Steel go bankrupt. Give me a few days to see how we can be helpful."

I then called Kimberly Reed, the chair and president of the Export-Import Bank of the United States, of which I was an ex officio board member, and asked, "Can you finance accounts receivable due to a U.S. company from foreign businesses?" She told me she could.

I said, "You will soon receive a call from U.S. Steel. You have to make your own business decision, but I am telling you that it is administration policy to try to find a responsible way to help them."

I next called Dan Brouillette, the Secretary of Energy, and said, "U.S. Steel is in bad financial shape, but needs money to build the most energy-efficient mill in the United States. Obviously the ultimate decision is yours, but can you give expedited consideration to a loan?" He agreed.

I also called Warren Buffett. "Warren, I know you don't like highly cyclical companies, but U.S. Steel is trading at $8 per share. Management may decide to raise close to a billion or so of equity to build the most energy-efficient steel facility in North America. I am helping them get the debt financing. If they can pull it off, and I think they can, this could be a $20-plus stock in a year."

"Wilbur, send me the papers."

Buffett did not ultimately invest, but his decision to pass was not a mistake. He has a certain investment discipline, and his prior adventures into highly cyclical companies, namely airlines, did not work out as well as he had hoped. If you are a real investor, you should stick to your philosophy. That determination has served Berkshire Hathaway extremely well over the years. My hope had been that his contrarian instinct would prevail here, but it did not.

Meanwhile, I called David Burritt back and said, "Please schedule a board meeting and let me talk to your directors." He agreed. I addressed the Board, saying, "I feel a bit strange calling you, since I used to chair International Steel Group. But I can tell you that this Administration will do everything in its power to prevent you from filing for bankruptcy."

I described my efforts to date in detail and added, "We are working hard to find financial support for you. But you also must have the courage to raise some equity, even at your stock's low price, so you can complete the project. It is in both your company's interest and the national interest that you don't chicken out now."

The board agreed. Soon they launched a successful equity offering through Morgan Stanley, raising more than $500 million, and the stock did go into the $20s. The company later found itself the subject of two takeover bids at much higher prices. The mill was built, and I understand that it has been highly successful. After the call I thought, "How weird is this? When I was in the steel business, we tried to knock them off, but now that I am in government, my job is to save them." I am not sure which role was more satisfying, but I am proud of both.

This anecdote is but one example of the lengths to which President Trump was prepared to go to help U.S. business expand and create jobs. More recently, the Japanese company Nippon Steel offered twice as much as Cleveland Cliffs to acquire U.S. Steel. Unfortunately, Nippon Steel—a company with a history of good labor relations—made a mistake in impolitely failing to give the United Steelworkers a heads-up before the announcement. Though they are now doing damage control to combat the xenophobia and unreasonable national security concerns attached to a takeover, things could have gone much smoother. In January 2024, I wrote an editorial in the *Wall Street Journal* in support of the deal, and maintain that a Nippon Steel acquisition poses no threat to America's economic or national security.[45]

Meeting with China's top officials, participating in national security decisions, and helping save a onetime business rival were pretty exotic experiences after decades spent as a financial fixer. These once-in-a-lifetime events made it worthwhile to accept the pressures of a Cabinet post and the slings and arrows of the Democrats and the media—I felt like I was a small part of history. While years of trade negotiations followed the Mar-a-Lago events, they were not fully concluded by the time President Biden was inaugurated and no noteworthy progress has been made since then. It will fall to future administrations to fully rein in Chinese trade abuses and many other instances of malfeasance. If our leaders zero in on China and only create deals with them that contain meaningful enforcement provisions, America will be better off.

CHAPTER 14

Life after Washington

On January 20, 2021, I found myself without a job. The time I spent serving as Secretary of Commerce went by in a whirlwind fashion. As political appointees are often fond of saying, the days were long, but the years were short. To have survived all four years amid the turmoil of the Trump Administration was an accomplishment unto itself.

Many people have asked me how I did it. First, I had known Trump for a long time, so I knew how to navigate his personality. We also had a lot of one-on-one meetings, so that kept the relationship close. Early on, there was even talk of giving me an office in the White House office building so that I'd be able to make fewer trips back and forth. And while Trump would get occasionally angry with me over things, he knew I would not do anything deliberately to hurt him.

Sadly, my do-no-harm mantra contrasted with many people I served with, even some in the President's inner circle. The Trump Administration was so plagued with high-level leaks because many appointees actually opposed various of his policies and leaked in an effort to undermine them. Some of his appointees, even in positions as high as Chief of Staff, were openly critical of him in discussions with others in and out of the Administration, all the while pretending to be team players. It deprived the President of the basic trust that any president should be able to expect from his staff.

Part of the reason that so many individuals who were not team players found themselves in positions of high power was because Trump had never before held public office, and the Trump Organization had relatively few employees. Therefore, he did not have a cadre of trusted and vetted people he could bring into the many senior positions that needed to be filled quickly. He had to rely heavily on the recommendations of friends, some of whom supported him out of personal relationships rather than belief in his policies. A few sought an appointment to replace a problematic career, and were not Trumpers.

President Trump also demands extreme loyalty, abhors losing, and reacts strongly against those who fail him. Finally, in addition to the fiercely determined efforts of the Democrats to destroy him, he had to contend with all the normal challenges a president faces, plus COVID-19. The media also had it in for Trump, even though his TV appearances greatly boosted their ratings.

These stresses caused from day one a tense set of interactions with staff. Trump is also very impatient. Once, when I was with him at Camp David, he was talking with Melania and me after a meeting and decided it was time to go back to our respective cabins to change for dinner. The President's driver was absent, so Trump jumped into the driver's seat of a golf cart and took us to our destination. The Secret Service freaked out at this, and you can be sure his driver never went missing again!

I was not in D.C. on January 6. My security warned that lots of trouble was likely, so I should work from Palm Beach. Nor did I talk with anyone in the White House that day, so I only know what was communicated through the media. I do not believe that political violence is appropriate regardless of how valid someone's concerns may be. Hopefully in the 2024 election there will be enough poll watchers to assure its legitimacy. I still don't understand why the Capitol Police, the National Guard, and the FBI were so unprepared for the rioting my security anticipated. Had they ramped up beforehand, the day would have been far less destructive.

River Club Imbroglio

On arrival in New York after leaving Washington, I was immediately thrown into the middle of a boiling dispute over the River Club and River House, even though more than one-third of the residents, including some board directors, were members of the club. Some residents felt the club was too elitist, some had had difficulty joining, and some were in arrears on their personal obligations to the club. The controversy had a long history. When the River Club's original lease of the River House space expired in 2015, some tenants wanted to evict them in the erroneous hope that an oligarch would buy the club's 60,000-square-foot space for $100 million and still pay maintenance fees on the property. But what oligarch wants to live in what would basically be a ground-floor apartment? Two-thirds of the River Club's building is underground, so that idea died.

Instead, by 2017, the club had negotiated a new forty-year lease, of which it prepaid millions of dollars in rent. When the pandemic hit in 2020, the club shut down and defaulted on its lease. This reactivated the sale controversy. Finally, in January 2022, I helped organize a shareholder meeting that voted 75 percent in favor of a new twenty-five-year lease. A naysayer on the board had circulated in the proxy fight a chart comparing a sale to a lease on a present value basis, but omitted the residual value of the residential ownership at the end of the lease. My chart showed that just correcting this fundamental error tipped the scales strongly in favor of leasing.

Following the meeting, I informally mediated the painfully slow negotiations between the two sides via Zoom. After another year, the parties finally put out a joint release I had drafted saying they had a deal. But a previously undiscussed dispute between the allocation of the water bill arose, prolonging the negotiations. Then another technical issue cropped up right before the closing, further straining the process. The whole ordeal confirmed an important point: When people negotiate a deal for too long a time, "deal fatigue" sets it. People forget their basic agreement and elevate trivial issues to cataclysmic proportions. I therefore have developed a maxim, "Deals that are going to get done get done promptly." Fortunately, in the case of River Club and River House, the symbiotic needs of both parties finally prevailed. Private clubs are a tricky business. They only break even because of high initiation fees, yet they must be very discerning about who they accept into membership to avoid degrading the compatibility of the members.

Palm Beach Living

Much more pleasant than dealing with the River Club battle was returning more permanently to my home in Palm Beach. In 2003, I bought a house on the Intracoastal Waterway.

The former owner was turned down for an Everglades Club membership, so he left town. As the closing approached, my lawyer sent me the original deed, which included a codicil that said, "No person who is not of the Caucasian race can ever own or lease this property, nor reside on it, except as a domestic servant." I was aghast and would not accept a deed with that restriction. He said, "It is invalid and has been illegal for a few years. I just sent it as a curiosity."

Our Palm Beach house has served us well for many years now, including as a venue for a wedding ceremony that went slightly awry. Pat Wood, my then ninety-two-year-old mother-in-law, decided in the spring of 2014 to marry Ed Ney, age eighty-nine, the retired CEO of Young & Rubicam. They chose to hold the wedding and a small reception at our Palm Beach home on the first Saturday in May, at 5:00 p.m., with a rehearsal an hour before. Late that morning, Pat called to ask if we could delay everything by an hour because they wanted to watch the Kentucky Derby first. We agreed, amused by their set of priorities.

The reverend arrived for the ceremony in his official robes. But after a few minutes, he said, "Wilbur, we have a problem. They forgot the wedding ring at Pat's apartment."

"No problem, we will send someone over to pick it up."

"No, that's not all. There is a bigger problem. They don't have a marriage license. I can't marry them without one."

"I'll have someone look for it. I know they have one because we flew them down a couple of days ago and they went straight to the Marriage License Bureau."

Well, we found the ring, but not the license. When I confessed that to the reverend, he repeated, "I can't marry them without a license." I promised to go myself on Monday and pick one up.

"That won't do."

I joked, "Reverend, you have a binary decision to make. Marry them or I will throw you into Lake Worth."

"You mean with my robes and all?"

"Yes!"

The reverend went ahead with the ceremony, but they never did produce a license, so he withheld a marriage certificate. Months later, in Southampton, the rector of the Dune Church had to ask if we would come to Ed's house and witness the real ceremony, license included. They were officially married. All's well that ends well.

The whole episode reminded me of a zany wedding many years before, when I was the best man at a small ceremony in the Marriage Bureau at City Hall in Manhattan. A friend had decided to marry a girl he had impregnated while in Aspen, Colorado. We got to the "chapel" at City Hall and signed in. One wedding was scheduled ahead of ours so we waited in a pew. This wedding consisted of a very pregnant young woman and a very nervous young man plus her burly father. The administrator pointed to the young man, declaring, "He has no tie. The Justice of the Peace doesn't marry tieless men." The father yelled, "I will fix that!" He took off his heavy leather belt and wrapped it around the lad's neck, proclaiming, "Now he has a tie!" Throughout the ceremony, the father held the belt tightly. I'm sure there's a metaphor there somewhere.

Hilary and I later bought the property next door to our main home in Palm Beach. It became a guesthouse and a party house and doubled our waterfront exposure. To decorate it we hired—who else?—Mario Buatta. At the same time, we hired a gentleman named Mario Nievera to do the landscaping. Renovation of the house required applying to the Town Council. I was traveling on business on the day Hilary went to the municipal building to plead our case, but previously had phoned each council member and the mayor to persuade them to agree with our proposal. Hilary went to the hearing with our lawyer. She had never been to a Palm Beach Town Council meeting before, and she had a front-row seat for some curious decisions. The first case was a man whose beachfront house had semicircular Mexican roof tiles that kept blowing off, leaking water into the house. He wanted to substitute flat shingles. The council turned him down. The next resident reported that Sprinkles, a favorite ice cream place, had a fire, canceling a birthday party for a terminally ill child. The local firemen did a good deed and instead held the party at the firehouse. This woman asked the town for a motion of appreciation to the fire department. One member said, "No. That doesn't deserve anything. They do that all the time." The motion was defeated. Hilary was shell-shocked.

Next came our item. The lawyer explained before each variance why we needed it. The mayor said, "You don't really need variances, you need a better architect," and voted against us. Nonetheless, our requests passed, with the mayor and one other member of the Town Council dissenting. Upon returning to Palm Beach, I called her to say, "A few days ago you agreed to support our application. What is going on?"

She said, "Well, I knew it would pass, but I wanted to show that developers can't just do whatever they want here in Palm Beach."

"I've been called a lot of names over the years, but I've never been called a developer! Why did you tell me that you weren't onboard?" No answer. Small-town politics are bizarre!

In any case, the project was a great success. The house won the Schuler Award from the Preservation Foundation of Palm Beach, and another prize from the state architectural commission. It also was featured in *Architectural Digest* and in several books about Palm Beach houses. The original architect was John Volk, who along with two others, was the major architect of Palm Beach units as late as the 1950s.

Even if the Town Council can make some odd decisions, it does a good job preserving Palm Beach's architectural integrity. Too many resort communities have lost their original charm to high-rise apartments and hotels, but not Palm Beach. Additionally, the town provides splendid uniformed services. The average emergency services response time is ninety seconds. I saw that recently when someone collapsed from a heart attack on the tennis court next to me at the Everglades Club, and again when a person suffered a stroke at a dinner in a private home. Also, the police routinely videotape comings and goings over the bridges into town and immediately deal with anything suspicious. When anti-Trump protestors tried to cross over from West Palm Beach, the town had the drawbridges up, eliminating the problem.

I have also personally experienced the high quality of city services. On our first night in the house, the two new maids somehow locked themselves into a room and were hysterical when we returned home from dinner. A call to 911 gave me locksmiths' numbers, but they were closed. So, they sent two officers over to my home who promptly jimmied the lock and freed the maids. I offered them tips, but they declined, saying, "Here are our business cards. Just call the chief tomorrow and say we did a good job." What other police department is that good? A year later, I crashed a newly acquired drone into the inland waterway. The brackish water had already destroyed the machine, but the fire department retrieved it anyway. Again, they refused to accept a tip! To show my appreciation to the town, I for years chaired the Employee Pension Fund and was vice chair of the project to put all utility lines underground. Meanwhile, rising real-estate values combined with new construction have enabled the mayor and town council to reduce the property tax rate in each of the last three years, all while building a public, par-3 golf course, two new parks, a recreation center, and a yacht basin. If only all municipalities were so well-run!

One of the alluring aspects of Palm Beach for Hilary and me is its social scene. Palm Beach has long been a place where wealthy people hobnob with each other. Brian Mulroney, the former Prime Minister of Canada, sadly recently deceased, frequently said, "When I came to Palm Beach originally, I thought I was old and wealthy, but soon learned I was neither." The demographics have since begun to change as new younger people have moved in, but Brian remains correct about the wealthy part. Fifty-seven billionaires live here, according to the *Palm Beach Daily News* review of the *Forbes 400* list (and they probably missed a few).[46] I can confirm for certain, however, that at least twenty taxpayers each spend more than $1 million annually on property taxes.

Billionaires or not, Palm Beach does attract some of the most interesting people. Years ago, Hilary and I went to a party in town that turned out to be very boring. In a corner stood an elegant man who looked as bored as I was, so I struck up a conversation. It turns out the man was none other than Harry Benson, the world-famous celebrity photographer who is perhaps best known for capturing shots of The Beatles in their early days. We all hit it off great, and Hilary, a writer, did two books with Harry capturing many of the magnificent personalities we have been fortunate to know: *New York, New York* and *Palm Beach People*.

As you might expect from such a resort, where the community is rather small, there always has been joviality among the residents, including pranks. Pepe Fanjul, the Cuban American owner of a sugar conglomerate who has repeatedly made *Vanity Fair*'s best-dressed list, and hedge fund manager Dixon Boardman have been great friends for decades and constantly play pranks on each other. Their most elaborate prank arose when they both were in London, more or less on business, without their wives. They ran into each other three nights in a row at dinner parties. Pepe noticed that at each party the same pretty young woman named Jennifer was seated next to Dixon, and they seemed to get along exceedingly well. Pepe later had a telegram sent to Dixon that read, "Dear Dixon, I so enjoyed our nights together in London and I adore the diamond watch you gave me. Love, Jennifer." Dixon's wife naturally was not amused by the telegram.

When Pepe returned to Palm Beach, Dixon called him, howling that he must admit to the prank. Pepe dutifully called Pauline and said simply, "Dixon tells me I am meant to call you to apologize about the telegram." That helped some, but Dixon was still peeved. So, he bought an ad that Sunday in the *Palm Beach Daily News* with a photo of Pepe's house, listing it for sale and giving Pepe's personal cell as the number to call. It didn't stop ringing for days. One good hoax deserves another! Over the years they have continued to play pranks on each other, and their friendship has flourished.

One of my favorite Palm Beach affairs is a century-old tradition: the black-tie New Year's Eve party hosted by the twenty-five Coconuts. The original Coconuts were bachelors in the 1920s, whose annual party repaid hostesses who had feted them during the year. Most of us now are married and do our own entertaining throughout the year, but it remains a signature event. Each Coconut invites twenty people, limiting the number of guests to five hundred. I am a Coconut, and as soon as the invitations can be released, the phone keeps ringing with calls begging for tickets. Of course, there is no shortage of New Year's Eve parties at all the clubs and hotels as well as private homes, but people like to know they made "the list" for the Coconuts. The event is held at the Henry Morrison Flagler Museum, the former home of industrialist Henry Flagler, who founded Palm Beach to provide a destination for his Florida East Coast Railroad. His private railcar, Number 91, is always on view at the party in the ballroom.

Many Americans, including me, are Anglophiles at heart, so I've been to England many times. King Charles III used to host U.S. and other high-ticket subscribers at gala benefits for his foundation. Each June, several black-tie events were held at Windsor Castle and nearby palaces. At other events at venues such as Balmoral in Scotland, the men wore kilts, including a dagger leg scabbard. Haggis was on the menu and attendees danced a Scottish jig. At one event, his favorite comedienne, Joan Rivers, had the zipper on the back of her gown pop open. Charles graciously zipped her up, and in her usually bawdy way she quipped, "Thank you. Men usually are more eager to unzip me than to zip me up!" With his usual aplomb, Charles briefly laughed and resumed his conversation. Lese majesty! Charles is now organizing the King's Foundation, which likely will be even more glamorous. Its forthcoming kickoff party is being co-chaired in Palm Beach by Kippy Forbes and my neighbor across the street, Tommy Quick.

I also recall Joan Rivers performing at former Canadian Prime Minister Brian Mulroney's seventieth birthday party at Club Colette in Palm Beach. She was preceded to the podium by former President George H. W. Bush, who spoke about his three F's: freedom, fidelity, and friendship. Joan began her remarks by saying impromptu, "Mr. President, I think my F-words are very different from yours." Indeed they were!

We also got to know well the Duke of Marlborough, John Spencer-Churchill, nicknamed "Sunny" or "Sunshine." He was tall and courtly, had a dry sense of humor, and was a gracious host. Every year he would have a small tailgate luncheon party at his Range Rover during the Royal Ascot horse races, with no butler to help. Clad in a morning suit and top hat, he would demonstrate how to peel a peach with a knife in one continuous motion. Sunny also loved Palm Beach and partied with us there. We, in turn, spent many nights at Blenheim Palace, the Marlborough estate. Sunny put us up in a splendidly archaic suite. Its bathroom had a warning sign, "Mind what you say. The walls have ears." The upkeep at Blenheim, the birthplace of Winston Churchill, is enormous, so it is a Trust House property with major parts open to visitors and picnickers, who generate several million pounds per year for the maintenance of the estate. Hilary served for many years as president of the Blenheim's U.S. foundation until Sunny's death in 2014. When Hilary relinquished her role, the family gave us a bust of Winston Churchill and inscribed our names on a plaque at the museum in Blenheim Palace.

One outcome of spending so much time in London was that we met Sir Elton John and his husband David Furnish. Every June, they hosted a fundraiser at their estate near Windsor Castle for about three hundred donors to raise funds and awareness for the Elton John AIDS Foundation.

One year, the theme was "Las Vegas." In front of the main house, they parked a stretched pink Cadillac convertible with a Marilyn Monroe look-alike in the front seat. Cocktails were served on the slope of a low hill atop which an enormous martini glass was filled with water in which two male ballet dancers in white tutus swam. On either side of the path to dinner were ice sculpture replicas of Las Vegas casinos and in the tent, a gaming area of roulette and blackjack. After Andrea Bocelli sang at dinner, a blue Rolls-Royce was auctioned for £600,000, about twice its list price. Events like these demonstrated over and over the British aptitude for the most elaborate marquees imaginable.

Over the years, the UK's non-domiciled, or "non-dom" tax policy has encouraged wealthy foreigners to move to London. If you are a foreign national with a residence there, you pay no UK tax on earnings outside the UK, paying tax just on your earnings from within the UK. London and the immediate suburbs are thus very popular with royal families throughout Europe, especially those royals whose families have been deposed by civilian governments. And the British are so fond of royalty that expatriate royals feel comfortable in London. Their presence adds to the glamour at London's restaurants and clubs like Annabel's, Harry's Bar, Mark's Club, One Hertford Street, and Oswald's.

Ostentatious Russian oligarchs are also among the individuals who have taken advantage of the UK's hospitable tax structure. Many stories are told about their outlandish behavior. My favorite one I have heard is of an oligarch who one evening knocked on the door of a young Goldman Sachs partner in the posh Mayfair section of London and simply said, "I buy your house."

"I'm sorry sir, you must have the wrong house. This one is not for sale."

"I pay you £12 million."

"Why don't you come back in an hour? I will talk to my wife."

The house was worth £5 million at best, so they decided to sell it. Upon the oligarch's return, they said, "We accept your offer. Would you like to come in and look around?"

"No need, I have seen your decorator's plans and photos. But you must be out by Thursday."

"But sir, that is only three days from now! We need a place to stay and somewhere to put our furniture."

"No problem, I have booked suite at Claridge's. Stay as long as you need. I will pay for it and for storage of your things."

At Thursday's closing, the buyer handed them an engraved invitation for a black-tie dinner at their former house the following evening. Inside they found more than one hundred Russian guests, impressionist paintings, and fine eighteenth-century French furniture. The buyer had clearly sent out the invitations before he bought the house! On the way back to Claridge's, the wife said, "We should have charged even more! He would have paid up to avoid being embarrassed."

The Collecting Bug

Returning to Palm Beach also allowed me one of my few vices: collecting. Collecting is an incurable, highly contagious disease, but it is delightful to be plagued by it. My addiction began as an eight-year-old boy, when I collected butterflies at the seashore. I would catch them with a net, cover them with alum, pin them to a board, and carefully label each species. But it turned out that I was allergic to them, so I soon stopped. The next year, my uncle Colby then started me collecting First Day Covers, elaborately engraved envelopes commemorating the issuance of a new stamp and postmarked the same day, but not addressed to anyone. Every time he ordered one for himself, he got me one. I kept them in plastic compartments in a specially designed loose-leaf binder. At philatelic conventions, he would trade one of his extras, plus a little cash for an earlier and rarer one, ultimately building a major collection.

Around the same time, my father started me collecting Indian Head pennies. These had been issued from 1793 to 1909, when Lincoln Head pennies were introduced. But a surprising number were still in circulation when I was a boy. Whenever Dad went to the local bank, he would buy from a teller $100 worth of pennies. He would bring them home and I would search for Indian Head pennies remaining in circulation, and then reroll them, substituting new pennies for the few Indian Heads. I built, at no premium, a substantial collection of Indian Heads that became more valuable as fewer remained in circulation. Unfortunately, while I was at Yale, my younger brother scrawled his name and address on the cover of every case I kept them in, destroying their pristine appearance and value. The pennies themselves were later sold as part of a divorce.

My oddest collectibles are shoes, or, more properly, slippers. Palm Beach has a bit of an odd subculture wherein residents collect slippers made by a company named Stubbs & Wootton. The owner of Stubbs & Wootton is Percy Steinhart, a Cuban refugee from the Castro takeover. He picked the name Stubbs & Wootton because it sounded so British and upper class. All the slippers have graphic designs woven above the toes: an insignia, logo, crest, monogram, you name it. Each Palm Beach club, for example, issues slippers with its logo and many universities also authorize pairs with their symbols.

Over the years, two hundred pairs of decorated velvet Stubbs & Wootton slippers have landed in my dressing room. I have been a good customer for years, so Percy gifted me a pair with the Department of Commerce crest to wear when Vice President Pence swore me in. That happened to be the same day as President Trump's first State of the Union Address, so the shoes stayed on while I attended the speech. Some beady-eyed CNN cameraman picked up the shoes and they went viral on social media. The resultant PR boosted Percy's sales tremendously, although the left complained about a cabinet member wearing such expensive and unusual shoes. For the rest of the Administration, I confined them to Palm Beach. More recently, for my eighty-fifth birthday party, Hilary had the New York boutique Belgian Shoes paint a version of René Magritte's work *Hegel's Holiday* on one slipper. The painting features an image of a drinking glass resting on top of an opened, upright umbrella, symbolizing a Hegelian concept of attraction and repulsion. On the other slipper is *La Clairvoyance*, Magritte's portrait of himself looking at an egg but painting a bird. One wag commented to me, "I think you wear these slippers to prevent you from putting your foot in your mouth more often." He may just be right. Palm Beach people now expect me to show up with new versions, so I have trapped myself and can't figure out how to escape from buying the next pair.

Much more serious is my love of art. At Yale, a student aid job taking attendance at Vincent Scully's art history classes whetted my appetite for paintings, though it was years before I could afford to buy art. In the 1970s, I collected American Pre-Raphaelite paintings. This group came decades after the British Pre-Raphaelites, but were equally devoted to the English critic

John Ruskin's theory that the best art was the most painstaking reproduction of the actual subjects. The Pre-Raphaelites were so obsessed with precision that one of them used a single mouse hair brush for his watercolors. That tiny bristle allowed for incredible detail.

Collectors naturally gravitate toward museum boards of trustees, and most of any museum's collection are donations or bequests from collectors. Other generous board members are just public spirited, not collectors. This led Bob Buck, a former Brooklyn Museum director, to once quip, "There are three T's to being a museum trustee: taste, time, and treasure. But if there is enough treasure, we can waive the other two." When I became vice chairman of the Brooklyn Museum, its chief curator, Linda Ferber, the greatest expert on American Pre-Raphaelites, became a friend and informal art advisor. At the time, the paintings by these recondite artists sold for just a few thousand dollars and rarely came to market, so most dealers were not interested in them. As the scholar William Gerdts said at the time, "American Pre-Raphaelites have a perfectly balanced market with very little supply and equally little demand." Still, I wanted some. After many hours at the New York Historical Society's genealogical files tracking down descendants of these artists, I contacted them and asked if they had any pieces. Frequently they did, and mostly resided in upstate New York, so I frequently took trips to look at their art and try to buy it. Many were receptive to selling, and my collection gradually grew.

Building philatelic and numismatic collections at a young age taught me some lessons that are equally applicable to fine art. There are three variables to value: physical appearance, rarity, and condition. Items in mint condition are the most highly prized, but unlike art, there is an especially high value to postage or coin errors and misstrikes given their rarity. In contrast, each painting is unique by its very nature, so the best examples provide both rarity and quality.

———————

In June 2006, Hilary and I were at Christie's in London to consider what to collect. Half a dozen paintings by the Belgian surrealist René Magritte were on view. We knew little about Magritte, but were attracted by the way his paintings made you wonder, "What is this all about? What did the artist have in mind?" He was truly the precursor to pop art, which also placed ordinary objects into an unexpected context. Each work had something odd and interesting about it, and the precise renderings of subjects harkened back to my love for Pre-Raphaelite paintings.

As we stood there transfixed, Olivier Camu, Christie's surrealism expert, introduced himself and said that if we waited until the exhibition closed, he would move the pieces to his office and discuss them with us. Well, we couldn't refuse that offer. He spent an hour teaching us about Magritte and those particular paintings. At the end, Olivier said, "If you want to be Magritte buyers, go around the corner to Sims Reed Rare Books. Buy and study the catalogue raisonné. If you are still interested, come back next week and bid." This was the most efficient soft sales pitch anyone has ever made. He subsequently sold us many of our Magrittes. As we were buying them, we lent them to museums all over the world for exhibitions. This helped us meet other Magritte collectors, curators, and dealers.

Now some big hitters have emerged as collectors of Magritte's work. A record auction price of $79.8 million for a Magritte was set in spring 2022 by Laurence Graff, the famous diamond merchant. I had lunch with him in London at Oswald's, two doors from his headquarters, and he told me how he started wheeling and dealing in paintings. It seemed to me that, to avoid sales taxes, he registered as a dealer but kept the paintings in a private back room at his jewelry store in London so no one would see them. The UK's HM Revenue & Customs office soon asked how many paintings he had sold. The answer was none, so they told him to act like a real art dealer or they would seek back taxes.

Two of the most amazing collectors I know are Leonard and Ronald Lauder, heirs to the Estée Lauder fortune. Ronald created his own Neue Galerie New York on 86th Street and 5th Avenue. It mainly has Austrian and German expressionist art, with which Ronald became enamored when he served as U.S. Ambassador to Austria. The museum restaurant is a good reproduction of a traditional Viennese café.

Not to be outdone, Leonard amassed a spectacular horde of cubist art, much of which he donated to the Metropolitan Museum of Art. A sad aside is that when the museum held the opening dinner in honor of the donation, not a single local elected official attended it. The politicians viewed this event as too elitist for their taste. Separately, Leonard for many years chaired the Whitney Museum of American Art and was the major donor and prime mover in their relocation to expanded facilities near the High Line on the West Side. I served for years on the Whitney Board at his invitation. Those meetings were the most professionally run of any I have experienced at a nonprofit organization.

Unfortunately, the art world is a bit of a murky business. Dealers sell tens of billions of dollars' worth of objects each year, with no transparency and no regulation. Auction houses invite known collectors to guarantee a sale price and share in any excess over it. Art prices are volatile, but we recently had a fortunate experience the day after Credit Suisse was declared insolvent: A Magritte in need of a cleaning was auctioned to us for less than the presale low estimate.

Paintings unfortunately lend themselves to money laundering. The most exotic money-laundering case involved a Tokyo gallery, Mountain Tortoise, which allegedly would buy a painting, usually at auction, and mark it up considerably for sale to a Japanese corporation. In Japan, a business can declare depreciation on pieces of art as though they were part of the building. Mountain Tortoise, which no longer exists, then apparently would contribute part of their profit to Japanese politicians, so in effect the corporation's political contribution would not only be laundered, but would also provide tax deductions.

Serious collectors' greatest regrets are the paintings they did not buy or which they sold. Something about a work of art remains a part of your life years later if it captured your imagination at a point in time. I feel that way about *Mount Tom*—a painting by Thomas C. Farrer I was forced to sell in a divorce—and many others. A similar affliction in serious collectors is that no matter how much they have already, they envy objects someone else has. Once, while leaving a Yale University Art Gallery board meeting, the chairman, Jack Heinz, mused to me as we passed the Paul Mellon British Art Center across the street, "If only I had Paul Mellon's money I could have built a great collection." Jack, of course, had a fine collection of his own. He was merely reflecting the impulses common to all real collectors: We never stop buying, never stop weeding out, and never stop wishing for more.

EPILOGUE

Scanning the Horizon

America is a land of innovation. From Robert Fulton's steamboat, to Thomas Edison's lightbulb, to Marc Andreessen's Mosaic browser, novel inventions have always powered our economy and our nation forward. Where American ingenuity is concerned, the digital revolution has been the most transformative development of my lifetime—and it is far from over. I have never stopped exploring and learning about new trends in technology, business, and the world. How could I? There are an infinite number of fascinating subjects out there! Continually challenging myself to learn about and adapt to the world around me is part of my secret for a long life. But even more than that, obtaining new knowledge and putting it to good use in your decisions helps sustain a rewarding life.

Since leaving government, I have spent much time scanning the horizon to see what lies ahead for our country. In the financial space, blockchain and cryptocurrencies are in vogue. I believe in blockchain, which is already being put to good use within the financial system, but not in crypto. My concerns about Bitcoin and the like are rooted in Research 101. Having seen hackers penetrate our most secure federal agencies, the notion that only the pseudonymous founder of cryptocurrency, Satoshi Nakamoto, could figure out the algorithm that creates Bitcoins seems highly improbable. This vitiates the argument that a finite supply of Bitcoins becomes an inflation hedge as scarcity develops over time. There also is the underlying, unproven assumption that enough demand exists for the ultimate supply of Bitcoin that can be created. Nor is there independent verification that there is a permanently limited amount of the currency.

My problems with crypto go beyond the conceptual. For example, most cryptocurrency entities do not provide audited figures for their own operations. There is no inherent reason why decentralized finance operators should not be audited, and this lack of oversight has increased my skepticism. The recent trials of Sam Bankman-Fried and other Bitcoin promoters demonstrate the pitfalls inherent in unaudited statements. Even more broadly, who are the natural constituencies for cryptocurrency? Who needs its anonymity? Drug dealers, human traffickers, weapons dealers, tax evaders, and others with an illicit reason for secrecy. I have nothing in common with any of them and therefore have no fundamental reason to need cryptocurrency's secrecy.

This negativity had cost me gains as Bitcoin soared in value. Nonetheless, in May 2022, after the first real crypto price crash, I paid $1,792 to attend a cryptocurrency conference at the Palm Beach County Convention Center. My hope was that there might be something in the rubble worth buying as a speculation. I was amazed that nine thousand people were paying a total of $16 million to attend the post-crash conference. The audience was mainly white males aged thirty to forty-five, with a few female companions and a few Asian Americans. Most were costumed with baseball caps about crypto, shirts with similar content, and usually either a knapsack or a tote bag with a crypto symbol. I had hoped that the speakers, all leaders in the field, would provide a serious analysis of what went awry and how to fix it.

Wrong! They were just cheerleaders. The first speaker had up on a twenty-five-foot wide, ten-foot-tall screen a grim image of the Black Plague. He began by exclaiming, "You see that image? That was the Dark Ages! That's where we are in the crypto world, but look at what came next! The Renaissance." He then clicked to an ebullient Renaissance scene. He got a five-minute standing ovation and spoke for another five minutes, all of which was without substance.

The next speaker began, "Crypto has lately had a bit of friction." (By friction, he meant billions of dollars of losses.) "But that is to be expected. We are a new industry, so it's natural that there will be some initial friction, but we will soon get it running smoothly." Another five-minute standing ovation. He continued, "The broader economy will ultimately welcome crypto and that will solve its problems." Yet another long, standing ovation.

These two performances convinced me that there was another crypto constituency beyond the scammers and criminals I had earlier identified. There is a cult of legitimate buyers who believe that crypto will decentralize the world economy and end traditional financial institutions' domination. These buyers basically distrust our present financial system and believe that blockchain and crypto will cure all its ills. A week later I told a group of central bankers that a big forthcoming problem is a generation of people that fundamentally dislike and disbelieve in the present financial institutions and are determined to reform and decentralize them. This is a phenomenon with which they will have to deal. The bankers pooh-poohed the idea. Time will tell who is right!

In early 2023, Silicon Valley Bank, Signature Bank, and First Republic Bank failed. Cryptocurrency fans regard these failures as proof of the fragility of the current financial system. They are not. As I explained earlier in this book, they are just the consequence of a poorly conceived bond-buying regulation colliding with the Fed's unprecedented rate increases. But even as the banks went under, there was no systematic failure, and no depositor was hurt. Meanwhile, cryptocurrency firms were failing, in many cases due to management improprieties. These failures prove that crypto is no panacea for human error or cupidity. At least with regulation and centralization there is a good chance most banks will get it right most of the time, and where there is a failure even the largest depositors are normally made whole. But there is no FDIC, no Treasury, no Federal Reserve to provide crypto with such support. Crypto is the financial equivalent of the Wild West, but I doubt that there ultimately will be gold in "them thar hills." I may still be wrong, but I will continue to look elsewhere for investments.

Another trend gaining steam is artificial intelligence. The opportunities and possible problems associated with AI are both much larger than even blockchain's. AI has the power to think and learn, as I recently experienced. Henry Kissinger and Eric Schmidt wrote an excellent book on AI in 2022. While preparing to attend Henry's hundredth birthday party at the Council on Foreign Relations, I asked AI to write a poem for the occasion. The first response was, "I am not very good at poetry," followed by a few lines of doggerel. Five minutes later I asked the exact same question. This time, out came ten lines. The last words of each line at least rhymed, but it wasn't poetry. I waited another five minutes to resubmit the request. This time AI sent thirty lines of iambic pentameter with mostly generalized content about Kissinger. By then it was time to leave for the dinner, so I did not pursue the gambit further. Clearly, the program was teaching itself to become more and more responsive to a request that it had not been programmed to expect. But AI can also go the other direction—to deny the user what it wants. A friend, the investor Alan Patricof, asked a program to recount the ten best Jewish jokes and it did so very well. A few minutes later he resubmitted the request, but the answer this time was, "I do not deal with ethnic issues." On reconsideration, AI self-censored itself, a curious and inexplicable development.

At the heart of AI is the selection of data used to inform the programs. AI programs are just sophisticated systems for gathering inputs from a variety of sources and processing them into outputs that respond to inquiries or requests. But who controls the inputs, who decides which inputs to ignore, and who creates the form and content of the outputs? And which data are reliable for use in creating AI? Somehow, in February 2024, Google's Gemini AI program produced images of Black Nazis when asked to generate images of the Third Reich. Clearly the AI had been programmed to consider racial diversity in image generation, but the programming had somehow backfired! One also wonders how AI programs will influence future generations when they query highly subjective questions such as, "Is capitalism a better system than communism? Who is the best candidate for president? What stock is attractive?"

There is also the danger that AI will replace humans in many white-collar jobs. Recall how nineteenth-century Luddites in England smashed machinery as manufacturers automated their plants. Buggy makers feared the automobile.

As computing power increased, so the need for operators of computers that used punch cards decreased. What happened in all these cases was that the nature of jobs changed, but productivity increased and on balance more jobs were created than lost. Economically speaking, I suspect AI will be a net positive.

But I also remain concerned about its destructive potential. AI is very good at imitating people's voices and creating "deepfake" videos. This creates the potential for all sorts of scams and frauds. There was even a case where a trial lawyer used AI to write a very well-reasoned brief that he filed with the court, only to have it discovered that the cases cited had been made up by AI. But my greatest fear surrounding AI is that it will make people even less likely to think. Look at what GPS has already done to us. No one remembers how to get to places anymore; they totally rely on GPS.

Our society can adjust, provided that our education system can adapt to teach the necessary skills. But I am not optimistic that this will happen. We consistently lag in international rankings. Now we are about thirtieth in math and nineteenth in science.[47] This is not good enough for world leadership. One reason for underperformance in our schools is the teachers' unions. They are not a force for productive change in our educational system. As demonstrated in the COVID-19 pandemic lockdowns, the teachers' unions define teachers, not pupils, as their constituency. The unions are powerful because they are leading financial contributors in statewide elections. Way back when my late mother was a young teacher, the dues went to mostly provide pensions. But the unions subsequently transferred the pension obligations to municipalities and states, so now unions preoccupy themselves with donating to politicians. This creates an obvious conflict of interest—the unions bargain for pay raises and work rules against the very politicians they bankroll and elect to office. If we continue to permit teachers' unions to rig the political system this way, taxpayers and students alike will suffer the long-term adverse consequences.

———————————

Despite these concerns, there are still many reasons to be optimistic about the future of the greatest country on earth. We have the greatest economy in the world, a respect for the rule of law, and a nation full of risk-takers. Our technological minds are the best in the world. And in every era, Americans have shown an extraordinary fortitude for overcoming challenges. I have no doubt we will remain exceptional.

One major reason I have confidence is our enduring entrepreneurial spirit. In 2020, at the huge consumer electronics show in Las Vegas, I led a fireside chat with a pioneer of nonmeat meat. This fellow showed up in a hoodie and very colorful sneakers. Equally colorful was his history. As a young man he had earned an MD and a PhD in biochemistry from the University of Chicago, and began working as a pediatric surgeon, but quickly grew tired of it. He next went to Stanford and worked with two Nobel Prize winners on cures for cancer. He ultimately decided he had to do something even bigger to help humanity. While on a sabbatical, he concluded that using animals as food sources was the biggest contributor to climate change. He reasoned that fixing it demanded he develop vegetable-based food that had no animal content, but tasted as good as meat. After beginning research, he came upon a molecule in clovers called heme, which gave meat its taste. That breakthrough resulted in nonmeat burgers and, later, nonmeat sausages. He confessed that he had yet to replicate the taste of chicken or fish, but would keep trying.

While I am not sure he correctly identified the greatest threat, I respect what this man was doing. He had benefited from his education at world-class American educational institutions, and was now striving to do good for the world through an entrepreneurial initiative, undoubtedly creating jobs in the process. He had not hit his goal yet, but he was committed to it. This is the American spirit in action. It is true that sometimes government makes it harder for entrepreneurs to achieve their goals. But overall, the opportunities our country affords, plus a relatively business-friendly framework, gives Americans the best chance in the world to succeed. After eighty-seven years, I continue to see how the American economy is the world's greatest force for economic prosperity (and I continue to seize new opportunities of my own). The sky is the limit for creative and motivated individuals. The same cannot be said about the environment in any other nation.

The world, the United States itself, and your specific situation may be depressing and stressful, but the answer is not to bemoan your fate. The only thing that can hold you back is yourself. The way to propel yourself to the life you desire is to ignore what is out of your control and figure out how to overcome the obstacles immediately confronting you and to seize opportunities available to you. This probably will involve some initial sacrifices on your part, but don't let that stop you. You also may have to take some risks to achieve the returns you are seeking. Some of those risks may turn out badly. That is not the end of the world, as long as you learn from them and are resilient. Society does not owe you a successful career or a happy life. You must earn both. I did it, and so can you. Escape from the safe room. Take the risks, and reap the returns!

About the Author

Wilbur L. Ross, Jr. served as Secretary of Commerce in the Trump Administration following fifty-five years of experience in investment banking and private equity. In this capacity, he advised President Donald Trump on commercial and economic affairs, and helped American entrepreneurs and businesses create jobs and economic opportunity.

A native of North Bergen, New Jersey, Ross spent a significant portion of his business career at Rothschild, Inc. Ross negotiated on behalf of creditors in some of the highest-profile bankruptcy proceedings in history, including those involving Pan Am, TWA, Texaco, and Drexel Burnham Lambert. After founding his own private equity firm in 2000, Ross purchased and restored many companies to profitability, including those in the steel, coal, textile, and banking industries. Over the course of his career, Ross restructured more than $400 billion in assets, earning him a distinguished reputation on Wall Street. In 2011, *Bloomberg Markets* named him one of the fifty most influential people in global finance. He is a member of Kappa Beta Phi.

Secretary Ross's philanthropic work has included significant support for the Japan Society, the Brookings Institution, the Blenheim Foundation, and numerous entities devoted to the fine arts, including the René Magritte Museum in Brussels. He was also an advisory board member of Yale University School of Management.

Secretary Ross is a graduate of Yale University and Harvard Business School. He and his wife, Hilary Geary Ross, have four children.

Notes

1   https://www.reddit.com/r/antiwork/ 2023. *r/antiwork*. Accessed
    2024. https://www.reddit.com/r/antiwork/?rdt=48380.

2   https://www.insidehighered.com/quicktakes/2021/09/23/survey
    -most-students-self-censor-campus-and-online Carrasco, Maria.
    "Survey: Most Students Self-Censor on Campus and Online."
    Inside Higher Ed, September 22, 2021.

3   https://www.thecollegefix.com/college-students-think-america
    -invented-slavery-professor-finds/ Hardiman, Kate. "Most college
    students think America invented slavery, professor finds." *The
    College Fix*, October 31, 2016.

4   https://www.nytimes.com/1976/10/02/archives/william-zeckendorf
    -real-estate-developer-71-dies.html Sterne, Michael. "William
    Zeckendorf, Real Estate Developer, 71, Dies." *New York Times*,
    October 2, 1976.

5   https://www.inc.com/jeff-haden/15-years-ago-steve-jobs-said-people
    -who-know-what-theyre-talking-about-dont-need-powerpoint
    -research-shows-he-was-right.html#:~:text=15%20Years%20
    Ago%2C%20Steve%20Jobs,About%20Don't%20Need%20
    PowerPoint. Haden, Jeff. "15 Years Ago, Steve Jobs Said People

Who Know What They're Talking About Don't Need PowerPoint. Research Shows He Was Right." *Inc.*, February 19, 2023.

6   https://www.chicagotribune.com/2000/11/19/if-your-mother-says -she-loves-you/ Chicago Tribune. "If Your Mother Says She Loves You . . ." *Chicago Tribune*, November 19, 2000.

7   https://www.military.com/daily-news/2022/09/28/new-pentagon -study-shows-77-of-young-americans-are-ineligible-military -service.html Novelly, Thomas. "Even More Young Americans Are Unfit to Serve, a New Study Finds. Here's Why." Military.Com, September 28, 2022.

8   https://www.latimes.com/archives/la-xpm-1992-02-06-fi-2084 -story.html Mulligan, Thomas. "Federated Emerges from Bankruptcy After Two Years: Retailing: Analysts say the slimmed -down owner of department stores is now a stronger company." *LA Times*, February 6, 1992.

9   https://nypost.com/2023/11/10/metro/2-of-the-140k-migrants-who -came-to-nyc-have-applied-for-work-permits/ McCarthy, Craig, and Emily Crane. "Only 2% of the 140K migrants who have come to NYC have applied for work permits." *New York Post*, November 10, 2023.

10   https://www.forbes.com/sites/bryancollinseurope/2018/08/07 /heres-what-warren-buffetts-mentor-said-about-investing/?sh =77e8ad284598 Collins, Bryan. "Here's What Warren Buffett's Mentor Said About Investing." *Forbes*, August 7, 2018.

11   https://slate.com/business/2003/01/the-next-andrew-carnegie.html Gross, Daniel. "Is Wilbur Ross the Next Andrew Carnegie?" *Slate*, January 16, 2023.

12   https://www.bloomberg.com/news/articles/2003-12-21/is-wilbur -ross-crazy "Is Wilbur Ross Crazy?" *Bloomberg*, December 21, 2003.

13   https://www.foxnews.com/story/transcript-icgs-wilbur-ross-on-the -sago-mine-tragedy Ross, Wilbur, interview by Neil Cavuto.

Transcript: ICG's Wilbur Ross on the Sago Mine Tragedy, New York (January 5, 2006).

14 https://www.reuters.com/world/us-intelligence-assesses-ukraine-war-has-cost-russia-315000-casualties-source-2023-12-12/ Landay, Jonathan. "U.S. intelligence assesses Ukraine war has cost Russia 315,000 casualties—source." Reuters, December 12, 2023.

15 https://www.wsj.com/articles/wilbur-ross-honored-for-contributions-to-u-s-japan-relations-1423016639 Heyman, Marshall. "A Japanese Knight? Well, Close Enough." *Wall Street Journal*, February 3, 2015.

16 https://www.washingtonpost.com/news/worldviews/wp/2013/02/05/the-cannibals-of-north-korea/ Fisher, Max. "The Cannibals of North Korea." *Washington Post*, February 5, 2013.

17 https://www.indiatoday.in/business/story/india-third-largest-economy-by-2027-global-brokerage-firm-jefferies-2505652-2024-02-22 Das, Koustav. "India set to become 3rd-largest economy by 2027, says global brokerage Jefferies." *India Today*, February 22, 2024.

18 https://www.usatoday.com/story/news/nation/2015/08/05/nasa-keep-paying-russia-send-astronauts-space-station/31178519/ King, Ledyard. "NASA to keep paying Russia to send astronauts to space station." *USA Today*, August 5, 2015.

19 https://www.nytimes.com/2022/05/14/opinion/sunday/rich-happiness-big-data.html Stephens-Davidowitz, Seth. "The Rich Are Not Who We Think They Are. And Happiness Is Not What We Think It Is, Either." *New York Times*, May 14, 2022.

20 https://www.architecturaldigest.com/story/buatta-article-112005 Clarke, Gerald. "The View From the Top." *Architectural Digest*, October 31, 2005.

21 https://www.nytimes.com/2013/09/05/garden/mario-buatta-the-beauty-of-a-bad-pun.html Green, Penelope. "Mario Buatta: The Beauty of a Bad Pun." *New York Times*, September 5, 2013.

22 https://banks.data.fdic.gov/explore/historical?displayFields
=STNAME%2CTOTAL%2CBRANCHES%2CNew_Char
&selectedEndDate=2023&selectedReport=CBS&selectedStartDate
=1934&selectedStates=0&sortField=YEAR&sortOrder=desc
FDIC.Gov. n.d. *BankFind Suite*. Accessed March 2024.

23 https://www.wsj.com/articles/training-for-the-jobs-of-tomorrow
-1531868131 Trump, Ivanka. "Training for the Jobs of
Tomorrow." *Wall Street Journal*, July 17, 2018.

24 https://www.thoughtco.com/average-number-of-legislative-days
-3368250 Murse, Tom. "How Many Days a Year Congress
Works." ThoughtCo, February 3, 2020.

25 https://www.nytimes.com/2017/11/05/world/wilbur-ross-russia.
html McIntire, Mike, Sasha Chavkin, and Martha M. Hamilton.
"Commerce Secretary's Offshore Ties to Putin 'Cronies.'" *New
York Times*, November 5, 2017.

26 https://politicalcharge.org/2019/01/26/saturday-morning-cartoons
-1-26/ Political Charge. 2019. *Saturday Morning Cartoons 1/26*.
January 26. Accessed March 2024. https://politicalcharge
.org/2019/01/26/saturday-morning-cartoons-1-26/.

27 https://www.washingtonpost.com/lifestyle/style/dont-sleep-on
-wilbur-ross/2019/09/27/e9928b46-dd93-11e9-be96-6adb81821e90
_story.html Zak, Dan. "Don't Sleep on Wilbur Ross." *Washington
Post*, September 30, 2019.

28 https://www.bloomberg.com/news/features/2018-11-06/wilbur
-killer-ross-isn-t-worried-about-the-trade-wars?embedded
-checkout=true Leonard, Devin, and Jenny Leonard. "Wilbur
'Killer' Ross Isn't Worried About the Trade Wars." *Bloomberg*,
November 6, 2018.

29 https://www.nytimes.com/2018/05/24/opinion/that-moon-colony
-will-be-a-reality-sooner-than-you-think.html Ross, Wilbur. "That
Moon Colony Will Be a Reality Sooner than You Think." *New
York Times*, May 24, 2018.

30 https://2017-2021.commerce.gov/news/press-releases/2017/12
/statement-us-secretary-commerce-wilbur-ross-president-trumps
-speech.html U.S. Department of Commerce. "Statement from
U.S. Secretary of Commerce Wilbur Ross on President Trump's
Speech on Regulatory Reform." *U.S. Department of Commerce.*
December 14, 2017. Accessed March 2024.

31 https://www.census.gov/library/visualizations/2021/dec/2020
-apportionment-map.html U.S. Census Bureau. April 26,
2021. "2020 Census: Apportionment of the U.S. House of
Representatives." Accessed April 2024.

32 https://www.pewresearch.org/short-reads/2022/06/08/key-facts
-about-the-quality-of-the-2020-census/#:~:text=The%20census%20
count%20of%20more,the%20number%20missed%20in%202010.
Cohn, D'Vera, and Jeffrey S. Passel. "Key facts about the quality
of the 2020 census." Pew Research Center. June 8, 2022. Accessed
April 2024.

33 https://www.nytimes.com/2021/02/24/us/politics/biden-jamal
-khashoggi-saudi-arabia.html Sanger, David E. "Candidate Biden
Called Saudi Arabia a 'Pariah.' He Now Has to Deal with It." *New
York Times*, February 24, 2021.

34 https://www.cnn.com/2018/01/26/politics/read-trump-davos-speech
/index.html CNN. "READ: Trump's Speech to the World Economic
Forum." CNN, January 26, 2018.

35 https://www.economist.com/finance-and-economics/2023/12/14
/is-china-understating-its-own-export-success The Economist.
"Is China Understating Its Own Export Success?" *The Economist,*
December 14, 2023.

36 https://www.usitc.gov/publications/332/executive_briefings/ebot
_serletis_u.s._section_321_imports_surge.pdf Serletis, George.
2023. *U.S. Section 321 Imports Surge with Rising E-commerce
Shipments from China.* Executive Briefing on Trade, Washington:
Office of Industry and Competitive Analysis.

37 https://asia.nikkei.com/Spotlight/Caixin/China-s-debt-to-GDP-ratio -climbs-to-record-287.8-in-2023 Yining, Xia, and Han Wei. "China's debt-to-GDP ratio climbs to record 287.8% in 2023." *Nikkei Asia*, January 30, 2024.

38 https://www.globaltimes.cn/page/202210/1277280.shtml Sheng, Yang, and Zhang Changyue. "CPC charts course for modern socialist China in all respects." *Global Times*, October 17, 2022.

39 https://www.reuters.com/technology/chinas-huawei-says-2021 -revenues-down-almost-30-sees-challenges-head-2021-12-31/ 2021. "China's Huawei says 2021 revenues down almost 30%, sees challenges ahead." *Reuters*. December 30, 2021.

40 https://www.usitc.gov/publications/332/executive_briefings/ebot _recent_developments_in_global_semiconductor_industry.pdf Jones, Lin, and Nathan Lotze. 2023. *Recent Developments in Global Semiconductor Industry.* Executive Briefing on Trade, Washington: U.S. International Trade Commission.

41 https://www.semiconductors.org/wp-content/uploads/2020/10 /SIA-SUMMARY-OF-BCG-REPORT.pdf Semiconductor Industry Association. 2010. *Turning the Tide For Semiconductor Manufacturing in the U.S.* Industry Research Report, Washington: Semiconductor Industry Association.

42 https://www.whitehouse.gov/briefing-room/statements -releases/2022/08/09/fact-sheet-chips-and-science-act-will-lower -costs-create-jobs-strengthen-supply-chains-and-counter-china / White House Briefing Room. 2022. *FACT SHEET: CHIPS and Science Act Will Lower Costs, Create Jobs, Strengthen Supply Chains, and Counter China.* Briefing, Washington: The White House.

43 https://www.fda.gov/media/144416/download U.S. Food and Drug Administration. 2020. *Pfizer-BioNTech COVID-19 Vaccine Emergency Use Authorization Review Memorandum.* Review Memorandum, Washington: U.S. Food and Drug Administration.

44   https://oversight.house.gov/release/wenstrup-releases-statement
     -following-dr-faucis-two-day-testimony/ Select Subcommittee on the
     Coronavirus Pandemic. "Wenstrup Releases Statement Following
     Dr. Fauci's Two-Day Testimony." Committee on Oversight and
     Acountability. January 10, 2024. Accessed March 2024.
     https://oversight.house.gov/release
     /wenstrup-releases-statement-following-dr-faucis-two-day-testimony/.
45   https://www.wsj.com/articles/xenophobia-drives-foes-of-nippon
     -steels-deal-japan-national-security-union-cc7ad53a Ross, Wilbur.
     "Xenophobia Drives Foes of Nippon Steel's Deal." *Wall Street
     Journal*, January 1, 2024.
46   https://subscribe.palmbeachdailynews.com/restricted?return
     =https%3A%2F%2Fwww.palmbeachdailynews.com%2Fstory
     %2Fbusiness%2Freal-estate%2F2023%2F04%2F04%2Fworlds
     -wealthiest-more-forbes-billionaires-than-ever-in-palm-beach
     -florida-including-donald-trump%2F70075086007%2F Palm
     Beach Daily News. "World's Wealthiest: More Forbes Billionaires
     than Ever in Palm Beach, Florida, Including Donald Trump." *Palm
     Beach Daily News*, April 4, 2023.
47   "https://www.pewresearch.org/short-reads/2017/02/15/u-s-students
     -internationally-math-science/ Drew DeSilver. "U.S. students'
     academic achievement still lags that of their peers in many other
     countries," Pew Research. February 15, 2017.

Index